MARK FENN
Foreword by Jack Cunningham, PhD

Narrative Jewelry

TALES FROM THE TOOLBOX

Schiffer Publishing Ltd

4880 Lower Valley Road • Atglen, PA 19310

To Jane,
my soul partner, for always being there.
I love you with all my heart and soul.

To Jerri and Sam,
you both have made me a proud father,
and Libby-Jane, you're the jewel in my eye.

To Grey and Murphy,
my studio companions.

Jacket design by Brenda McCallum
Type set in Baskerville and Frutiger

Jacket image, front: Dauvit Alexander, *Blood Will Have Blood: A Macbeth Brooch.* Courtesy of Andrew Neilson/Neilson Photography.
Jacket images, back: Center: David and Roberta Williamson *(Dan Fox)*. Clockwise from top left: David Brand. Nick Palmer. Xu Chen. Ginger Meek Allen. Aleksandra Vali. Mary Hallam Pearse *(Walker Montgomery)*.
Spine image: Mark Fenn *(Mike Blissett)*.
Front flap image: Heather Croston *(Victor Wolansky Photography)*.

ISBN: 978-0-7643-5414-4
Printed in China

Published by Schiffer Publishing, Ltd.
4880 Lower Valley Road
Atglen, PA 19310
Phone: (610) 593-1777; Fax: (610) 593-2002
E-mail: Info@schifferbooks.com
Web: www.schifferbooks.com

For our complete selection of fine books on this and related subjects, please visit our website at www.schifferbooks.com. You may also write for a free catalog.

Schiffer Publishing's titles are available at special discounts for bulk purchases for sales promotions or premiums. Special editions, including personalized covers, corporate imprints, and excerpts, can be created in large quantities for special needs. For more information, contact the publisher.

We are always looking for people to write books on new and related subjects. If you have an idea for a book, please contact us at proposals@schifferbooks.com.

CONTENTS

FOREWORD

Wearable objects have, for thousands of years, been imbued with meaning. We may never know the significance of early examples, understood to be jewelry, which date as far back as 135,000 years to the Middle Paleolithic period. A deliberate intent by the maker to convey a particular narrative or story is, however, a more recent aspect of body adornment.

Narrative, as a specific identifiable genre of contemporary studio jewelry, has increased in popularity since its early origins, which was most probably in the United States approximately a century ago. That it has exponentially flourished in the last twenty years or so is perhaps testament to how makers increasingly direct their creativity towards making some meaning of the world in which they live, exploring universal themes through the objects that they make. This allows the viewer, and ultimately the wearer, to interact on a personal level, investing these small objects with their own interpretation and meaning, which may or may not resonate with the original intent of the maker.

In *Narrative Jewelry: Tales from the Toolbox*, Mark Fenn, himself an experienced exponent of narrative jewelry, wanted to bridge an information gap, which he felt existed whilst studying as a mature student at the University for the Creative Arts. With 241 contributors featured here, the audience, from students to academics, makers, and collectors, will find *Narrative Jewelry* insightful and informative, a little curious, and an enjoyable read.

Professor Jack Cunningham, PhD

PREFACE

This book is a response to the dissertation I wrote when I undertook a bachelor of art honors degree in silversmithing, goldsmithing and jewelry at the University for the Creative Arts in the United Kingdom. My dissertation analyzed the different ways narrative is used in contemporary jewelry and as I researched this subject I found there was a gap in the literature available on the subject. Yes, I could find one or two books that had examples of narrative jewelry, but no books that had narrative jewelry as a central theme.

During my research I was trying to find narrative jewelers to interview and I was given an introduction to Professor Jack Cunningham, who at that time was head of the Birmingham School of Jewellery and is one of the foremost narrative makers. Jack kindly agreed to an interview and was a wealth of information; he not only pointed me in the direction of other narrative jewelers, he gave me a number of catalogs of his work. My learning from my undergraduate research process was the springboard to a successful dissertation, and also had a major impact on my studio practice.

After university I was invited by Brigitte Martin from Crafthaus to run an online exhibition on narrative jewelry. The response I had for calls to the exhibition was fantastic and allowed me to run the online exhibition in two parts. Through the process of curating that exhibition I developed the idea of putting together a book about narrative jewelry. This idea has come to fruition with the help of over 240 makers who shared their beautiful work and the narratives that go with them. I hope you find the book interesting and informative and that it helps you understand the genre of narrative jewelry a little better.

ACKNOWLEDGMENTS

Professor Jack Cunningham, thank you for your support and encouragement.

To Dauvit Alexander aka The Justified Sinner and Jo Pond, who make the most amazing work and agreed to contribute essays to the book, thank you.

I am eternally grateful to Beverly Hayward. Thank you for supporting me as a student with dyslexia and giving me a voice.

To the jewelers who kindly shared their stunning images and insightful words and who have supported me in this endeavor.

Thanks to the jewelers who helped with my original research and helped plant the seed of an idea.

To my very good friend Mark Ansell of SPC Design & Print who helped with my endless questions about Photoshop, cheers my friend.

To my tea drinking friend Brigitte Martin of Crafthaus for her continued support for my quest to bring narrative jewelry and makers to a wider audience, thank you.

Pete Schiffer of Schiffer books, thank you for the opportunity. And thanks also to Karen Choppa, Catherine Mallette, Jesse Marth, and all members of the team at Schiffer for their help and support, with special thanks to Sandra Korinchak for her unending support and guidance.

To the Association for Contemporary Jewellery for their support and help many thanks.

Thanks to James March for the photograph of me on the inside cover and to Shelly and Garrie Keeys of Ruskins outfitters in Whitstable for making me look so smart for the picture.

INTRODUCTION

This book is an illustration of narrative jewelry in action, including the stories attached to each piece by the maker and the potential stories you, the reader, will project onto the pieces as you view them.

Narrative jewelry usually elicits some response, verbal or emotional. The genre of narrative jewelry is new to many, and this book will be of interest to those in the jewelry field—students, makers, or suppliers—as well as more generally to the public, the wearer, and the curious.

There is no single widely-accepted definition of narrative jewelry, but my purpose with this book is to engage people, generate interest, and possibly open discussion. This quote from Jack Cunningham gives one definition of narrative jewelry: "A wearable object that contains a commentary or message which the maker, by means of visual representation, has the overt intention to communicate to an audience through the intervention of the wearer."* The pieces in this book show how jewelry can be more than what is first seen, more than we expect and not just about shiny pretty things. The beauty of narrative jewelry is in its levels of engagement, from first view, to understanding, to reconsideration, and for some, simply in owning or wearing and in the story they generate around their purchase. The themes of narrative jewelry cover a broad spectrum of thought and feeling and show the links between storytelling and making.

The makers and their work are presented alphabetically. I have left the makers to decide how much or how little they say, and I have kept their words, their stories, as close to their original contribution as possible. Most prominent makers in the field of narrative jewelry have contributed to the book and I have respected the wishes of those prominent makers who chose not to contribute. Sometimes the missing ones help highlight their own work by not being present and at other times their absence can feel a loss. However, the book contains amazing images and stories and I feel proud to have collated it.

I contacted narrative jewelers through a general call through several sources including Crafthaus, the Association for Contemporary Jewellery, Facebook, and Twitter. I also asked for recommendations of other artists who might be appropriate to include in the book. So from a baseline of personal contacts, through the power of social media and recommendations, I received over 350 jewelers and over 1,500 images and texts. They were selected down to the 241 makers and 450 images included in this book.

During the process of approaching makers to contribute to the book, I asked each for an explanation of why the maker worked with narrative, a short description of the narrative of his or her work, as well as images of his or her pieces. Some makers gave answers to these questions and some did not. Some choose not to explain the narrative of their work in order to let their work talk and let the reader/viewer interpret the work with his or her own narrative.

The desire to tell a story or to share one's own narrative is a human trait and the reasons for telling are manyfold. This is because now, in a postmodern society, there are many forms in which that narrative can be expressed. With the meta-narratives of, for example, the early cave paintings of prehistoric man, to the early propaganda of the Bayeux Tapestry, with its modern-day counterpart of the political cartoon, they have paved the way for the lesser, but one might argue, the more important narratives of postmodernism.

One sees how the narratives of the past are given a modern-day, contemporary makeover and thereby given a new narrative, a new tale from the toolbox. In the jewelry of Keith A. Lewis, he comments on the impact of AIDS with his reinterpretation of the martyrdom of St. Sebastian (see page 154). With Jack Cunningham's work the more personal narrative is at the forefront of the design, and this leads into the argument of the importance of the maker in the relationship with the wearer and viewer.

My work *White Horse* (see page 93) makes a symbolic reference to death, one taken from Revelation 6:8: "And I looked, and behold a pale horse: and his name that sat on him was Death, and Hell followed with him." This is the fourth and final horseman, named Death. The color of Death's horse in the Greek text is written as *khlôros*, which is frequently translated as "pale," though "pale green" and "ashen" are other translations. Nevertheless, whatever translation the reader wishes to use, the colors conjure up the sickly pallor of a cadaver. So although my work does not explicitly reference death, the connotations are there, if the secondary subverted narrative is made known. Of course, one might glance at the image and observe an illusionistic representation of a horse and envisage a depiction of strength and loyalty. Once a piece is sold the narrative from the maker's toolbox is laid dormant and, to a degree, lost, and it is then the viewer who lays their own claim to the new narrative/tale.

This book shows that the use of the personal lesser/minor narratives is a valid starting point with which to embark on the design process within the context of jewelry making and design. Where a maker might be drawn to a

* From "Maker Wearer Viewer," practice-based PhD thesis, 2007.

quasi-modernism approach to making, in the sense that the specific medium of a piece is paramount, just as the purity of form is dominant, today it appears that the context is simultaneously a governing principle. This process has brought to the fore the requirement of visualizing the context in which one is working, that is the narrative.

Hence, there are many tales from the toolbox. One might consider that just as there are many facets of a gemstone, there are many facets to a person's persona. The analysis of narrative within jewelry shows that the subject matter or starting points are as many as there are makers. Accordingly, the different ways in which narrative is used in contemporary jewelry are fluid.

Narrative Jewelry: Tales from the Toolbox highlights that narrative makers use known and traditional symbolic references within their work, but conversely that they build their own visual language to convey their narrative. Therefore, when a postmodern jewelry piece is crafted from a postmodern overflowing eclectic toolbox, the tale from that toolbox will be as diverse as the postmodern society that created it.

IDENTIFYING WITH THE NARRATIVE

As makers, we tacitly or explicitly convey a story, or respond to a given story by design, through compositional arrangement and material choices. However, the value of communicating in this way is defined by how this story is experienced by the maker and the viewer. These interpretations evolve through nostalgic connection, emotional response, or a perception of value. The latter of which is influenced by trends, materials, artist notoriety, sustainability, ethics, or the symbolic values which the artifact represents.

The origin of the narrative may well have been the maker, but it is the wearer and viewer who complete the story.

A jewel is designed for consumption, however the art jeweler who typically adopts the contemporary narrative genre, designs artifacts which are not necessarily created to be sold, or to be given to others, as is tradition for jewelry. When the art form is a jewel, it is usually intended for another person. It could be argued that it is not the story conveyed by the maker which bears importance. The narrative jewel replicates the recital or rendering and requires the viewer to piece the story together for themselves. A piece of narrative jewelry is displayed or worn, but not necessarily articulated. Therefore there is a psychological connection with the viewer which is not explicitly defined. Narrative suggests the story is portrayed in the context of jewelry through the maker and that it is physical, implied, or unspoken.

Narrative is a spoken or written account of a story. It is the storytelling which accompanies and conveys the message. The narrative within an exhibition of jewelry may actually be the accompanying catalog, or the showcase descriptor. The works themselves give meaning through the use of symbols and visual communication. They are the symbol/sets of symbols used to represent the story; however the interpretation of this story is determined by the viewer.

We process symbols from our own viewpoint. Some individuals may interpret them as the artistic creator anticipated, whereas others do not pick up on the intended communication and instead draw their own conclusions, just as body language can be misinterpreted. Groups of people who share underlying beliefs and traits are likely to experience symbols from a common perspective. Color, form, symbol, and material can all convey different associations, even words can be subjectively interpreted, invoking different responses.

So why do we adopt the narrative genre? Identifying with a group, a set of makers, a culture, provides a sense of belonging. Many of us identify with a collective of makers, giving clarity and direction to the commonality within the approach of our practice, wearing a label which feels comfortable, appropriate, even justified. It could be argued, the word narrative in the jewelry world has been reappropriated as a noun; a personal approach to generating outcomes which communicate a story. These outcomes may or may not be intended wholly for public consumption. For some, the narrative umbrella is the motivation behind the creativity. The story can provide emotional stimulation, something with which to start the creative process.

What motivates us to make, if creating decorative objects for decorative sake does not feel justified? The majority of makers are compelled to create, but we all employ different stimuli. A key stimulus is the potential for items created to elicit a response or have purpose. The reciprocal relationship is one of communication and even recognition. Physical, emotional and intellectual engagement, alongside the expression of skill and an opening for dialogue, can be conveyed through a jewel. A static inanimate object therefore has great potential for psychological connection. The desire to create any artifact or jewel, which in turn creates an emotional response within ourselves and others, brings reward. Fulfilment through our creations motivates further creativity, and momentum subsequently enables us to generate a voice and establish an identity.

In adopting the narrative genre, we are choosing to define ourselves and our creations and must therefore consider this assumed identity. Narrative is in essence, descriptive, however from the makers' perspective; the pieces may actually be prescriptive. Could the term narrative therefore be otherwise described as responsive jewelry; implicit jewelry; organic jewelry? The word *organic* is commonly characterized as a harmonious relationship between the elements of a whole. The jeweler carefully and deliberately considers the harmony of the elements which create their composition. The viewers make the story complete through their own interpretations. This harmonious relationship forms the narrative and is the sum of cultural, social, emotional and environmental experiences relating to the composition.

The viewer or wearer brings meaning to their experience of a piece. The focus of the narrative jeweler may well have been political, cathartic, historical or otherwise intended, but the outcome provides a shared experience, which, although potentially communicated at cross-purposes, has a value. A powerful harmonious (or un-harmonious) composition embodies the energy and thoughts of the artist and draws the viewer in. Curiously, sensing that there's more to know, the conversation begins.

NARRATIVES OF MATERIAL

My own work is necessarily material-driven. I work with "found objects," very often found materials (1) and these materials have inherent narratives derived from its history: what it is, where it was found, how it was previously used. There are social and political histories embedded within these materials. It is important to my practice that these inherent histories are kept intact and that the material is used in a manner which respects both the material itself and the origin of the material. Over the last few years, I have found that my work is increasingly coming to foreground the inherent narratives of material over any enforced narratives that are given to the materials. Those latter narratives, on reflection, sometimes overwhelm the work.

Contextualizing the materials using the eponymous components of Jack Cunningham's seminal *Maker, Wearer, Viewer* (2), these materials in themselves generate engagement responses which are in addition to the responses generated by the forms, concepts, titles, etc. Everyone who engages with the materials, whether in the raw state (maker) or in the context of the finished work (wearer, viewer) contributes to the narrative, a narrative which is unstable, open to change and interpretation.

In response to Cunningham's ideas, Liesbeth Den Besten questioned, "How can a jewel, that often has no coherent figurative representation, and (has no) decorative function, tell stories?"(3) and then goes on to discuss how much of the concept of narrative jewelry is often seen to be ". . . illustrative, like the rather novelistic storytelling that is so characteristic of American jewelry." (4) Indeed, one of the masters of this "illustrative" style is a maker who has influenced me greatly, Kevin Coates. Coates takes a metaphorical and animistic approach to his materials, weaving the narrative of material closely into his finished works, ". . . it is a profoundly held, prime condition-of-existence for anything I make (and by make I mean both create, and then allow to exist) that it should incorporate something 'other' in addition to the collected and worked materials from which it is formed." (5) Helen Clifford suggests that this approach works because he not only "understands the physical qualities of his materials, but also their 'implications, associations and potential meanings'" (6), an approach similar to that taken by the Renaissance makers (7).

A lot of my mature work has been led by this type of—often complex—"narrative" (for example, *Blood Will Have Blood: A Macbeth Brooch* after Shakespeare, shown on the cover of this book; *A Forest*, based on the lyrics of a song by The Cure; or *20,000 Leagues Under The Seas* after

the book by Jules Verne) which, on reflection, are much more "illustrative" than "narrative." Although the jewelry still has material narrative, it is distant, referenced, subsumed by the illustration. Over the last few years as my work has become more social, gendered and political, I have become increasingly uncomfortable with this obliquely-applied storytelling: the material of my work—discarded iron from industrial sites—tells its own story of society, gender and politics and it is this very human narrative which has always drawn me to it. (8,9)

Some contemporary makers such as Bob Ebendorf and Jo Pond have taken the approach of liberating the material narratives completely; Keith Lo Bue allows the materials to dictate the form of the final illustrative work, writing the narrative from the materials. These approaches create a material poetics which destabilize the relationships between maker/wearer/viewer and which require a different sense of what is meant by "narrative jewelry." Jo Pond describes her process as, "Using found objects is like starting the process of creating with part of the story already written. I am able to choreograph, make introductions and interventions." (10) Bob Ebendorf says, "Many of the objects I find generate the ideas for the jewelry. I don't go out to find things to make the execution of any idea possible" and that "intuition and a bit of chance do come into it." (11)

Exposure to the found-object works of these makers has shown me that it is possible to move away from the reliance of imposed—"novelistic"—narrative and allow the materials to develop a much freer narrative which, in turn, allows the wearer-viewer to read their own stories into the work much more than when I (the maker) try to impose complex narratives. This, perhaps surprisingly, is liberating. It allows the materials to bring their own history to the fore and allows the material some control, guiding the narrative as opposed to being bombastically directed by the maker.

For me, this has meant the development of not only a new way of working but also of a new poetics of material (12), a poetics which is felt instinctively by the maker/wearer/viewer but which may not generate the same meaning in each. Elizabeth Moignard asserts that whatever the maker's intent, it is "one component in what becomes a network of intentions and readings" and that the piece "acquires archaeological deposits of other thoughts about it" (13). Keeping the work removed from "novelistic" narratives enhances this deposition of thought, a process appropriate to the industrial-historical background to my own work.

By distancing myself from specific and detailed illustrative narratives and by allowing the materials to simply be themselves, I do not "interpret" either the materials or the finished works but seek to liberate the inherent historic narrative of the materials. This requires me to find a new approach to making, one which treats the materials as improvising musicians treat musical notes. Writing about John Coltrane, David P. Brown explains, "In such works as 'My Favorite Things,' he obliterates the song as a sound object [. . .] in order to use fragments of the song as raw materials and resources." (14) My most recent approaches to found materials work in this improvisatory (15) way, the original material being broken up and fragments becoming poetically allusive resources in the new narrative which builds outward from the source components. This use of materials is not a mere post-modern agglutinative bricolage but rather—as Coltrane was expressing with his free jazz improvisations—a statement of optimistic modernism. In rejecting the applied illustrative narrative, I have found a way of creating pieces of narrative jewelry which respect and enhance the historic, social and political narratives of the original material.

NOTES

1. The two are not the same: found objects are left more or less intact and identifiable; found materials are transformed, rather as traditional jewelers transform silver or gold.

2. J. Cunningham, *Maker, Wearer, Viewer*. Glasgow: Scottish Arts Council, 2005.

3. L. Den Besten, "Reading jewellery. Comments on narrative jewellery." Last modified February 25, 2006. https://klimt02.net/forum/articles/reading-jewellery-comments-narrative-jewellery-liesbeth-den-besten.

4. Ibid.

5. Elizabeth Goring, quoting Kevin Coates in *Kevin Coates: A Hidden Alchemy, Jewels and Table-Pieces*. Stuttgart: Arnoldsche, 2008.

6. Helen Clifford, in *Kevin Coates: A Hidden Alchemy, Jewels and Table-Pieces*. Stuttgart: Arnoldsche, 2008.

7. See Yvonne Hackenbroch, *Renaissance Jewellery*. New York: Sotheby Parke Bernet, 1978.

8. My first found-object works date from around 2006 when I found some discarded, rusted tools and materials in an abandoned factory in Glasgow and I was immediately struck by a sense of loss, both social and political.

9. More overtly political works include *Empire State Human*, 2012; the untitled works for the *Enough Violence* show, 2013; and *Walk Like A Man (Sex Crime)* for Boris Bally's *Imagine* show, 2016. See also Dauvit Alexander, and Simon Murphy. *ENOUGH Violence: Artists Speak Out.* Pittsburgh: Society for Contemporary Craft, 2013. Further references to the political nature of the work can be found on my weblog, http://wringhim.blogspot.co.uk/.

10. Jo Pond, *In.Ti.Mate* exhibition catalogue. San Francisco: Velvet Da Vinci, 2015.

11. Bob Ebendorf, quoted in Vigna, Caroline, et al. (Eds.), *Robert W. Ebendorf: The Work in Depth*. Racine: Racine Art Museum, 2014.

12. NOT "a new language of material"—the language has not changed but the use and disposition of the elements of language has.

13. Elizabeth Moignard, *Narrative and Memory*, from J. Cunningham, *Maker, Wearer, Viewer*. Glasgow: Scottish Arts Council, 2005.

14. David P. Brown, *Noise Orders: Jazz, Improvisation and Architecture*. Minneapolis: University of Minnesota Press, 2006.

15. Historically, the role of improviser in jewelry has been taken by the wearer: the traditional "charm bracelet" in which the wearer intermittently adds charms with personal symbolism as they can be afforded; rockers' rings, lying somewhere between the symbolic and protective, both figuratively as an amulet and literally as a knuckle-duster; hip-hop neck-chains strung freely as symbols of power, sexuality, and wealth. In these cases, the wearer creates a personal narrative from the juxtaposition of jewelry made by others.

NARRATIVE
WORKS

RODRIGO ACOSTA ARIAS

My work is based on investigating the connection that can be established between jewelry and the diversity of garments, and jewelry's relationship with memory and the body.

People's relationships with their bodies through the garments they wear, being seen and concealing, being and not being. States of being and feelings are reflected in the garments that shape the body. Garments, memory and the traces—both physical and mental—they leave on those who use them.

A process of deconstruction, only to rebuild again. I am interested in fashion as a social phenomenon, as a construct of culture, as a part of the identity of a person, the reason why people choose what they choose to wear. In this way, artistic jewelry allows me to combine two different worlds, by using classic jewelry techniques and garment production techniques, creating pieces that border between jewel-art and fashion-art.

Chaos is needed for new creative vision. Many times, my search for the new has led me to disorder, to chaos . . . . I need to be carried away by what I feel, what I have experienced, by the natural or inner impulse that provokes an action or a feeling . . . free of prejudice, without awareness of reason.

Maker: Rodrigo Acosta Arias | **Title:** *Desformas* | **Materials:** Fabric, brass, cotton thread and steel wire | **Size:** 190 mm × 100 mm × 50 mm | **Image credit:** Adolfo López

RAMEEN AHMED

Trained in architecture, Rameen currently works as a studio metal artist. Her work incorporates the concept of jewelry as contemporary wearable art, akin to sculpture. As part of her creative vision she uses non-traditional materials such as rusted iron, perforated steel, and cactus ribs and pairs them with traditional silver, gold and other semi-precious materials.

Her narrative pieces tend to delve into the geopolitical nature of where she lives. In particular her personal perspective on the border issues between the southwest deserts of the USA and northern Mexico.

Maker: Rameen Ahmed | **Title:** *Desert Talisman* | **Materials:** Sterling silver, found plastic water bottle cap sealers, Sonoran desert devil's claw and found bullet casing with nickel pin-back | **Size:** 127 mm × 127 mm × 114 mm | **Image credit:** Rameen Ahmed

Narrative: Survival in the extreme desert has one solitary barometer: water. Water literally predicts life or death, especially during the long trek of (Mexico-USA) border crossing on foot, where there is no "found" water. The current symbol of that instrument is the container. It is the plastic water bottle that each "journey(wo)man" and child has to carry and use judiciously. And the discarded "sealer" of that container denotes the quenching of thirst, real and metaphysical.

A talisman, by incorporating the objects one fears and/or wants to attract, through the process of creation endows the wearer with magical properties against harm. The entwining bottle sealers are emblematic of the stark practicalities of hope and salvation amidst the beautifully desiccated but dangerous forms from the desert. The pollution of these objects reminds the viewer/wearer that, on the border, even the noblest aspirations can come at a cost.

MAE ALANDES

Mae Alandes works with different metal, enamel and recycled materials, such as pencil shavings.

I think that narrative jewelry is not only ornamental, it can take advantage of the opportunity that other arts do not offer: jewelry goes to the street, on the hand as a ring or in the lapel as a brooch. I conceive narrative jewelry as an artistic tool to express myself. In my work I employ humor to make a critical social comment.

Maker: Mae Alandes | **Title:** *Why Is the Middle Finger [in Spanish, the "Heart" Finger] the Favorite of Women? Because It's the Longest* |
Materials: Brass | **Size:** 75 mm × 5 mm × 15 mm | **Image credit:** Mae Alandes

Narrative: The middle finger (in Spanish, "heart" finger), a ring-shaped heart, how it changes everything with another point of view. As love and sex go hand in hand.

DAUVIT ALEXANDER

Rusty bolts lie by the side of the road. A coffee jar filled with corroded spring washers sits on the windowsill of a disused engineering works. Someone throws a cast iron fencing spike into a skip. A piece of pitted steel washes up on the beach.

These are not the images normally associated with the worlds of either "commercial" or "art" jewelry but they are the sources of the material for most of my work. Combining these materials—especially corroded steel and iron—with precious metals and gemstones, using the skills of the traditional fine jeweler, I aim to make pieces which are aesthetically pleasing, technically interesting and, if possible, humorous: if they happen to be not just a little unsettling or disturbing, so much the better.

My jewelry is primarily aimed at men. Even in the supposedly free world in which we now live, jewelry for men is circumscribed by what footballers and actors wear, reported by magazines, filtered through a corrupting veil of media; men dare not strike out for fear of being tagged an outsider, a loser, effeminate . . . . Using what *would traditionally be seen as masculine materials—iron, steel—from traditionally masculine backgrounds—the road, the building site, the machine shop—I look back to the last time men could freely wear jewelry: the Renaissance.*

Renaissance jewelry was a glorious, allegorical, blackly humorous, alchemical mess. It was a triumph of skill and material over taste. It mixed precious with semiprecious with worthless, a riot of color and shape. It was huge and overblown. It verged on the unwearable, comfort sacrificed, preferring to make statements about the wearer's beliefs, power and money. So it is with my own work: it takes a bold person to wear a piece by The Justified Sinner.

I did not originally train as a jeweler—but as a gardener—and largely taught myself the skills of metalsmithing, something that I view as an ongoing process, constantly learning, improving and expanding, pushing both what is considered possible and what is considered acceptable in jewelry.

Maker: Dauvit Alexander | **Title:** *Blood Will Have Blood: A Macbeth Brooch* | **Materials:** Found, corroded iron cap from an oil-tank; silver; pure iron sheet; polycarbonate reflector material from a crashed car; carved obsidian skull; garnets; strawberry quartz; black spinels | **Size:** Approx. 70 mm × 85 mm × 22 mm | **Image credit:** Dauvit Alexander, The Justified Sinner. Image courtesy of Andrew Neilson/Neilson Photography

Narrative: For many years, I have wanted to make a piece based on Shakespeare's *Macbeth* and this was the result. Taking the line from Act 3, Scene 4, "It will have blood; they say blood will have blood," I created this Gothic brooch in the form of a traditional "penannular" kilt brooch, reflecting the darkness of the play.

Maker: Dauvit Alexander | **Title:** *I Put a Spell on You* | **Materials:** Found, corroded iron conduit; corroded iron nut; silver; amethyst; mandarin and tsavorite garnets; zircons; included quartz | **Size:** 75 mm × 45 mm × 45 mm | **Image credit:** Dauvit Alexander, The Justified Sinner. Image courtesy of Andrew Neilson/Neilson Photography

Narrative: A terrible pun on the idea of "hex," a hex nut becomes a spell and a tribute to one of my absolute favorite songs, written by Screamin' Jay Hawkins and performed by Diamanda Galás. I created this piece imagining that it was for Diamanda to wear as she sings the song of love and insanity.

Maker: Dauvit Alexander | **Title:** *20,000 Leagues Under the Seas* | **Materials:** Laser-sintered, bronze-infused steel; large found, corroded iron washer; found steel CO2 cylinder; sterling silver; fine silver; 18k gold; opalised fossil squid; carved pink opal starfish; diamonds; jadeite; tsavorite garnets; pearls; porcelain faux coral; blue zircons; chrysoprase; blue and green chalcedony; paraiba tourmaline; peridots; blue topaz; rough peridot and apatite crystals | **Size:** Collar approx. 400 mm outside diameter; pendant approximately 90 mm × 110 mm × 40 mm | **Image credit:** Dauvit Alexander, The Justified Sinner. Image courtesy of Andrew Neilson/Neilson Photography

Narrative: I made this piece based on Jules Verne's amazing book, *20,000 Leagues Under The Sea*. The body of the squid is made from opalised fossil squid body! The beast is described in the book, "It swam crossways in the direction of the Nautilus with great speed, watching us with its enormous staring green eyes. Its eight arms, or rather feet, fixed to its head, that have given the name of cephalopod to these animals, were twice as long as its body, and were twisted like the furies' hair" and I have combined this description with the beast in the James Mason film [version] of the book to create the one here, departing from zoological accuracy by giving it Verne's "eight arms" rather than the correct ten (which would have driven Carol, who carved the wax, to distraction!). The eyes are jade with tsavorite garnets set over and the steel Nautilus has peridot portholes and a garnet-set propeller which was made using CAD/CAM processes and which really spins when blown.

JULIE ALLISON

Julie Allison is a jewelry designer and maker. She is currently based in Edinburgh at Coburg House Art Studios where she gets lots of inspiration from the beautiful Edinburgh architecture. Julie describes her work as a quirky, narrative collection of hand drawn memories.

I have been fascinated with narrative jewelry since art college. When visiting galleries I was always drawn to the narrative work and was overcome by my reaction to seeing a memory or story captured in a piece of jewelry. I always saw jewelry as very personal and what's more personal than telling your story through a piece. When I began creating and exhibiting my collections I loved watching people's reactions to my work, when they connected with it and how it made them feel. I love nothing more than creating a piece of jewelry that is very personal to the wearer, encapsulating their memories. As much as I love making I so enjoy seeing their face when they see their memory piece for the first time, it brings me such joy. There is so much beautiful jewelry in the world to look at but I feel that narrative jewelry is so interesting and will never go out of fashion. It's a piece that can last a lifetime and when you are gone your jewelry can be passed down and they will always think of you and the stories/ memories that you had told about the piece when they wear it.

Maker: Julie Allison | **Title:** *Let's Go Fly a Kite* | **Materials:** Drift wood, silver, steel, Lazertran | **Size:** 105 mm × 70 mm | **Image credit:** Julie Allison edited by Ejike Wosu

Narrative: A favorite childhood memory of flying a kite that I'm sure most people have. The excitement of seeing it soar into the air for the first time, the noise of it flapping in the warm summer breeze. The spectacular scene of lots of kites in the air, flying free like giant colorful birds.

INÊS VESPEIRA DE ALMEIDA

Inês Almeida was born in Lisbon in 1977. She sought (and found) new languages in the field of jewelry at the Escola Massana Centre d'Art i Disseny in Barcelona, the city where she lived for seven years. In 2003 she returned to the Portuguese countryside and a year later started working as a teacher of Project and Goldsmith Technologies at the Antonio Arroio Artistic School in Lisbon, where she remains today.

Maker: Inês Almeida | **Title:** *Invisibilidade II* | **Materials:** Alpaca, brass, silver, glass, paint, coral beads and agate stone | **Size:** 35 mm × 22 mm × 5 mm | **Image credit:** Vitor Loureiro

PATRICIA ALVAREZ

Patricia Alvarez is a jeweler and a member of Joyeros Argentinos. She studied with different silversmiths and participated in many exhibitions.

When jewelry tells a story it is magical.

I am passionate about nature, colors, feelings, stories, of life itself.

My jewelry allows me to capture all I feel and show it to others. These works are for me a journey of discovery, of meetings, an order of the soul, an internal release. To tell stories through my jewelry I surrender my intimacy, and the wearer will feel part of it and of the story.

Maker: Patricia Alvarez | **Title:** *Time Tenderness* | **Materials:** Silver, cooper, frozen agate, ceramic paint | **Size:** 420 mm | **Image credit:** Patricia Alvarez

Narrative: "In times of violence, I have time tenderness for you."

In this piece I represent my concern for my grandchildren because of the violent times we live in, and try to compensate with time tenderness towards them.

PETER ANTOR

Peter Antor is a metalsmith who uses jewelry as a platform to discuss architectural forms and concepts. Peter is currently working at Haystack Mountain School of Craft in Maine.

Maker: Peter Antor | **Title:** *Architectonic Rings #1* (right) | **Materials:** Sterling silver, cement, ebony, plexiglass, 24k gold leaf, powder coat | **Size:** Approximately 64 mm × 67 mm × 25 mm | **Image credit:** Peter Antor | **Title:** *Architectonic Rings #2* (left) | **Materials:** Sterling silver, cement, ebony, 24k gold leaf, powder coat | **Size:** Approx. 76 mm × 76 mm × 76 mm | **Image credit:** Peter Antor

Narrative: *Architectonic Rings* uses jewelry as a platform to explore my passion for architecture both past and present. By combining the spatial and structural qualities of architecture with the intimacy created between jewelry and its wearer, I encourage the viewer to explore, discover, and question the work.

Architecture allows viewers to immerse themselves completely within it. It can be appreciated for its artistic aesthetic and functional integrity. Jewelry is also functional, but instead of engulfing the viewer, it becomes an extension of the body. By fabricating with mixed materials I can decisively create, conceal and reveal physical spaces.

Small intricate sculptures draw the audience in close to view the work intimately. This closeness can create a quiet atmosphere allowing the viewer to reminisce about the past or daydream for the future. The architectural elements reference, but do not point to specific buildings. Instead the juxtaposed components encourage the audience to place them in an imagined environment.

ALAN ARDIFF

Stories connect people, and that is what gives me the greatest pleasure in making narrative jewelry. Narrative jewelry is not just attractive pieces of jewelry to wear, both the wearer and admirer get to be part of the story. My work also has another dimension in that it is kinetic—as the wearer moves, the chain activates the mechanism within the piece. People are naturally attracted to movement and this *invariably ensures reactions to the work as it is worn—creating random connections between strangers and from this new stories are started. This piece was inspired by my friendship with "Red Mole" aka Paul Preston, as we have taken many, many journeys in our imaginings.*

Maker: Alan Ardiff | **Title:** *Out of This World—Mole and I in Space* | *Kinetic Pendant—Spaceship Rocks on Its Journey through Space* | **Materials:** Gold, silver, diamonds and gem stones | **Size:** 5 cm diameter | **Image credit:** David Cantwell

HEBE ARGENTIERI

Hebe Argentieri is a jeweler based in Junin, Buenos Aires. She intends to communicate ideas, emotions and memories through her pieces. Transformation, whether of the environment or her most private world, is of particular significance in her work. Also important are the materials chosen to convey her ideas—these may include debris from a fire, plastic, paper or flowers.

Maker: Hebe Argentieri | **Title:** *Voices* | **Materials:** Oxidized nickel silver, plastic, paper | **Size:** 220 mm × 150 mm × 40 mm | **Image credit:** Damián Wasser

Narrative: Forty years ago the military seized political power in my country, Argentina. This dictatorship, that lasted until 1983, carried out a plan against the media in order to control all the information that could reveal the massive human rights violations and economic disaster that was taking place. Thirty-thousand people were abducted, tortured and killed during this time. Among them, many writers and journalists who tried to inform and alert the people about what was going on. My necklace *Voices* includes the names of all these journalists and writers.

CHRISTINE ATKINS

Christine Atkins is an Australian sculpture artist predominantly working in metal and timber. Atkins work is layered with personal and collective experiences, environmental awareness and the use of nature as metaphor.

For many of us it is not a matter of making a conscious decision to create from a narrative perspective, rather it is an inability not to that drives us. Personally, when working from a narrative I have a deeper more personal connection with the work as it is created with meaning and purpose rather than an object created purely for aesthetics. Narrative practice encourages expressive freedom, yet paradoxically allows for complete control. It is the creator who decides if the story is fantasy or fact, how much or how little is shared and if the narration is past, present or future. This freedom allows the narrative to be representational or abstract, overt and confrontational, subtle or perhaps even slyly hidden. Each body of work, each individual piece provides an opportunity to learn more about the world, human nature or one of many infinite possibilities. It is inevitable from this immersion to gain a sense of how, why and where we ourselves fit within this retelling.

Maker: Christine Atkins | **Title:** *In Real Life I Am Less Than 1 mm* | **Materials:** Bronze, recycled sterling silver, mica, cotton thread, wood, synthetic diamonds, recycled gold | **Size:** 340 mm × 130 mm × 16 mm | **Image credit:** Christine Atkins

Narrative: Beetles are intriguing, ranging in color from rich velvety reds, iridescent blues and greens to metallic browns and blacks. With around 450,000 identified species, beetles represent approximately forty percent of the insect world and make up around a quarter of the whole animal kingdom. With beetles so colorful, diverse and prevalent how is it we do not often notice them around us? Growing to less than a minuscule 0.5 millimeter featherwing beetles provide us with one possible answer.

SHIRI AVDA

Shiri Avda is a jewelry designer and an artist who creates on the borderline between the philosophical and the wearable. Shiri is an award-winning designer who exhibits worldwide and whose work has been published in several art and design books. Her studio is located in the fashionable Noga neighborhood in Tel Aviv, Israel.

Narrative is the force behind my creations.

It always starts with an initial story or thought that I want to explore. And my way to figure those thoughts out is the process of making jewelry. It is a non-literal way of thinking; it is exploring thoughts through materials, colors and shapes. Hence, some of the pieces reflect the discussion happening within me and some are the resolution.

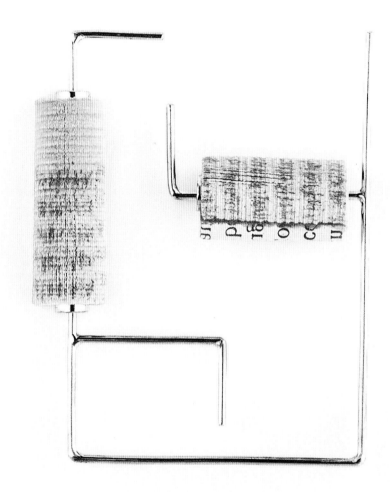

Maker: Shiri Avda | **Title:** *A-Maze (Conceptual Two-Fingers Ring)* | **Materials:** "Fur" fabricated from an old book, brass | **Size:** 60 mm × 45 mm × 13 mm | **Image credit:** Nir Slakman

Narrative: This year I found myself thinking a lot about the role of religion and prayer in an instant pop culture era. Making jewelry helps me to reflect and figure out my thoughts. This conceptual two-fingers ring holds a secret. It combines elements from several religions: the pagan maze, the Buddhist praying wheels, the monotheist praying book. Further inspection reveals that the praying wheels are made of "trash literature."

ALISON BAILEY

I believe that objects can vividly revive one's memories and have the power to evoke comfort and nostalgia. Most of my work involves a narrative revolving around places of comfort, most specifically my grandmother's house. The contrast, color, repetition and tactile qualities of my pieces preserve my memories of these places and experiences. I work in metal because of its preciousness and its permanence. I use fabric in combination with metal because of the contrasting properties of the two materials. The fabrics in my work come from various sources: from my grandmother, some are found, and others designed and printed by me.

Maker: Alison Bailey | **Title:** *Pebbles of the Mississippi* | **Materials:** Roller-printed and hollow-formed pewter; vintage, hand-dyed, and digitally designed and printed fabrics; freshwater pearls; sterling silver and embroidery thread | **Size:** 19 mm × 254 mm × 76 mm | **Image credit:** Alison L. Bailey

Narrative: When I was young my parents would take my brother and I to visit my grandmother. She lived in a small town in Wisconsin located in the bluffs overlooking the Mississippi River. I remember investigating the rocks along this majestic river. This necklace is in honor of my grandmother and the times I spent in her house. She was a quilter and she taught me how to sew and I cherish the memories I have of her, her house and the rocks along the banks of the mighty Mississippi.

HAZEL BAKER

Hazel Clarrie Baker is a jewelry and object maker from Wales. Hazel's work focuses on aesthetic; texture and color play a particularly important role, while underlying narratives invite the wearer to explore.

I am a bit of a hoarder. I love found objects, particularly those that remind me of something. The objects I use, usually have a narrative directly related to my personal experiences. My collection "Mabandod and Things" takes inspiration from my early childhood memories, and my current home in rural Wales. Both dwellings are smallholdings, which is where my rustic and unrefined aesthetic springs from. Most of the narratives in my work are very personal. I don't need the wearer/viewer to understand them. In fact I like the idea of new narratives being put onto them depending on who is wearing them.

I start with the object and create compositions with other objects and bits of metal. When I am happy with the composition I put it together, and then I can build it up, or work into it, or add another composition. I hate writing . . . . But I love talking and communicating so my jewelry gives me a voice and individual elements inspire me to tell a story through the creative process of jewelry making. My pieces are all individual and many are unusual in that they do not conform to many western ideas of jewelry as "neat shiny items." My pieces don't deliberately challenge the usual formats but neither do they conform. I am using the narrative of individual elements to help express the emotions of the wearer.

Maker: Hazel Baker | **Title:** *Mushroom* | **Materials:** Copper, found objects, thread, beeswax, paper | **Size:** 70 mm × 40 mm × 35 mm | **Image credit:** Hazel Clarrie Baker

Narrative: An underlying theme throughout "Mabandod and Things" is my eating habits as a child. The piece reminds me of mushrooms, which I used to hate. The papers inside the copper containers are recipes from an old recipe book I found on the farm. The recipes I have chosen are things I would never have eaten as a child. One of the found objects is a medicine canister, which I have used to symbolize being ill with asthma as a child.

MELISSA BALDOCK

Melissa Baldock is an art jewelry maker and silversmith. Her studio is located on a rural property in the hills of Snug, Tasmania, Australia. Her background in horticulture and land conservation has led to her look to the natural environment and its symbolism, aesthetics, local history and culture for inspiration. Her intention is to create meaningful art jewelry pieces, which are anecdotal of her home, are sympathetic to her heritage and culture and are an indication of the preciousness and wonder of the many World Heritage areas in her own home state.

Narrative: I created this ring with the intention of bringing back to life a convict brick re-sourced from the demolition of a dilapidated convict-built outhouse. The shape and form are important aspects in the story that are associated with this piece. I wanted to preserve a piece of history, open up a conversation about the past while simultaneously showing respect to the original maker of the brick. The original maker being one of the many convicts who were transported to Tasmania, to colonize and build the island state to what it is today. By recycling the original convict brick, which is imbued with the energy of the original maker, the piece is more a collaboration of the past craftsperson and myself. Tasmania's convict history tells a story of crime, punishment, toil, endurance and survival in some of the severest, yet most beautiful environments in the world.

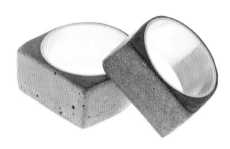

Maker: Melissa Baldock | **Title:** *Convict Brick Ring* | **Materials:** Found convict brick, sterling silver, resin | **Size:** 20 mm × 20 mm × 11 mm | **Image credit:** Melissa Baldock

COLLEEN BARAN

Colleen Baran is a Canadian artist who has exhibited in eleven countries and has been widely published.

My continued inspiration by words and narratives comes from a lifelong love of books. As a child libraries were always my favorite places, in them I could always find my favorite authors, magical worlds and exciting new facts. I read voraciously. That love of stories has always stayed with me, inspiring works that explore stories based on my own life.

Narrative: In the "Like Wearing a Love Letter" series I wanted to make jewelry that was like a love letter; like preserving a memory or a thought of love.

Pieces include small phrases, letters or words that evoke stories and cumulatively tell ongoing narratives. Little stories of love that can be: sincere, ironic, deep, passionate, conflicted, uncertain, comfortable, simple or complex. Possibly a permanent record of a fleeting thought, a declaration of a permanent bond or an artifact of a love no more.

you make my heart beat faster

Maker: Colleen Baran | **Title:** *You Make My Heart Beat Faster* | **Materials:** Sterling silver, custom made rubber stamps, ink | **Size:** 5 mm × 43 mm × 23 mm | **Image credit:** Colleen Baran

HEBA BARAZI

American-Syrian artist Heba Barazi is a metalsmith and polymer clay artist. She maintains an active studio practice making and selling wearable art objects through local retail galleries and internationally.

Humans are the only living species on this planet concerned with beautifying their world with art. For me, making beautiful objects of art is to experience my humanity. Making beautiful objects of art loaded with meaning and purpose is to bring humanity to the experience of my world. Recognizing the strong bond we form with objects, especially jewelry, I choose to express my art through wearable objects telling stories and changing hearts. In doing so, I hope that my creations resonate with people more intimately than art and more lasting than thoughts.

Maker: Heba Barazi | **Title:** *Syria . . . Told Through Rings, the Pomegranate* | **Materials:** Polymer clay, sterling silver and glass beads | **Size:** 36 mm × 36 mm × 36 mm | **Image credit:** Heba Barazi

Narrative: "Can't speak of Damascus, without the Jasmine trailing up my fingers

And, I can't say her name, without my mouth brimming with apricot juice, pomegranate, berries and quince"

—poet Nizar Qabbani

This work is part of the "Syria . . . told through rings" story, a reaction to the disturbing conflicts that brought Syria to the forefront of our daily news, erasing its glorious legacy and imprinting it with images of war, destruction and savagery.

The story is inspired by one of Syria's most famous poets, Nizar Qabbani, who wrote "I am a ring jeweled by Damascus . . . ." With this story, I am trying to remind people that Syria is not just war, it is a rich land of natural beauty and a people with a long history of literature and culture.

GILLIAN BATCHER

Gillian E. Batcher owns Jewel Envy, a collaborative studio located in the heart of the Roncesvalles Village in Toronto, Canada, where she designs and makes jewelry marketed under the label PASH Jewelry Design. In addition to making jewelry she teaches classes from her studio, George Brown College, and OCAD University.

I often work in narrative as I find jewelry has an almost limitless ability to be manipulated and transformed by the creator for storytelling.

There are few restrictions on materials, dimensions, and scale except those imposed by the maker. By its very nature it invites interaction between the piece and the wearer as well as viewers. The body as display takes a story out of the personal home domain, where much art is privately appreciated, and invites interaction with anyone we encounter in our public lives; giving those around the wearer a glimpse of more than just a sense of one's fashion.

Maker: Gillian Batcher | **Title:** *Pumping Heart* | **Materials:** Sterling silver, 24k gold leaf, synthetic rubies and sapphires, plastic, resin heart | **Size:** 70 mm × 90 mm × 30 mm. Necklace 640 mm in length, hanging portion with pump 650 mm long, fabricated | **Image credit:** Paul Ambtman

Narrative: Red needs only to be mentioned and stylized hearts spring to mind. This commercially inspired notion of love has facilitated the creation of an entire language of feelings and emotions tied to this simple symbol. *Pumping Heart* reflects the sentiments of the heart that red inspires in us. These feelings are illogically connected to the actual heart muscle but are ingrained in our society's views and beliefs.

The symbolic heart allows us to paradoxically both associate and disassociate with our feelings in order to embrace and accept them. These pre-packaged sentiments depict how we interweave our life, made possible through blood, with our emotions made possible by life.

HARRIETE ESTEL BERMAN

Harriete Estel Berman uses postconsumer, recycled materials to construct artwork ranging from jewelry, Judaica, sculptures and installations of social commentary. Her work is included in the permanent collections of sixteen museums and featured in over thrity-eight books.

Maker: Harriete Estel Berman | **Title:** Silicon Valley: *Circuit Board Bracelet with Plums Bracelet, Circuit Board Bracelet with Cherries Bracelet, Bead Bracelet with Resistors Bracelet* | **Materials:** Recycled tin containers, 10k gold rivets, aluminum rivets, wood, handmade paper, recycled computer transistors and computer circuit boards | **Size:** 270.5 mm × 290.5 mm × 270 mm depth | **Image credit:** Philip Cohen

Narrative: The fruit crate and bracelets symbolically represents the past, present and future of Silicon Valley where I live. Only decades ago Silicon Valley was covered with fruit orchards. Blossoms covered the ground like snow. Now it blooms with inventions and enterprising ventures.

ROBERTA BERNABEI

Roberta Bernabei is a jewelry maker and historian whose work has been exhibited at various national and international venues, including Victoria & Albert Museum; National Museum of Modern Art, Tokyo and the Museums of Decorative Arts in Berlin and Turin. She has been an academic at Loughborough University in the School of the arts since 2004. Her theoretical research into the history of "contemporary" jewelry has enabled the recent publication of her first book: *Contemporary Jewellers: Interviews with European Artists.*

My latest work has dealt with an interactive exhibition to imbue memory with jewelry. Participants are asked to talk about their memories and therefore the narrative and visual images provided by them become the main source of inspiration. The final brooches attempt to imbue their personal memories and my experience of working on a participatory project. The short narrative next to the piece of jewelry complements the work as it enables the viewer to be involved in the act of sharing the project.

Maker: Roberta Bernabei | **Title:** *Father and Son* | **Materials:** Engraved copper, glass beads, nickel, silver, 3-D printed nylon frames | **Size:** 70 mm × 45 mm × 15 mm | **Image credit:** Roberta Bernabei

Narrative: My work is based on people's memories. In *Cedar House project* every participant was invited to share her or his memory through narration and visual aids such as images or objects. The final brooch attempts to imbue personal memories and the experience of working on a participatory project. The narrative complements the work as it enables the viewer to be involved in the act of sharing the project.

This brooch represents a memory of father and son of a memorable day dedicated to the Remembrance Day in the UK. The sky was peppered with bright red poppies. This fragile but strong flower has been a source of inspiration to depict the relationship between "father and son" described by the person who took part at the participatory project.

CHIARA BET

A contemporary designer and jeweler—but an old artisan at heart—Chiara works in Sheffield (UK), thriving on the vibrant communities of fellow makers that are Yorkshire Artspace and the Academy of Makers.

Chiara's pieces clearly mirror her intrigue with the human body, folklore and mythology, inevitably morphed by personal narratives and fantasies. Dark regional tales from northern Italy, her native land, also provide inspiration, adding a further layer of meaning and zest to the artist's fanciful creations.

I have a deep fascination with the human figure and the fantastic, which inform my jewelry. The playful use of body forms and the rich palette of silver, gold, and black are evocative of fanciful creatures of a Classical Grotesque nature and opulent artworks of Renaissance times, a reflection of my Italian background. In my work, I aspire to recreate the sense of wonder and amusement so peculiar to such styles by embedding my own myths and legends in figurative pendants, brooches, earrings, and rings—offering bite-size escapism from a disenchantment of reality.

Maker: Chiara Bet | **Title:** *The 7 Deadly Sins (Neckpiece—Main Body)* | **Materials:** Silver, gold; garnets, freshwater pearl, opal | **Size:** Main body: Height: 230 mm; Width: 250 mm (at its widest—forged wires at the top); Depth: 50 mm. Necklet length: 300 mm | **Image credit:** Nigel Essex

Narrative: Meant to be understood in the tradition of ornamental grotesque, *The 7 Deadly Sins* represents exactly what it states. The carnal quality of its characters, each portraying a specific sin, displays the artist's fascination with teratology, both in its scientific context as well as its folkloristic aspect—a narrative created by word-of-mouth and flamboyant reports of bizarre human beings, before science could provide a logical explanation to the "frightful sightings."

KELVIN BIRK

Kelvin Birk trained as a gold- and silversmith in Germany and London, setting up his studio in London in 1998.

He has been teaching jewelry making and art related subjects at several colleges in Britain, Europe and Asia since 1999.

Within my work I am consciously disregarding what is traditionally considered precious and valuable. I revel in a lack of control, allow chaos to take over and the nature of the precious materials to dictate the final outcome of the pieces.

Maker: Kelvin Birk | **Title:** *In Memory* | **Materials:** Old engagement ring 18k gold, crushed onyx | **Size:** 25 mm × 20 mm | **Image credit:** Kelvin J. Birk

Narrative: This was one of my mum's rings, where she lost the pearl and she asked me to replace it. I never managed to do it before she died. After her death I crushed up some onyx beads, which came from a necklace of hers, and stuck it on the ring instead of the pearl.

LISA BJÖRKE

In Lisa Björke's works, which she does not always refer to as jewelry, she explores the relationship of objects to the human body and how the objects relate to the room.

By combining copper, brass, leather and different kinds of wood with more unconventional materials, she creates objects that in different ways are linked to the body and celebrate the craftsmanship and the worker as a phenomenon.

Lisa Björke works and lives in Stockholm. She has participated in both Swedish and international exhibitions and has received several grants.

Is there a borderline between reality and fantasy, and can we tell the difference? Is it straight, floating, vague or sharp? What is real and what is not; do we really need to know? Do I need to know? My work is about the balance or unbalance between the real and the fantasy. The pieces can be seen as a micro cosmos on the border, and they represent a portal to either of the two worlds: the real or the fantasy land. The pieces can be seen as characters in a play in an unexciting reality; they belong in the same family but play different parts. If this was a fairy tale who would be the evil stepmother and who would be the hero saving them all from despair? Whatever part they are playing I want them to be on the borderline where jewelry ends and imagination begins . . . .

But is it necessary for them to be jewelry? The easy answer to that would be yes, because I'm a jeweler . . . but the real answer for me would be that they need to be jewelry because I want the piece to be in a direct contact with the viewer or wearer, where it can be explored and investigated without any gap in between that can take some of the information away. When worn on the body we have the direct contact and it is easier to relate spontaneously and directly.

Jewelry can be a portal to journeys within the mind. We can say the beauty lies in the eye of the beholder, so we might as well say the journey will be in the mind of the same. Maybe they didn't grow out of my hand, but out from a dream into a scenery where they seem to belong. Are they what they look like, or do they keep a secret inside, are they what the hole was in Alice in Wonderland or the wardrobe was in Narnia, the portal to a surreal world? I sure hope so . . . . Only if I dare cross the border, if I drop the control, can I start a travel within the mind, in a land where reality and dream blend in with each other and the order of things is subverted and unpredictable, and you are invited to come along. Enjoy your journey!

Maker: Lisa Björke | **Title:** *Inner Nomad, Baby Blue* | **Materials:** Iron, iron powder, resin, lacquer | **Size:** 115 mm × 130 mm × 40 mm |
Image credit: Lisa Björke

Maker: Lisa Björke | Title: *Inner Nomad, Cream White* | Materials: Iron, iron powder, resin, lacquer | Size: 135 mm × 120 mm × 45 mm | Image credit: Lisa Björke

Narrative: Iron, Fe (from Latin *ferrum*)—atomic number 26

Iron is the cheapest and one of the most abundant of all metals, the most common element forming the planet Earth as a whole, forming Earth's outer and inner core.

I value the iron for its industrial features. It is hard and sustainable and to me precious . . . I invest time, thought and stories and I raise the value with every minute.

Iron is buildings, transportation, weapons, jewelry and a lot more. Iron is inside us and around us. Iron is society.

A traveler, a nomad, a human, an animal, a bird.

To settle, to nest, to find a home.

Maker: Lisa Björke | Title: *Inner Nomad, Dirty Yellow* | Materials: Iron, iron powder, resin, lacquer | Size: 120 mm × 90 mm × 50 mm | Image credit: Lisa Björke

GITTE BJØRN

Gitte Bjørn is a Danish goldsmith, apprenticed from 1986 to 1990.

Gitte has a seat on the board of the Goldsmith's Guild, and she is also the guild's only accredited Schaumeister (Show champion). Gitte's artistic career spans four decades, with works ranging from intricate jewelry across hollowware and contemporary silver sculpture to large bronzes in the public domain and even entire playgrounds, including an underwater divers' playground measuring approximately 50 by 200 meters.

Given the vast range of techniques that Gitte employs, her methodologies are necessarily many and diverse. However, all her works are sharply narrative and often figurative, and they are conceived of through a many-tiered process of runaway association, which is usually shaped into a surreal and humorous expression.

Maker: Gitte Bjørn | **Title:** *Love Sounds (Sonorous Rings)* | **Materials:** Silver, "valves" in 18k gold and diamonds | **Image credit:** Ole Akhøj

Narrative: The *Love Sounds* rings are an expression of that inflated, infatuated feeling that is being in love. Inside each ring, a nickel-silver comb is mounted which is played by a small steel ball. The sound is a beautiful tingling, reminiscent of that hopelessly in love feeling of the gut, triggered by a shaking of the hand wearing the ring.

The rings are finished in a glossy polish. The distorted images that are mirrored in the rings is an allegory of love's distorted reality.

Finally, some of the rings are equipped with a socket, set with a diamond. The sockets are shaped to resemble a valve, the association being to the inflated, ballon-like feeling of being in love, which is prone to sudden puncture. Using the valve it is theoretically possible to adjust the level of inflation, infatuation, the level of being in love-ness.

NISA BLACKMON

Nisa Blackmon is a vigorous hybrid of artist and biologist; she has been a practicing metalsmith since 1992. Her areas of interest and research include the relationships between jewelry, the body and the land, the collecting culture of natural history museums and the mediation of scientific instruments between "knowers" and knowledge.

My jewelry tells stories because I believe that objects have great power to shape, inform and illustrate our lives and memories. I use a lot of found objects and domestic materials, sometimes fragmented or transformed, to add the stories they bring with them to my own. When I am crafting my jewelry, the story I want to tell is at the forefront of my thinking, whether it is obvious in the finished piece or more in the background. Lately I have been trying to use narrative in a more subtle way, as I think this leaves more room in my work for other people to layer their narratives over mine. The coexistence of these narratives in a piece can create a connection with viewers of my work that I find very satisfying.

Maker: Nisa Blackmon | **Title:** *Autopsy* | **Materials:** Copper, freshwater pearls, cotton thread, glass microscope slide | **Size:** 240 mm × 750 mm × 25 mm | **Image credit:** Nisa Blackmon

Narrative: *Autopsy* focuses on the moment when the researcher's technician views the opened body of Henrietta, in which the tumors had become so widespread that "it looked as if someone had filled her with pearls." (Skloot, 2011)

This brooch is from a series based upon scenes from the book *The Immortal Life of Henrietta Lacks* by Rebecca Skloot. Henrietta Lacks was a poor black woman from Maryland who was diagnosed with, and later died from, uterine cancer. While being treated at Johns Hopkins Hospital, tissue samples from her tumor were sent (without her knowledge) to the labs of a researcher there, who developed them into one of the most famous and long-lived cell culture lines in history,

called HeLa cells. Despite the fame of the cell line and its widespread use in endeavors such as the development of the polio vaccine, Henrietta Lacks remained unknown for more than twenty years. Until then, her siblings and five children had no idea of the role their sister and mother had unwittingly played in the history of medicine.

This work was my attempt to interpret several of the moments in the book that struck me most deeply and express them in the language of jewelry. Traditional jewelry materials were combined with domestic materials and scientific lab paraphernalia to create a three-dimensional tableaux referencing the impactful moments.

IRIS BODEMER

Jewelry as an object of decoration does not attract my interest. The works, one after the other, turn into a picture story like a diary, notes about happenings and experiences.

Maker: Iris Bodemer | **Title:** *Untitled (Neckpiece)* | **Materials:** Bronze, diamond crystal, onyx, garnet, wool, thread | **Size:** 130 mm × 150.5 mm × 10 mm | **Image credit:** Julian Kirschler |

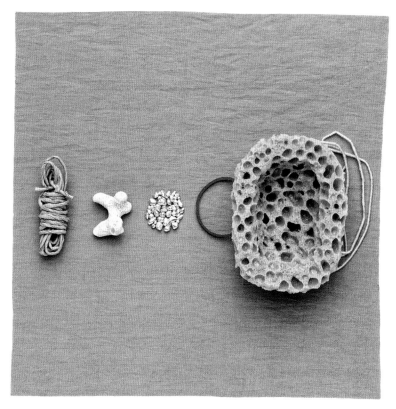

Maker: Iris Bodemer | **Title:** *Untitled (Neckpiece)* | **Materials:** Gold 999, coral, serpentine, sponge, string, rubber, textile | **Size:** 190 mm × 190 mm × 30 mm | **Image credit:** Julian Kirschler, Courtesy of Rotasa Trust Collection

KRISTINE BOLHUIS

Kristine Bolhuis is an independent jewelry maker. Her work explores form and structure resulting in minimalist, kinetic jewelry that moves and shifts as it is worn on the body.

It is unusual for me to turn toward narrative in my jewelry, as I tend to think more about structure than a story. However, in 2004 I gave birth to my first child. He was born with Treacher Collins Syndrome, a rare condition that causes significant hearing loss. This series of brooches derived from my experiences with using sign language to communicate with my son during his infancy. Individually, each of the small, metal brooches represents a thought communicated and as a whole they refer to the experience of trauma and the transformative power of art to mediate life experience. These pieces are signs, gestures, a narrative of hands.

Maker: Kristine Bolhuis | **Title:** *Talking Together* | **Materials:** Sterling silver, nickel alloy | **Size:** 90 mm × 30 mm × 10 mm | **Image credit:** Katie MacDonald

Narrative: Mother and son. Long worn fingers and little chubby fingers talking together, being close.

TORIL BONSAKSEN

Toril Bonsaksen is a metal artist who works with jewelry, sculpture and public art. She is based between the capital of Norway, Oslo, and Tåvær in the north of Norway.

I collect nature's treasures. Seedpods, corals, twigs and stones and choose those who contain a certain personality, for example a shape that resemble a bird. The association is enhanced by adding precious stones or other elements. This gives further shape and life to the story of the bird. The birds; Thinking about the Flyway II is made from radish seed pods. I have used phenomena in bird migration to illustrate stories about identity, belonging and inner turmoil.

Maker: Toril Bonsaksen | **Title:** *Thinking about the Flyway II* | **Materials:** Organic material, oxidized copper, ruby, silver | **Size:** 30 mm × 60 mm × 30 mm | **Image credit:** Kirsti Reinsberg Mørch

Narrative: Many birds migrate long distances along a flyway. The most common pattern involves flying north in the spring and returning in the autumn to warmer regions in the south.

KEN BOVA

Ken Bova is a past president of the Society of North American Goldsmiths (SNAG) with work in the permanent collections of the Smithsonian National Art Gallery, The Philadelphia Art Museum, and The Georgia Art Museum among others.

He combines the two areas of his training, jewelry and metalsmithing, in one-of-a-kind mixed media wearable assemblages focusing on narrative content.

As a kid I used to take the seeds from mimosa pods and string them with a needle and thread into long heishi-like strands for necklaces. I kept them in cigar boxes, along with bits of colored paper, drawings, feathers, small bones, stones, colored shards of glass and treasure maps that I drew myself—relics of an imaginative and active childhood.

In addition to art, I studied philosophy and religious studies in graduate school with Dr. Lynda Sexson. In her book Ordinarily Sacred *she says that inventories of children's treasures and those of religious holy places are remarkably similar; that the "junk" that's precious to kids, and adults, is the stuff of the sacred.*

She writes, "The sacred, when not bound by politics and economics, is nearer to something we call the aesthetic."

My work is, in part, the result of this heritage. It seeks to convey my fascination with the "sacred aesthetic" through story-telling; through color and line, objects of intimacy, elements of the landscape both external and internal and the wonder of small things that attract my attention. It is about mapping the treasures in my life. It is about precious junk becoming sacred, becoming aesthetic.

Maker: Ken Bova | **Title:** *In Mortem Memoria* | **Materials:** Sterling, 23k gold leaf, liquid enamel on copper (sgraffito, overfired), hair, dried miniature rose petal, Madison River garnet, baby teeth (human, canine), butterfly wing, beetle leg, armadillo shell | **Size:** 76.2 mm × 63.5 mm × 6 mm | **Image credit:** Ken Bova

Narrative: This brooch is one of three memorial pieces created after the loss of friends and family one year. This particular piece recalls aspects of my younger brother coupled with mementoes from our childhood.

JONATHAN BOYD

Jonathan Mathew Boyd is an artist, researcher and jeweler working from his studio in the Barra's in Glasgow. Jonathan has exhibited and given lectures about his work internationally. In 2014 he was the designer and lead manufacturer of the Glasgow 2014 Commonwealth Medals, estimated to have been seen by an audience of well over 2 billion.

I am an applied artist and jeweler working in a variety of material specializing in conceptual work and complex lost wax casting techniques. The works I create and exhibit look to explore relationships between the sculptural, art, design and the wearable. My aim is to create jewelry as an art form. To explore these relationships I use language and its connection with the environment, the person and the object as a set of complex narratives.

My work is inspired by our relationships to language and our environments. I am interested in how language can shape thoughts about an object and its context with works often being inspired by a text's narrative, structure, context and meaning. My most recent works have started to look at how language and environment overlap and the effect that modern advertising and information overload has on our daily reality. My works have now started to incorporate images next to text and the imagery comes from photographs I take in and around the city. This urban photography is inspired by the text and vice-versa.

Other narratives and themes that run through my work are value, perception, craft, film and the digital.

I create work through an extensive period of research and a rigorous artistic methodology. As an art form jewelry connects with us on a visceral, emotional level. We embed memories in the objects we choose to adorn us, because of this I have always believed that jewelry is a perfect medium for exploring narratives and themes which explore the human experience. I believe the audience cares not only how an object is crafted but also why it is made.

Maker: Jonathan Boyd | **Title:** *All My Own Thoughts and Words* | **Material:** Silver | **Image credit:** Jonathan Boyd

Narrative: When we are surrounded by a constant barrage of signs and imagery when can we ever produce an original thought? This piece explores the life of the city living artist.

DAVID BRAND

As a youth, I had the run of a 1920s steam powerplant managed by my engineer father. Thus, I'm attracted to old technology, and as an engineer myself I enjoy using found objects and technical elements in jewelry to tell fantastical stories about how the world is measured and how information is transmitted.

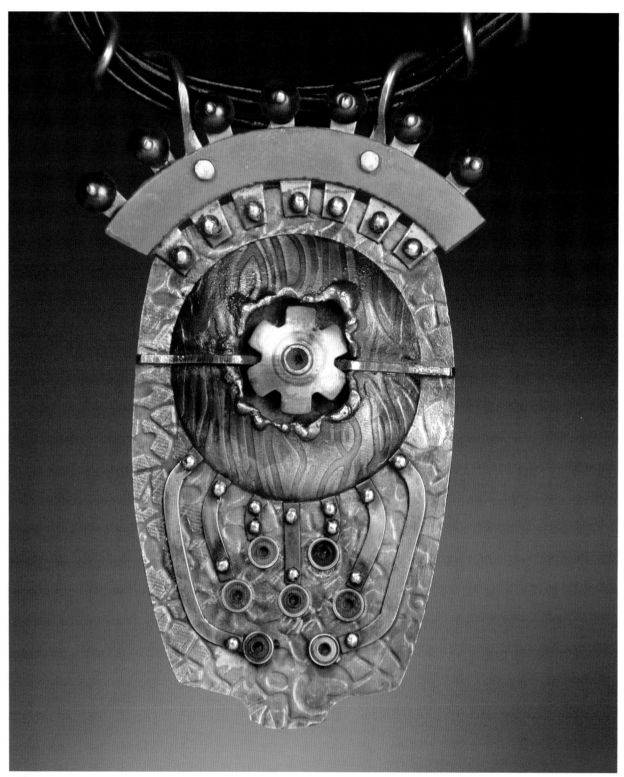

Maker: David Brand | **Title:** *Enigma Decoder* | **Materials:** Copper, bronze, silver, switch element from electronic device, pearls, friction washer from instrument, sapphire bearings from machinist dial indicator. Roller printed, solderer, and riveted |
Size: 88 mm × 55 mm × 6 mm | **Image credit:** David Brand

Narrative: Bombe was the name of an electro-mechanical machine developed in the UK by Alan Turing and others to defeat the Enigma code machine used by Germany in WWII to command its U-boat fleet. Further development occurred in my own city of Dayton, Ohio, USA. In this piece, the data arrive at the coiled structure at the top and are routed through the central spinning disc (many discs in the actual machine). The decoded results are sent out through the sapphire jewels at the bottom.

Maker: David Brand | **Title:** *Commentary on Current Economic Conditions* | **Materials:** Copper, bronze, steel, button from 1940s J.C. Penney's overalls, game token, lamination from electric motor, switch element with gold contacts, US penny | **Size:** 97 mm × 37 mm × 5 mm | **Image credit:** David Brand

Narrative: One view of economics is the effective management of labor and resources for the greater good. A more cynical view is that of a continuing argument about who gets the money. Currently there exists a growing disparity between rich and poor and as expressed in the piece, pay day somehow comes with the feeling that the value of our money is being hollowed out.

Maker: David Brand | **Title:** *Captain Midnight Weather Predictor* | **Materials:** Copper, bronze, steel, Captain Midnight member's pin and spinner advertising pieces, lamination from electric motor. Roller printed, soldered and riveted | **Size:** 95 mm × 60 mm × 5 mm | **Image credit:** David Brand

Narrative: During the 1930s and '40s, adventure-hero stories were popular radio entertainment and most featured advertising premiums to maintain continuing interest. In this piece, the propeller element (top) contains a litmus paper behind the "S" that changes color with humidity. In case that proves unreliable, one can do at least as good as the weatherman by spinning the disc at the bottom and reading the number appearing in the window on the back and looking in a table of predictions for the result.

SANNA BRANTESTAD

Sanna Brantestad is a jewelry artist whose work shows a great diversity of expressions and emotions. To Sanna, it's all about the narrative and personal.

Sometimes it's like a game I play; to tell stories without saying a word.

The narrative is always the starting point, the process and result in all my work. It starts maybe with a direction, an emotion and then the urge to be released and told. *It's a search after its purpose, its own expression. To fit pieces, to cut and glue, to break and mend a story together, something new is to be told. I can think that I choose to tell a story but in the end it is always the story that tells me its own tale. That is what it's all about for me.*

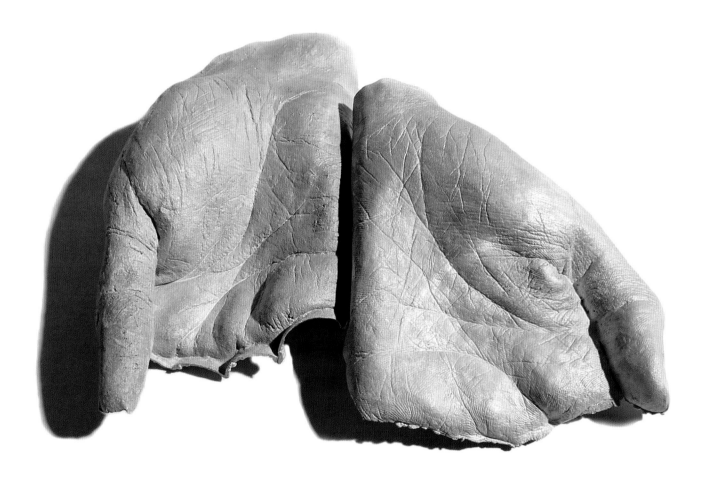

Maker: Sanna Brantestad | **Title:** *To What Remains When Everything Else Disappears—Brooch* | **Materials:** Copper, silver | **Size:** 160 mm × 120 mm | **Image credit:** Sanna Brantestad

Narrative: This is a work about days of grief. Lost grip. It's about memories. Imprints.

A tribute to the small things that mean the most. To what remains when everything else disappears. This work is a tribute to my dear mother Birgitta.

JULIE BROOKS

Julie Brooks is a native of North Carolina, currently residing in Seattle, Washington. Julie has been published in *1000 Rings*, *The Art of Enameling*, *500 Wedding Rings*, and *Humor in Craft*. She exhibits nationally and is included in the collections of David Freda and Rancho Obi-Wan in Petaluma, California.

The advantage of the emotions is that they lead us astray.
—Oscar Wilde

My work is a conversation between my past, present and future.

Through making, a method emerges to guide me during instances of contentment, conflict or longing for what may never be. Metalsmithing has influenced a way to delve into these vulnerabilities and uncertainties. The use of tools and handwork slows the immediacy of emotions to reflect on decisions I've made and ponder new possibilities. A facilitator of strength and transformation leading to the creation of narrative vignettes that serve as intimate witnesses to my life. They are expressions that embrace the beauty of the inherent value of emotions and states of awareness.

Maker: Julie Brooks | **Title:** *The Empty World (Brooch)* | **Materials:** Copper, enamel, oxidized sterling silver, 18k gold plate, stainless steel | **Size:** 69.85 mm × 57.15 mm × 12.7 mm | **Image credit:** Jason Dowdle

Narrative: It took several years for my divorce to be finalized, and I felt imprisoned by a person who wouldn't let me go. In 2010 I was granted my life back. A fresh start. I was relieved, but my mother voiced anxieties about the future. She believed that in my mid-30s I had missed the chance to have a family, a house, and a settled lifestyle. I didn't understand where this was coming from, as it was not the representation of my thoughts on the matter. But her loss was a different experience than mine and it sparked an idea for a new body of artwork. This collection was based on what becomes of expectations versus reality, the antiquated notion of the nuclear family, and what it means to "really have it all." I decided to make everything that this version of idealism would provide and its realistic disintegration.

The work is white enamel with sugar fired surfaces. They have the look of white Jordan almonds: sometimes used for symbolic wedding favors in Italian and Greek cultures, and adopted at weddings here in the United States. The bitter almond and the sweet sugar symbolizing the bitterness of life and the sweetness of love. I wanted to make something beautiful out of loss. Loss is sobering and reflection allowed a healing that I did not receive in the years leading to my divorce.

This is the perfect house, cast from a Monopoly game piece that serves as the dream house in symbolic form, set in an aerial view above a sprawling suburban cookie cutter neighborhood. The structure of the neighborhood is an abstracted grid pattern and references DNA. Specifically the nature versus nurture conversation as to the biological urge for women to settle down and have children.

SARA BROWN

Sara has exhibited nationally and internationally, and has recently had work published in *Showcase 500 Art Necklaces*, and *On Body and Soul: Contemporary Armor to Amulet*s. Her work, which integrates a variety of mediums and techniques, is largely influenced by and assembled from the examination of lived experiences.

For me, every piece is a story, and through making wearable objects I found that my work had slowly become my diary. Each piece is an entry made for reasons that vary from commemorating a moment or person of significance to the most mundane daily activities.

A phone call from a friend,
playing cards at the kitchen table.

The sudden death of someone dear.
Picking burrs out from shoelaces,
or dandelions from the cracks in the sidewalk.
Discovering an old poem my mother had written.

Breaking surroundings down into generalized patterns and shapes, moments into tightly cropped drawings or brief glimpses of text, I then reassemble these elements into a wearable object that I can carry with me. The starting points for each piece may vary in intensity, but when I approach each piece individually, those often forgotten moments in between it all are always treated as importantly as those with more significance.

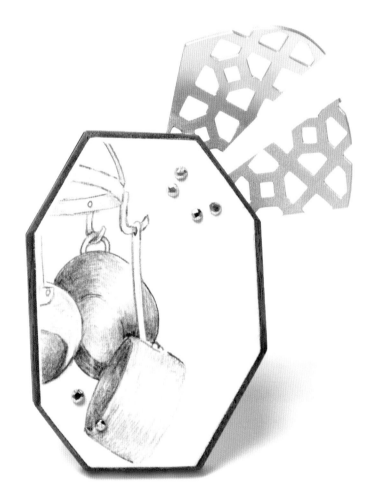

Maker: Sara Brown | **Title:** *Pots and Pans (Brooch)* | **Materials:** Sterling silver, walnut, paper, 10k gold, brass, copper, graphite | **Size:** 70 mm × 50 mm × 20 mm | **Image credit:** Sara Brown

Narrative: Those pans set at that angle. That pattern, poking out, barely visible from under the sink. From my seat in the kitchen these are a few of the details that will stick.

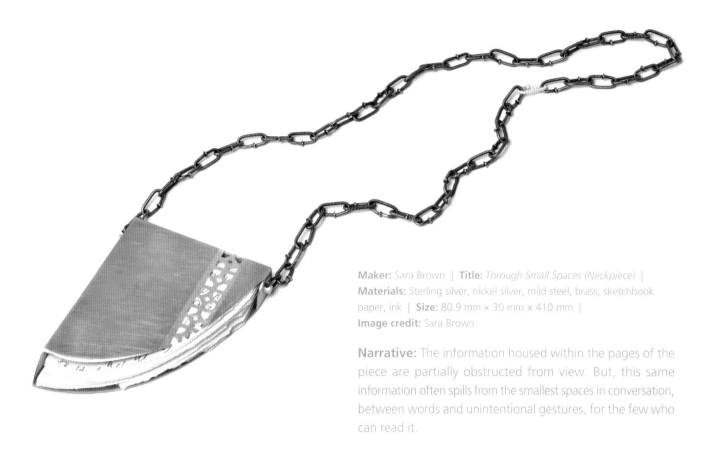

Maker: Sara Brown | **Title:** *Through Small Spaces (Neckpiece)* |
Materials: Sterling silver, nickel silver, mild steel, brass, sketchbook
paper, ink | **Size:** 80.9 mm × 30 mm × 410 mm |
Image credit: Sara Brown

Narrative: The information housed within the pages of the
piece are partially obstructed from view. But, this same
information often spills from the smallest spaces in conversation,
between words and unintentional gestures, for the few who
can read it.

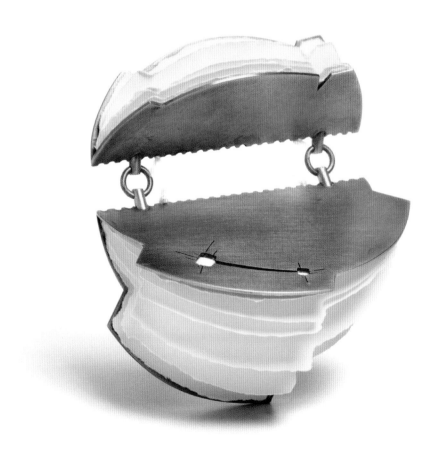

Maker: Sara Brown | **Title:** *Blanks (Brooch)* | **Materials:** Stainless steel, mild steel, brass, sketchbook paper, thread |
Size: 80.9 mm × 80.3 mm × 50.1 mm | **Image credit:** Sara Brown

Narrative: Being speechless, over and over again.

KATHLEEN BROWNE

Kathleen Browne is a metalsmith/jeweler who headed the Jewelry/Metals/Enameling Department at Kent State University until her recent retirement. Her artwork has been exhibited widely both in the U.S. and abroad and has been published and/or reviewed in numerous journals, books and catalogs. Kathleen is the recipient five Artist Fellowship Grants from the Ohio Arts Council.

I am at heart a storyteller. My work over the years has reflected a careful observation of human interaction, and often uses photography and its manipulation to provide commentary, sometimes with humor, about the human condition. For the creation of my jewelry, I have used photographic processes in very different ways—the anachronistic hand-painted black and white photo for its object quality, the appropriated and manipulated xeroxed image, and the digital and sometimes, pixelated image.

Maker: Kathleen Browne | **Title:** *Mood Swing (Necklace—front view)* | **Materials:** Fine silver, sterling silver, vitreous enamel, 24k gold, 18k gold | **Size:** 508 mm × 76.2 mm × 12.7 mm | **Image credit:** Shawn Wood |

Maker: Kathleen Browne | **Title:** *Mood Swing (Necklace—reverse side)* | **Materials:** Fine silver, sterling silver, vitreous enamel, 24k gold, 18k gold | **Size:** 508 mm × 76.2 mm × 12.7 mm | **Image credit:** Shawn Wood

Narrative: The images used in this work are appropriated from a pulp magazine printed during the 1950s titled *Secrets*. The magazine photos were overly dramatic and stagy, both tragic and unintentionally comic, but somehow they captured the zeitgeist regarding female transgression. These reconfigured and manipulated images freeze a moment in the daily drama of our lives and, set as jewels, they serve as paeans to the mundane.

Maker: Kathleen Browne | **Title:** *Limen (Necklace)* | **Materials:** Copper, sterling silver, vitreous enamel | **Size:** 584.2 mm × 88.9 mm × 12.7 mm | **Image credit:** Shawn Wood

Narrative: This work uses commercially-made ceramic decals made from photographs I have taken that describe liminal spaces or the spaces that exist in between. These threshold spaces serve as metaphors for transformation—a crossing over from one state to the next. By incorporating these images into my jewelry, they serve to commemorate the transitional nature of all things.

EMMA CAHILL

Emma Cahill is a jewelry designer who makes wearable objects using new technologies informed by her mother's love for gardening and the tools that create a beautiful garden. Emma is an award-winning designer and is a member of the Association of Contemporary Jewelry.

I make wearable objects and have an innovative approach to jewelry making. I make brooches and neckpieces from 3-D printed plastic which I then dye by hand. The color inspiration comes from the graduating hues of tulips, hydrangeas and the deep hues of beetroots.

I'm working with this narrative to celebrate my mother's creativity. I wanted to represent the process of gardening by creating a visual representation of garden tools. By working with multiple disciplines from new technologies, traditional metalwork skills and textile techniques, I challenge preconceptions of the materials used for jewelry and I challenge old-fashioned ideas of the garden.

Maker: Emma Cahill | **Title:** *Dipper Neckpiece* | **Materials:** Hand dyed 3-D printed plastic, rubber tubing, silver | **Size:** 280 mm × 240 mm | **Image credit:** Damien Maddock

Narrative: My work deals with the process of gardening, the main source of inspiration comes from my mother's garden and the hard work that she puts into it. Gardening is a tiring process of hacking and cutting but the results are beautiful and rewarding. My focus is on the gardening tools that aid this process.

JESSICA CALDERWOOD

Jessica Calderwood is an image-maker and sculptor who works in esoteric craft media. She uses a combination of traditional and industrial metalworking processes as a means to make statements about contemporary life. Her works are imbued with personal stories and vibrant color.

My most recent series combines botanical forms with fragments of the human body in order to address the narrative of human life cycles: growth, metamorphosis, aging, death. The choice to use flower and plant forms is multi-layered. Flowers have been used throughout history as symbols of the feminine: "she is as delicate as a flower." It can be found in mythology, literature, folklore and visual art. Western culture has an intricate system of flower symbolism that has been a way for humans to express and communicate complex emotions. I am interested in using these symbolic references in order to talk about issues of gender and identity. I choose to work narratively because my work is inspired by personal everyday experiences and beliefs. I enjoy compressing an event or emotive experience into a singular image to imply a before and after, leaving the viewer to fill in those moments that are not explicitly defined.

Maker: Jessica Calderwood | **Title:** *Wallflower* | **Materials:** Enamel, copper, sterling silver, China paint, stainless steel | **Image credit:** Jessica Calderwood

Narrative: *Wallflower* references both the flower itself used in the image, as well as the cultural reference to a person who feels shy or awkward, wishing to blend in with the wallpaper pattern, to become a chameleon. In order to make this piece, I conjured up vivid memories of seventh grade school dances and reinterpreted them through the lens the adulthood.

MELISSA CAMERON

Australian-born artist and writer Melissa Cameron lives and works in Seattle, Washington. Her works are in the collections of the National Gallery of Australia, the Cheongju City Collection in South Korea and The Arts Centre Melbourne.

Through the jewels I make, I work to forge an intimate connection between the viewer and wearer of my pieces, and an external narrative. This I do in the hope that through my practice I might facilitate an *understanding and respect for the interconnectedness of all humanity. I recognize and respect the narrative embedded in both new and used materials, and leverage the inherent meaning of domestic objects throughout my art. Interleaving my patterns among the signs and symbols of utilitarian objects to drive the forms, I share stories through my jewels, with the benefit that my message is conveyed directly to an audience, in a portrayal that I hope is richer than the sum of the parts.*

Maker: Melissa Cameron | **Title:** Ruchnoy Protivotankovy Granatomyot Works: *RPG @ 1:9 (Pin), 22m radius @ 1:9 (Neckpiece), Anti-personnel Round (Pin), Un-handle (Pendant)* | **Materials:** Powder-coated new steel trowel, stainless steel, poly cotton ribbon | **Size:** Largest: 440 mm × 125 mm × 35 mm | **Image credit:** Melissa Cameron

Narrative: The RPG series tells a story about the Rocket Propelled Grenade launcher (RPG is the Russian acronym), depicted here at 1:9 scale. The chosen scale echoes the nine million of these weapons that have been made so far, and the nine countries that still currently manufacture the weapon. The necklace that unfurls from the former hand-trowel is in a strip 2.444 meters in length, or 22 meters at the reduced scale, representative of the over 22 meter lethal radius of this weapon. The RPG is capable of four to six firings per minute. The smallest pin takes the form of an anti-personnel round, cut into four pieces to show the minimum rate of fire, and is also scaled at 1:9.

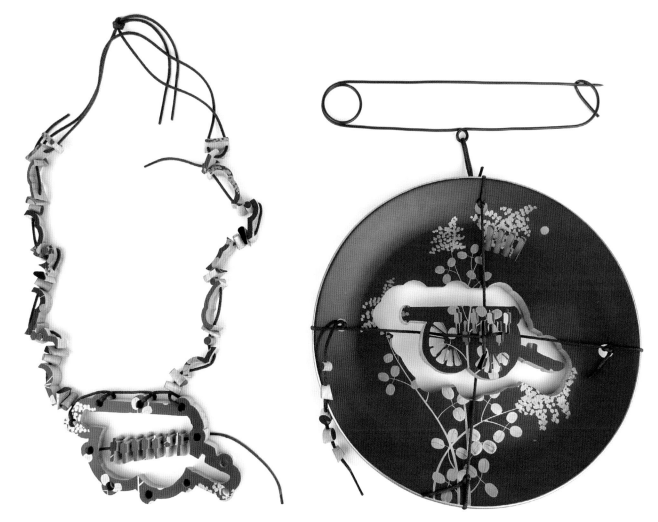

Maker: Melissa Cameron | **Title:** Cannon Works: *Tank—Cannon—Seven Personnel (Neckpiece)* and *11 RPH Cannon (Brooch)* | **Materials:** Vintage Japanese lacquer ware plate, copper, cotton cord | **Size:** Largest 400 mm × 110 mm × 10 mm | **Image credit:** Melissa Cameron

Narrative: *Cannon* presents a twenty-four pound cannon from the American Revolutionary War. Seven personnel were generally assigned to fire this piece, with which it was possible to fire approximately eleven cannon balls per hour. The face of the large brooch work depicts a clock face, while in the smaller neckpiece a silhouette of the cannon is bordered by a pattern of eleven circular holes.

Cannon and *Tank* form a part of my ongoing research into military technologies, entitled the Escalation Series. Conceived to present a historical continuum, the series pits similar ancient and modern military technologies against one another, in an attempt to question humanity's continuing relations with itself.

Maker: Melissa Cameron | **Title:** *Tank—M1 Abrams (Neckpiece)* and *1100 Shot Round (Breastplate)* | **Materials:** Non-stick coated pan, stainless steel | **Size:** Largest 400 mm × 110 mm × 10 mm | **Image credit:** Melissa Cameron

Narrative: The M1 Abrams is a battle tank produced by the US army and used by many nations, including Australia. It is generally configured to host at least forty rounds for the main cannon inside the cabin, alongside the four personnel. Amongst others, it fires the M1028 120mm anti-personnel canister cartridge (depicted coming out of the muzzle), which holds approximately 1,100 tungsten balls, each around one centimeter in diameter. There are 1,100 holes in the work between the neckpiece and the breastplate; a testament to the M1028 round's ability to effectively make the cannon into a shotgun.

BIFEI CAO

Bifei Cao is a cultural maker in metalsmithing and jewelry-based objects. Bifei was raised in a small mountain village in Southern China.

Bifei's multi-piece objects are a series of narrative pieces that are a fusion of his Chinese aesthetic with an expressiveness of contemporary life experience. Those objects can be worn on the body or stand alone, and embody stories gleaned from his childhood memories as well as those culture negotiations between both his native culture of China and other cultures. He hopes those objects could capture the attention of the viewer and engage them in a dialogue by utilizing materials.

Maker: Bifei Cao | **Title:** *Hide and Seek* | **Materials:** Sterling silver, 14k yellow gold, decal on enamel, clear coat finishing | **Size:** 40 mm × 18 mm × 114 mm | **Image credit:** Bifei Cao

Narrative: *Hide and Seek* also has a theme of children's games. A Chinese traditional brush painting was put on decal paper and set into the prepared form. Applying Chinese painting on enamel was the primary concern, but more important it became an essay to record my feeling of a child's life.

Maker: Bifei Cao | **Title:** *The Memory of Chinese New Year—Drum Play* | **Materials:** Sterling silver, copper, decal on enamel, thread, plastic, acrylic painting, powder coating | **Size:** 135 mm × 45 mm × 105 mm | **Image credit:** Ken Yanoviak

Narrative: Drum Play is an important activity in Chinese New Year and is in my memory. *The Memory of Chinese New Year—Drum Play*, applied both the drum form and the red color of the Chinese New Year ceremony to reflect both my nostalgic memory of homeland and a context of Chinese history. I morphed this drum form, Chinese architecture and Chinese well forms together to be the main form. A frog has a meaning of fortune and also has a narrative meaning of my personal life, a frog grows in a well symbolizing how I grew up in a small village.

FAUST CARDINALI

I am a sculptor, painter and jewelry maker.

My work in multiple media is conceived in relation to four personal Cardinal-Cardinali points, corresponding to the four points of the compass:

North—drawing and theory / South—painting and liquidity / East—sculpture and plastification / West—jewelry making, technology.

Worn, exhibited on the body, decoded, jewelry-sculpture becomes the disjunctive synthesis of thought. Even the most cryptic, sensual, astounding stories in metal become new languages. They emerge, take form as objects, become the source of installations, or the material where archaeology, science fiction, psychology, and the history of art come together.

Narrative jewelry dispels inhibitions from the world, just as the artist does.

The artist frees us from the grip of our inhibitions; he is a "disinhibitor."

Maker: Faust Cardinali | **Title:** *Mein Martin* |
Materials: Silver, 18k gold, aluminium, ruthénium, ruby, jade, plastic |
Size: 60 mm × 170 mm × 25 mm | **Image credit:** Faust Cardinali

Narrative: The niece of a well-known philosopher, orders from the artist a perfume flask as a gift for her uncle. A long process transforms the object, which becomes a waterproof container. In this way, it will keep forever the fragrance of the jewelry owner.

Maker: Faust Cardinali | **Title:** *Dissiparsi in Love* | **Materials:** Silver, 18k gold, diamonds, lapis lazuli, emerald, plastic, polyester | **Size:** 90 mm × 90 mm × 30 mm | **Images credit:** Faust Cardinali, courtesy of Galerie MiniMasterpiece, Paris

Narrative: Two screens are pierced by an arrow. Fuzzy images of human bodies appear, the resin covers the lascivious details. Like a science fiction film, the brooch turns into an architectural object frozen by time . . . .

Maker: Faust Cardinali | **Title:** *Santa Stradina* | **Materials:** Silver, 18k gold, plastic, enamel, polyester, photographs | **Size:** 53 mm × 100 mm × 15 mm | **Image credit:** Faust Cardinali

Narrative: Each photograph is interchangeable in this compass pendant jewel. This allows the traveler collector to choose his own way, without losing the North. In any case, the "stradina," which means "little road," will be always "santa," which means "holy." In this case the artist has chosen Ilona Staller (Cicciolina) as his icon.

SOPHIE CARNELL

Sophie Carnell is a jeweler splitting her time between working from her studio in Hobart, overlooking the Derwent River and living on Bruny Island, being inspired by the stunning landscape of Southern Tasmania. Having initially completed short courses in jewelry design after finishing her Fine Arts degree Sophie has gone on to teach herself an array of skills in jewelry creation using a diverse range of media.

My jewelry practice explores relationships to landscape, place and interconnections with our environment—whether my own or of people long gone. Precious metals and natural and found materials are combined and transformed into objects and wearable tokens that carry an essence of this beautiful land in which we live. My works speak of the effects that landscape can have on people and conversely the effect that humans can have on their landscape.

Maker: Sophie Carnell | **Title:** *Treasures for Our Daughters* | **Materials:** Plastic tubing, beachcombed nurdles, plastic fork tines, faceted TV screen, recycled sterling silver, freshwater pearls | **Size:** 200 mm × 170 mm × 30 mm | **Image credit:** Sophie Carnell

Narrative: This necklace is modeled on nineteenth century precious jewelry akin to that brought to Van Diemen's Land (Tasmania) with the colonists. Originally Victorian jewelry would incorporate prized coral from far-off lands, however the "coral" in this piece is created from plastic tubing; beads are replaced with beachcombed plastic "nurdles" (pellets used in plastics' production); and crystal drops are substituted with plastic fork tines. A precious gem is faceted to the television screen.

Plastic was not invented when the first settlers came to Tasmania yet now with only just over one hundred years of existence it is all pervasive and we are absolutely destroying our planet and its life forms with it. With our escalating usage of single-use plastics what legacy do we leave for generations to come? Are these the sort of treasures that will be passed through the generations?

TIM CARSON

Tim Carson is a London-based badge maker and co-founder of Timothy Information Limited. He makes, teaches, plays in a band and occupies himself with a number of other pursuits that coincidently offer similarly limited financial reward. But, if just for one minute, Timothy could stop trying, so desperately, to be funny. Failing. And instead think about taking himself, and his work, just a little bit more seriously, then maybe even you might have heard of him.

Jonathon Coe's What a Carve Up!; *Crass LP liner notes; all Raymond Chandler, Bill Hicks scripts; books on Jean Tinguely (okay, I look mostly at the pictures of these); Kingsley Amis's* Lucky Jim; *Goon* Show *scripts; every Kinky Friedman, John Cooper Clarke poem; John Wain's* Hurry on down; *Carter USM lyrics. That's the backstory and backbone of my work. That's what I strive to materialize.*

Maker: Tim Carson | **Title:** *Two Geezers* | **Materials:** Acrylic, Brass, Stainless Steel, Yellow Plate, White Metal | **Image credit:** Simon B Armitt

Narrative: "Are you sitting comfortably? Then we'll begin . . . ."

MARIANNE CASMOSE DENNING

Marianne Casmose Denning lives in Copenhagen.

Maker: Marianne Casmose Denning | **Title:** *Medal for a Painter* | **Materials:** Found iron, fabric, thin nylon cord, stuffing, steel | **Size:** 200 mm × 250 mm | **Image credit:** Federico Cavicchioli

Narrative: I was doing pieces for an entry test to a jewelry school—create contemporary medals for persons you admire—and in the street outside a shop I found the remnants of an old and rusty iron lamp shade. I was with my parents at the time; they saw an odd piece of iron, but I saw the potential for beauty. The situation reminded me of a fairy tale by the Danish author H.C. Andersen, "Jack the Dullard."

CRISTINA CELIS

Cristina Celis is a Mexican artist whose work has been exhibited at museums and galleries in Mexico, Europe, the US and Argentina. Cristina has been interested in Contemporary Jewelry since 2010 and has taken part in the "Travelling Workshop" organized by Otro Diseño, as well as workshops given by Shari Pierce, Jiro Kamata, Tanel Veenre, Jorge Manilla, Hanna Hedman, and Mia Maljojoki, who have greatly influenced her work.

Cristina's work speaks about memory, daily rituals and intimacy. Her pieces are made essentially from stoneware, porcelain and silver.

I dare to speak in silence.

I think my work should represent my ideas on life. It should stand for the way I am, the way I behave and what I believe in. Jewelry is the mediator between the world and me, an instrument that allows me to claim fragments of reality, to legitimate memory and to speak out through the materials I love.

Maker: Cristina Celis | **Title:** *Earth from My Land Pendants* | **Materials:** High-fired red stoneware, oxidized silver | **Size:** 70 mm × 20 mm × 20 mm, chain 280 mm long | **Image credit:** Francisco Velazquez. Piopics Photography

Narrative: Clod of earth from my land,
and from my corn field.
Path my people walk on,
adobe, brick and tile,
plate, pot and pan.
Oh how I long for you!
　　—Cristina Celis

Not forever on earth:
just a bit here.
If gold breaks,
If quetzal plumage tears.
Not forever on earth:
just a bit here.
　　—Prince Nezahualcoyotl, Aztec poet

JICHANG CHAI

Jeweler Jichang Chai studied fine art in China before coming to the UK in 2009, to study jewelry making and design. In 2013 he returned to Shanghai to open his own studio and launch his personal brand.

Why do we have "art"? As humans we have a desire to record, and maybe that is the most primitive reason that made people hold a rock and draw in the caves. Until photography was invented, people used a paintbrush to record family, stories and history. That is art. Contemporary art uses abstraction to express, and sometimes the understanding between audience and artist is lost. Works of art become not that straightforward.

I understand the difference between contemporary and classic art. My job is the former, but even so, I do not want my pieces to be incomprehensible; they need to give some space to the audience. Otherwise works are too arrogant. Material is not the first thing I will consider. I prefer to put my energy on the narrative, using the direct element to communicate. Randomly finding objects and stones is the interesting part in my making process.

With each piece I hope people can "feel clues" and elements that relate to me or themselves. My themes come from my own life, they work more like a diary, they record the stories I read, the memories I live through, the dreams I dreamed, not because my life is special. Just the opposite, I am ordinary and that means I can narrate as an objective traveler. People can find resonance and centering in my pieces. Nevertheless, making good looking pieces is the first thing, always.

Maker: Jichang Chai | **Title:** *Conqueror (Brooch)* | **Materials:** Aluminum, copper, resin, found object | **Size:** 120 mm × 80 mm × 25 mm | **Image credit:** Jichang Chai

Narrative: Traveling to Rome was an amazing experience for me, seeing the art and many other things that I had only read about in books. Lots of sculpture talking about high civilization and ancient Rome's powerful military strength. They conquered many lands and became the source of European culture. In that period they used military might; now that time is gone, but they are still conquering—they conquer an young Asian man's heart and they conquer people from all over the world who come see their art and culture.

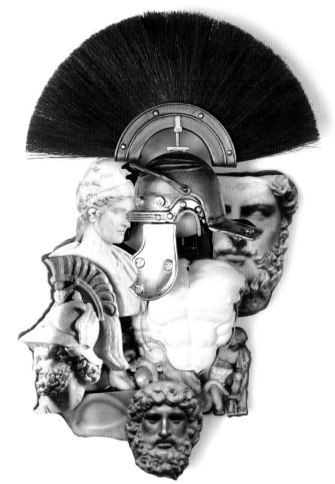

Maker: Jichang Chai | **Title:** *Dressage (Necklace)* | **Materials:** Aluminum, copper, resin, found object | **Size:** 130 mm × 150 mm × 60 mm | **Image credit:** Jichang Chai

Narrative: "Knight" is one word I like, and motorcycles are the new saddle horses, they are some kind of artificial organism. I talked with many riders, and they all said "they are not just machines." I love horses, animals have intelligence, but from these many conversations I too became interested in these beautiful machines. I used the best part I like in the equestrian event called dressage. Repetition, an old method, but the element is the motorcycle, a modern way to rebuild chivalry.

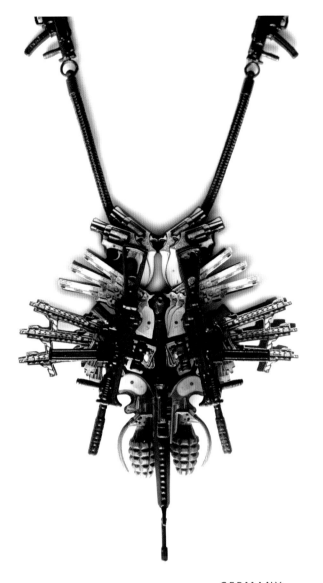

Maker: Jichang Chai | Title: *Jungle Law (Necklace)* | Materials: Aluminum, copper; resin; found object; silver | Size: 90 mm × 110 mm × 25 mm | Image credit: Jichang Chai

Narrative: *Jungle Law* is a nice story book, but in the real world what kind of law or rule should we keep? Different jobs built different circles, people are in there, people met people, circle crosses circle. It is a web, it is a jungle, everyone can hurt anyone, or use money, power or sometimes just words. Hair trigger nervous narrow complex relationships grow in this concrete jungle. I used direct elements to express this atmosphere; the front is an exposed power, the backside is an invisibility power; which one is more powerful . . . ?

GERMANY

ATTAI CHEN

Attai Chen is a jewelry artist. Born in 1979 in Jerusalem, Israel, Attai has lived and worked in Munich, Germany, since 2007.

I believe that every artwork has its story, whether it is known and defined by the artist, or whether it is a tail hard to pin. The story is there from the moment the connection is made between material and maker. The material brings its characteristic substance and form, its history, its inclinations, and so does the maker.

Most often I find that I am seeking to create pieces of jewelry composed of fragments that ceased to be defined or belong to one context or another. I try to create work that reflects different and sometimes contradictory concepts, notions and ideas.

In that way I hope to invite the viewer to create and interpret the objects' narrative in his or her own manner.

Narrative: This is in homage to the actual and somewhat gruesome story of the Grimm brothers, in which the princess, instead of kissing the frog, tosses him on the mirror attempting to smash him. The commercial distortion of the story is an allegory for our protected but somewhat decadent culture, a distortion that sweeps the dirt under the very soft and colorful synthetic carpet.

Maker: Attai Chen | Title: *The True Story of Prince Frog (Pendant)* | Materials: Frog, gold, diamond, sapphire, granite | Size: 85 mm × 70 mm × 35 mm | Image credit: Attai Chen

XU CHEN

Xu Chen has dedicated herself to jewelry art for nine years. She is known for the alternative expression in her silver projects. Xu is based in Shanghai, China.

The narrative nature of jewelry, in my view, is not as simple as telling a story, but addresses the true affections or attitudes toward *life. I prefer to interpret art in a simple, refined, abstract way, so some parts of life status and attitude under a certain age is my target, instead of a full story with beginning and ending.*

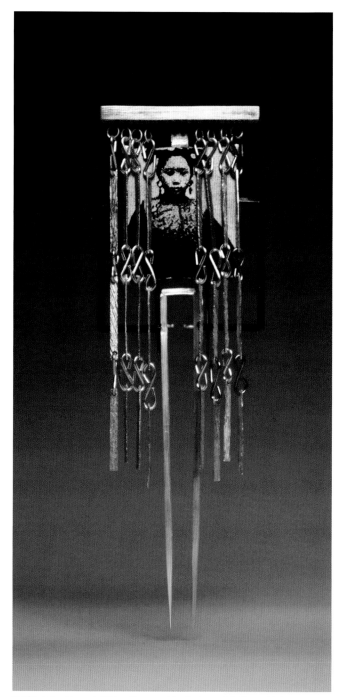

Maker: Xu Chen | Title: *Drowned in Autumn 02 (Hairpin)* | Materials: Silver, cupronickel, pearl | **Size:** 70 mm × 115 mm × 5 mm | Image credit: Xu Chen

Maker: Xu Chen | **Title:** *Drowned in Autumn 03 (Brooch)* | Materials: Silver, cupronickel | **Size:** 40 mm × 125 mm × 8 mm | Image credit: Xu Chen

Narrative: The design's theme is the female face behind the door. In ancient China, a female was born to be confined in a courtyard for a lifetime, isolated from the outside world. But in this case, the glimpse through the door slot implies a meaningful story of her life; and the use of a hairpin shaped like a gravestone is meant to present depression. The woman is an embodiment of the tragic life of females in ancient China.

Maker: Xu Chen | **Title:** *Drowned in Autumn 01 (Brooch)* | **Materials:** Silver, cupronickel, feather | **Size:** 275 mm × 75 mm × 15 mm |
Image credit: Xu Chen

Narrative: This series of three works, "Drowned in Autumn," reflects rethinking of people's inner world and self-examination: imprisoned by one's own soul and no more steps forward. People are living in their own world, where an external boundary exists for self-relief and protection, but on the other hand, it is an obvious way to restrict self-development as well as weaken themselves.

In this case, ancient female profile and accessories, such as *buyao* (a kind of tassel on traditional Chinese hairpins) and a hairpin, are employed as the metaphor of depressive affections. However, the expectation of creating these items is to break down those walls locking people's real feelings deep down in their inner world, causing them to get through a tough life and come to a destination full of inner peace and light.

EMILY COBB

Emily Cobb is a jewelry designer and maker living in Philadelphia. Emily utilizes 3-D printing technology and traditional jewelry-making techniques to create her work.

The illustration enchants me; it has a title and caption, but no story.

I feel compelled to envision the narrative . . . to create the before and after . . .to solve the mystery.

An enduring fascination with Chris Van Allsburg's book, The Mysteries of Harris Burdick, *inspires me to produce illustrative jewelry.*

I generate each piece from personal fables that often contain animals as central parts of the imagery. When the body becomes part of the composition it animates the work, and I want this interaction to spark creative discussion and dialog. The descriptive titles and captions are meant to encourage further interpretation of the objects, and through the juxtaposition, metamorphosis and abstraction of representational forms, my work is intended to captivate the imagination.

Maker: Emily Cobb | **Title:** *Thaw Out: The Dark Frog* | **Materials:** Nylon, white pearl, acrylic | **Size:** 38 mm × 64 mm × 19 mm | **Image credit:** Emily Cobb

Narrative: "When the frogs finally met their fateful demise, their bodies simply became one with the pond."

In this parallel universe aging proves both beautiful and haunting, which in the end is not far from the truth. In the case of this frog brooch, the amphibian slowly thaws like an icicle on a warm day, its skin succumbing to gravitational pull.

JAKI COFFEY

Jaki Coffey is a designer/maker. Her work is informed by color and narrative and often encourages users to interact with the pieces. She is a based in Dublin, Ireland.

I love working with narrative but I never want it to be so literal that the viewer can't transfer their own stories onto the work. The relationship between wearer and work is enhanced when no specific narrative is forced on them—sometimes even titling a piece is enough to imbue meaning.

To this effect the narratives I create are often more present in the beginning of the making process—at the design stage I love the way color can be used as a subconscious narrative tool. I work a lot with yellow. It is a color that means many different things to many people: spring, warning, heat, joy, energy.

Maker: Jaki Coffey | **Title:** *Pippet Neckpiece, from Lust in Found* (Neckpiece with Brooch attached) | **Materials:** Gold plated copper, magnets, found objects, tubing | **Size:** 250 mm × 550 mm × 10 mm | **Image credit:** Damien Maddock

Narrative: The narrative of the Lust in Found project worked back to the place that I most enjoy exploring and finding my found objects: the skip [trash dumpster]. By their contents, skips tell a story about what is happening inside a house. Mourning grown-up children gutting their parents house—children's toys which are no longer needed—the avocado bathtub which has seen its day.

In Lust in Found I have constructed wearable, yellow skips and taken advantage of the skip aesthetic by utilizing found objects.

The wearer is invited to "fill their own skip," which encourages my idea of wearer as curator.

Skip brooches act as the common element but they are also transferable to the neckpieces which I have constructed. The necklaces are constructed of found objects, furthering the skip aesthetic, but also contain gold plated metal elements which contrast with the "rubbish" but also question the notion of preciousness.

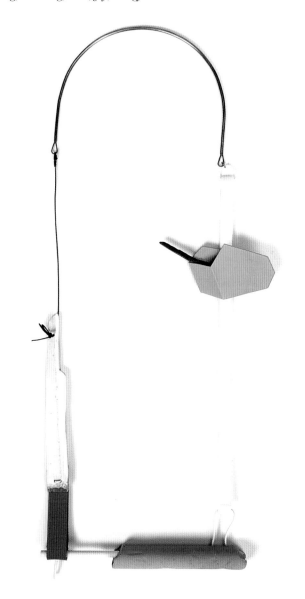

LINDA CONNELLY

Linda Connelly is an enamel artist and jeweler. Linda's work is inspired by the narrative and the personal. She lives in Sanderstead, Surrey, UK.

Maker: Linda Connelly | **Title:** *Fairy Elephant Pendant* | **Materials:** Fine silver, sterling silver, fine gold, enamel | **Size:** 31 mm × 33 mm | **Image credit:** Linda Connelly

Narrative: My late father always told me that I danced like a "fairy elephant." I made this in memory of him. Here she dances with huge enjoyment and sense of fun.

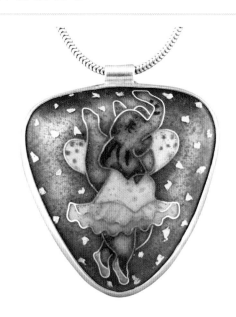

ANDY COOPERMAN

Andy Cooperman is a metalsmith, writer and educator living in the Pacific Northwest of the United States where he builds jewelry and objects for exhibitions and private clients.

Am I a narrative maker? I've never really considered myself to be. But others have, and looking back over my body of work I realize that there are pieces that could, indeed, be characterized as narrative or iconographic (my term).

The two terms are close, but different in my eyes. I think that narrative is the more directed of the two, more invested in a specific

communication. Narrative work is revelatory whereas iconographic relies on a more subliminal understanding. Iconographic work leaves more room for the viewer to bring their own associations to the table.

When I build a piece like the Cataract, Chicken Chokers, Tel, *it's because I want to tell a specific story and for that I need a physical object. More accurately, it's not so much a story, it's more an exchange that I want to create. An informational back-and-forth that centers around the unfolding meaning or underlying character of the piece. Without the object to react to and with, there's no way for that to happen.*

Maker: Andy Cooperman | **Title:** *Chicken Choker #2* | **Materials:** Sterling, guitar string, magnets (clasp), pearls, plastic chickens | **Size:** Chicken: 20 mm | **Image credit:** Doug Yaple

Narrative: I am an inveterate punster and I made the two *Chicken Chokers* (this is the second iteration) because I had to: it was the only way to set up the joke and watch as it unfolds. The chokers are built around two (somewhat racy) puns. Many people are familiar with one or both and just as many are not. The sweet spot is binary. It's either the satisfaction of understanding and being in on the joke or the discomfort of needing to have the pun(s) explained.

I took care to make the pieces beautiful and engaging to both begin the conversation and to ensure that the chokers could stand on their own as (albeit improbable) objects after the joke is revealed.

Maker: Andy Cooperman | **Title:** *Cataract* | **Materials:** Sterling, 18k, 14k, Roman glass fragment, diamond | **Size:** 40 mm | **Image credit:** Doug Yaple

Narrative: *Cataract* is a more personally narrative piece concerning the mechanics of vision and the surgical instruments involved in restoring it.

Maker: Andy Cooperman | **Title:** *Tel* | **Materials:** Sterling, bronze, gold, concrete, lens | **Size:** 75 mm | **Image credit:** Doug Yaple

Narrative: I'm suspicious of blatant iconography and things that may be construed as trite or manipulative. But sometimes you just have to let that go. *Tel* was built for "Anti-War Medals," an exhibition inspired by the pins and brooches worn by Madeleine Albright during meetings and negotiations. A *tel* is a mound or hill in the Mideast, often just the tip of the archaeological iceberg.

CAPPY COUNARD

Cappy Counard makes jewelry and vessels that honor detail, interconnection and nuance. The content of her pieces reflect on memory and observation, potential and realization: what we notice, what persists, the things we hold and the things that hold us.

The narratives I communicate in my work tend to be more elusive than specific. They are like the stories of memory, a gathering of impressions that connect into moments of clarity. I work in metaphors. Interconnecting parts speak about relationships, a seed represents potential, a bundle of sticks symbolizes the day's many tasks, and a kitchen vessel conveys the value of domestic labor and maternal care. Space is left in my narratives with intention.

Maker: Cappy Counard | **Title:** *Other* | **Materials:** Sterling silver, copper, horse hair, glass beads | **Size:** 600 mm long with 40 mm × 30 mm pendant | **Image credit:** Cappy Counard

Narrative: Today, in our culture and in the media, our differences are emphasized far more than our similarities. This creates a divide that often feels insurmountable and disregards our interconnection and numerous commonalities. These two necklaces are intended to be worn together. Initially distinguished by their polarities, closer observation reveals that they actually share the same visual language of holding and letting go, effort and acceptance.

Maker: Cappy Counard | **Title:** *Balance 1* | **Materials:** Mahogany, silver, soapstone, beads, grommet | **Size:** 600 mm long with 125 mm × 150 mm pendant | **Image credit:** Cappy Counard

Narrative: I once imagined balance as the equilibrium found when two weights aligned. In reality, two now seems like such a small number. Instead, life's responsibilities, commitments and tasks tend to be measured in heaping mounds and never-ending lists. Perhaps, some semblance of balance might only be attained in welcoming chaos and accepting the weight of so many cumulative parts. The ability to adjust allows for the tenuousness of a moment's stability.

Maker: Cappy Counard | **Title:** *Reach* | **Materials:** Copper, holly wood, rusted refrigerator, seed, beads, horse hair, fabric from a file card | **Size:** 45 mm × 45 mm × 25 mm | **Image credit:** Cappy Counard

Narrative: Securely burrowed in the back of this brooch is a single sweet pea seed, which represents the best of human nature and potential. This promise is being funneled through tiny tubes to be distributed by delicate bristles. It is about reaching beyond safety to find possibility.

HEATHER CROSTON

Heather Croston is a studio jeweler based in the Philadelphia area of Pennsylvania.

Through making narrative jewelry I illustrate stories of transformation. My most recent series uses historical references, flora and fauna to explore the meaning of legacy. The works are meant to be worn as a symbol of remembrance.

Maker: Heather Croston | **Title:** *Forever Known* | **Materials:** Oxidized sterling silver, 14k gold, enamel on copper, glazed porcelain, carved tagua, Corian | **Size:** 228 mm × 152 mm | **Image credit:** Victor Wolansky Photography

Narrative: This piece is the result of my exploration into how those who came before us become part of our personal identity and narrative. It is contemplation of what traces people leave behind as their personal legacy and how their memory is honored, remembered or forgotten.

BECKY CROW

Becky Crow is an illustrative jeweler. She has been creating narrative pieces of jewelry, three dimensional illustrations and wall pieces since graduating in 1999. She continues to live and work in Brighton, UK.

My work has always been influenced by storytelling whether acting as a direct illustrative interpretation to a piece of poetry or prose, alluding to folktales, or drawing on my own life story, experiences and memories. The pieces often feature figures but are also inspired by the wonder of wilderness and nature. My hope is that people can connect their own life stories and experiences to the scenes represented, that they act as triggers for memories as well as the collective unconscious of oral storytelling traditions.

Maker: Becky Crow | **Title:** *In the Tree (Brooch)* | **Materials:** Sterling silver | **Size:** 40 mm diameter | **Image credit:** Becky Crow

Narrative: Memories of childhood days playing in the trees, where the woods became kingdoms for our imagination, the testing ground for daring and bravery.

Maker: Becky Crow | **Title:** *After every hope has been set free* | **Materials:** Sterling silver, 18k gold wire | **Size:** 40 mm × 50 mm | **Image credit:** Becky Crow

Narrative: *After every hope has been set free* is one of a group of four brooches, illustrating a short poem considering the fragility of hope and what carries us and keeps us during the dark times.

"When darkest clouds press down on me
After paper prayers on stormy seas
After every hope has been set free
Still golden thread you tether me."

Maker: Becky Crow | **Title:** *After paper prayers on stormy seas* | **Materials:** Sterling silver, 18k gold wire | **Size:** 40 mm × 50 mm | **Image credit:** Becky Crow

JACK CUNNINGHAM

Jack Cunningham initially studied interior design before undertaking his degree in jewelry and silversmithing. He and his wife divide their time between their apartment in Paris and home in the Charente region of France.

Relationships, family and place are factors of particular significance in the narrative dialogue present in the work of Jack Cunningham. Equally important in the process of communicating his ideas are the materials incorporated, most recently, found objects and readymades. Through the process of association and personal viewing methodologies, Cunningham is interested in the dialogue that is consequently established between the maker—the originator of the artifact's statement, the wearer—the vehicle by which the work is seen, and the viewer—the audience who thereafter engages with the work.

Maker: Jack Cunningham | **Title:** *Fragments and Curiosities (Series) Brooch* | **Materials:** Oxidized silver, Perspex, cultured pearl, 18k Y gold detail, readymades | **Size:** 100 mm × 155 mm × 20 mm | **Image credit:** David Withycombe

Narrative: In the series titled Fragments and Curiosities, the assemblage of objects and imagery allude to museum cataloging and our fascination with the natural world and its manifestation in "Cabinets of Curiosity."

Maker: Jack Cunningham | **Title:** *Fragments (series) Brooch* | **Materials:** Silver, tiger's eye, green coral, nephrite, cultured pearl, readymade | **Size:** 120 mm × 90 mm × 20 mm | **Image credit:** David Withycombe

Narrative: The readymade section of ruler is a useful visual metaphor for time, age, or perhaps depth. This composition of objects is intended to suggest place, emotion, a sense of being, which the viewer is invited to engage with and assimilate through his or her own experiences.

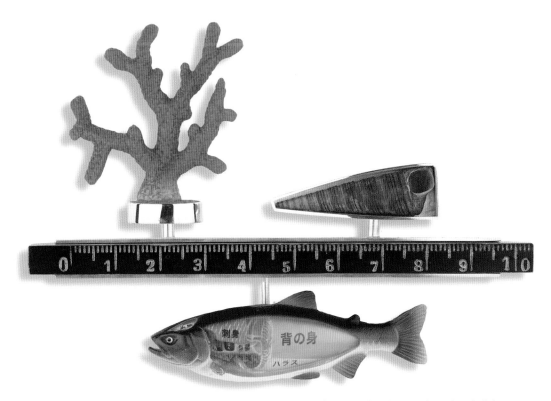

Maker: Jack Cunningham | **Title:** *The Great Barrier (Series) Brooch* | **Materials:** Silver, readymades, shell | **Size:** 105 mm × 90 mm × 20 mm | **Image credit:** David Withycombe

Narrative: Beyond the peripherique at the extremity of one's family tree, lie the hidden, the forgotten and the unknown, even the ex-communicated. The Great Barrier series acknowledges the migration of family members to the New World. The courageous decision, so common in 1950s Glasgow where not only were great oceangoing liners built on the Clyde, but one could sail from the city on a £10 one-way ticket to any part of the globe. With its hope, promise and anticipated wealth, these pieces reflect on those seeking a new beginning in Australasia.

LISA & SCOTT CYLINDER

Lisa and Scott Cylinder have been collaborators for the past twenty-eight years, after meeting in 1984 as undergraduates at Tyler School of Art, Temple University, in Philadelphia. Since that time, they have lived and worked mostly in rural Pennsylvania while raising two children and refurbishing three houses. They began to make one-of-a-kind sculptural jewelry pieces together in 1998.

Lisa and Scott continue to work in many varied styles and materials. The common thread throughout their work has been a hunger to explore, utilize and manipulate a multitude of materials. Often starting with found objects, they reinterpret these objects as materials, removing them from their original context.

They work with narrative themes as their way to convey ideas about their time as makers, referencing twentieth-century art, craft, and design, and as a means of the preservation of objects that otherwise may have been discarded or forgotten.

Makers: Lisa & Scott Cylinder | **Title:** *Rig Necklace* | **Materials:** Sterling silver, bronze, nickel silver, vintage Monopoly game pieces, epoxy resin, sand, rubber, patina, paint. Fabricated, cast and carved | **Size:** Overall 235 mm × 158 mm × 13 mm. Pendant 64 mm × 64 mm | **Image credit:** Scott Cylinder

Narrative: *Rig* is a statement about the fossil fuel industry and how we have been dazzled by the trappings of the automobile culture. Vintage Monopoly car tokens circle a very large gemstone which distorts and aggrandizes a silhouetted oil rig. The irony is that the gemstone is not a gem at all, it is cast and carved epoxy resin. This creates an illusion, much like the premise that consumption of fossil fuels is never ending. The rubber neck cable and gas pump closure hang around the wearer's neck like a metaphorical albatross.

Makers: Lisa & Scott Cylinder |
Title: *Perfect Day Brooch* | **Materials:** Sterling silver, copper, vintage bone scrimshaw, linoleum, epoxy resin, patina. Fabricated, cast and carved | **Size:** 57 mm × 64 mm × 6 mm | **Image credit:** Scott Cylinder

Narrative: *Perfect Day* is from the series "20th Century Cameos (Created in the 21st Century)." It depicts an idyllic scene of a ship on the water, created around a vintage found scrimshaw carving. We have placed the scrimshaw in our frame, created from flooring linoleum, epoxy resin, silver and copper, all made to look like a Polaroid photograph.

This illusion of the past, both in materials and memories, is further punctuated by the carved copper thumbtack, complete with tromp l'oeil drop shadow. Things are not always what they seem.

Makers: Lisa & Scott Cylinder |
Title: *Sentinel Brooch (He Died For Your Bins)* | **Materials:** Sterling silver, bronze, brass, linoleum, epoxy resin, hematite, patina, paint. Fabricated, etched, cast and carved | **Size:** 70 mm × 51 mm × 13 mm | **Image credit:** Scott Cylinder

Narrative: *Sentinel Brooch* is from the series "20th Century Cameos (Created in the 21st Century)." The narrative refers to the 19th- and 20th-century concept of using a canary to test oxygen levels in a coal mine and how that concept translates into our 21st-century lives. The ideas of both animal rights and how we pillage the planet have become far more relevant and dire. This cameo is memorializing the birds that died so that humans could mine and profit from fossil fuel and how a once simple idea has become such a powerful and loaded concept.

ADRIANE DALTON

Adriane Dalton is an enamelist, metalsmith and illustrator currently based in Logan, Utah. Working in a range of mediums, she creates both jewelry and works on paper contemplating the permeability of our physical and social bodies and memory as a folkloric medium.

Maker: Adriane Dalton | **Title:** *Capacity for Dreaming* | **Materials:** Antique silver-plated spoon, sterling silver | **Size:** 76.2 mm × 25.4 mm × 6.35 mm (chain 600 mm long) | **Image credit:** Adriane Dalton

Narrative: Daydreaming is a radical act of self-care. The ability to survive is equal in proportion to one's capacity for dreaming.

This silver spoon is severed from its intended function. The form is rendered incapable of feeding. The object is dismembered but it is also transformed. It moves from an artifact of gendered social roles and classed rituals nearing extinction to a commemorative emblem of the layered histories of use and user. Reassigned as a pendant, this new object serves as a meditation on the ephemerality of women's labor and the power of holding space for dreaming in all of its forms. Reclaimed from expected function, the new form honors the object with an afterlife. Freed from service and given new dignity, the object provides the slightest pull to remind bodies in the present of the weight of the past.

ANNETTE DAM

Danish artist Annette Dam has received various grants and awards for her work, where the artistic, conceptual and handcraft meet. Her focus is on creating unique pieces of jewelry, producing exhibitions and demonstrating jewelry as an art form.

My jewelry is created in a sensual and narrative universe with layers of both seriousness and humor, ideally considered through a both loving and critical perspective.

My work method includes a lot of questions to myself and through an investigative and reflective practice, the goal is to discuss and communicate with the world around me.

Maker: Annette Dam | **Title:** *Life Unexpected* | **Materials:** Silver, freshwater pearls, resin, elastic band | **Size:** 350 mm × 180 mm × 40 mm | **Image credit:** Dorte Krogh

Narrative: In the necklace *Life Unexpected* I used an old-fashioned towel hanger, from the time before we spent 20,000€ on our bathrooms, propping it with design items.

I connected it with a graduated pearl necklace, which comes from another cultural layer and then also an undefinable stonelike "thing" (which is really a resin cast of a piece of asphalt). All three elements come from different times and cultures, and linked together they tell a story from our current, faceted and complex time.

Maker: Annette Dam | **Title:** *Happiness Comes in Many Forms (Necklace)* | **Materials:** Oxidized silver, rose quartz, black obsidian, resin, Milliput, elastic band | **Size:** 500 mm × 180 mm × 30 mm | **Image credit:** Dorte Krogh

Narrative: In the piece *Happiness Comes in Many Forms* I use the familiar form of the classic medallion, the oval shape and the hinge, to imply that the two forms on each side are somehow supposed to fit together. It is quite obvious that they don't. One of them is a fist-mark cast in silver and the other oval is a resin cast of a piece of asphalt with a gemstone stuck on it with a gum-like chunk of pink Milliput. The necklace might say something about relationships being hard work but with a bit of sparkle sometimes, to one person; to another it might talk about how opposites attract; and to the next person watching it might say something totally different.

Maker: Annette Dam | **Title:** *Transcendence (Brooch)* | **Materials:** Oxidized silver, copper, resin | **Size:** 80 mm × 90 mm × 45 mm | **Image credit:** Dorte Krogh

Narrative: The brooch *Transcendence* also plays on an ambiguity, drawing similarities to a pink balloon. However, the balloon has become a little flat, morphing into a faceted shape on one end. The balloon, which would otherwise be associated with lightness and an elevation, now has a heavy feeling to it. Still nice and pink but containing less air and sharper edges.

With this piece, I would like to emphasize that not everything is what we expect and prefer. Managing expectations is a difficult art!

A friend who saw this brooch associated it with women's breasts as they age. They are flabbier, yet with more form and character. It is just typical for women as they get older, not quite as firm as they used to be, but much more interesting!

This was not my intention when I made the brooch, but I appreciate that it inspired such an unexpected narrative.

ANNA DAVERN

Anna Davern's practice straddles the visual arts, jewelry, fashion and education. She teaches, writes, curates and primarily makes jewelry and objects from the Northcity4 studios in Brunswick, Melbourne.

My practice involves an intervention into the iconography of the kitsch souvenir to question long held ideas about Australia's cultural identity. Issues of colonialism, multiculturalism and racism and are all tackled in a process of filtering, selecting, intervening and reassembling images found on old biscuit tins and ephemera.

The use of narrative in my work comes from a desire to tell stories and create personalities for the objects that I make. I believe that if a viewer is able to imagine a story about an object, this enables a greater connection between the object and the viewer.

The incorporation of humor into my work acts as a buffer, a kind of cushioning around the more difficult elements of Australia's dark history. This is not to say that I want to make light of serious issues, rather that humor puts the viewer at ease and in so doing, they're more comfortable to investigate the ideas further.

Maker: Anna Davern | **Title:** *Liz* | **Materials:** Re-worked biscuit tin, copper | **Size:** 120 mm × 90 mm × 5 mm | **Image credit:** Terence Bogue

Narrative: This brooch is from a group of works titled "Intervention," which marked the beginning of my use of the printed imagery from old biscuit tins for a narrative purpose. I used these images to construct fantastical hybrid creatures and strange altered landscapes. The wall-works and brooches from "Intervention" were part Aussie folkcraft, part comment on cultural intervention and part humorous acknowledgement of the hybrid nature of contemporary Australian culture.

Maker: Anna Davern | **Title:** *Nag* |
Materials: Sublimate printed steel, re-worked
biscuit tin, copper, garnet beads |
Size: 120 mm × 80 mm × 5 mm |
Image credit: Terence Bogue

Narrative: This brooch and his partner,
Nagaina, are named after the two
indigenous snakes that inhabit the
Indian garden of the English family in
Rudyard Kipling's *Rikki-Tikki-Tavi*. They
are fantastical hybrid creatures that can
be imagined to inhabit an alternative
colonial dimension. These creatures are
disfigured and mutated monsters that
appear to have been born of an
absinthe-fueled liaison between May
Gibbs and Hunter S. Thompson.

Maker: Anna Davern | **Title:** *Nagaina* |
Materials: Sublimate printed steel,
re-worked biscuit tin, copper, garnet bead
| **Size:** 120 mm × 80 mm × 5 mm |
Image credit: Terence Bogue

ROSIE DEEGAN

Rosie Deegan is an artist and jeweler, with a fascination for tools and their inherent links to narratives of creation, craft and use. Since her graduation she has been exploring aspects of luxury, purpose, function and craftsmanship heritage. She lives and works in Nottingham, UK.

"Have nothing in your house that you do not know to be useful or believe to be beautiful." —William Morris

Having worked with the concepts of masculine and feminine values in objects of luxury, I wanted to turn my focus to the nature of craft. William Morris' work was a particular inspiration for these pieces. His work encapsulates the beauty and value of traditional craftsmanship, which "with the onset of the industrial revolution . . . began to suffer an irreversible decline" (G. Adamson, The Craft Reader, 2010). As an artist and in particular a craftsman, I strongly believe that craft should be integral to any creative process and that the value within a handmade object cannot be replicated as a mass produced commodity.

Maker: Rosie Deegan | **Title:** *Impotent Tennon Saw (Strawberry Thief)* | **Materials:** Found handle, hand-pierced brass, ebony, cattle bone, ebony and brass inlay | **Size:** 400 mm × 135 mm × 22 mm | **Image credit:** Emma Allen, Luna Photography

MARION DELARUE

Since 2010, French maker Marion Delarue has developed a strong relationship with Asia and is deeply influenced by the Asian culture and aesthetic, as well as by its traditional craft techniques. Marion experiments with different materials within her practice such as porcelain, Chinese feather marquetry and Korean natural lacquer.

Because I do not favor any particular material, I am keen on choosing the most appropriate material and developing its properties as much as possible for each project.

Fascinated by highly developed techniques that I use in a traditional or experimental way, I strive to bring together traditional savoir faire and contemporaneity; handcrafted techniques and critical thinking.

Maker: Marion Delarue | **Title:** *FengHuang* | **Materials:** Casted rice paper pulp, steel, feather marquetry of natural feathers of crane, rooster, duck, peacock and pheasant | **Size:** 110 mm × 70 mm × 30 mm | **Image credit:** Marion Delarue

Narrative: To make this collar fastening, I used FengHuang—an altruistic bird who brings good fortune to anyone who glimpses at him—as inspiration. In the Chinese mythology, the very symbolic description of this imaginary bird compares him, mostly, to five existing birds: the crane, the rooster, the duck, the peacock and the pheasant. It is also said that his plumage is made of the five colors that represent harmony: blue, red, yellow, green and white. This feather marquetry has thus been created with natural feathers of those five birds in those five colors. The fastening rod can move, allowing the FengHuang to swing when its wearer moves to make the ever-changing plumage play with the light.

MARTINA DEMPF

Martina Dempf is a professionally trained jeweler and designer with a master's degree in social anthropology and philosophy. Combined, her scientific studies and creative work are strongly related and complement each other.

In my jewelry creations, I work with different narrative codes and connotations, focusing on the human being, daily challenges and spiritual life.

I have always been fascinated by rock paintings and hieroglyphs. I have traveled to several places in Africa in order to see them in their original environment, and as an anthropologist I have researched the context and the message behind them.

The aesthetic quality and the fact that such icons convey meaning and exciting stories triggers my imagination and enables me as a jeweler to transform all kinds of material and found objects into jewelry.

I find objects in different places and study their character and the history of the material. By combining found items like driftwood, waste metal, anthropomorphic pearls, mammoth-ivory and other materials I create new notions and connotations that leave space for the viewer and her or his own personal imagination.

Maker: Martina Dempf | **Title:** *Snowden (Brooch)* | **Materials:** Mammoth ivory, copper, silver | **Size:** 115 mm × 70 mm | **Image credit:** Sebastian Ahlers

Narrative: The circa-20,000-year-old mammoth ivory from Siberia features an abstract representation of Edward Snowden, who is in exile in Russia. For me Snowden is a modern hero, comparable to astronauts entering dangerous and unknown territory for the sake of mankind.

AMANDA DENISON

I am a jeweler living and working in London. My work is inspired by the traces of what once was—dilapidation and decay, curios and fragments, the remnants of things that were well used. I am inspired to repurpose these relics and to give them a new life.

Maker: Amanda Denison | **Title:** *Virtues Necklace* | **Materials:** Bone gaming chips, bone corset rings, sterling silver (oxidized), linen scraps | **Size:** approx. 1220 mm l. | **Image credit:** Amanda Denison

Narrative: *Virtues* necklace is inspired by a photograph of Patience Henderson-Drew who after being widowed worked as a seamstress and lady's maid, a role that she hated and resented in spite of her seemingly demure and timid nature.

Virtues girls' names (Faith, Hope, Charity, Patience, Fortune, Silence, Temperance) are "needle pricked" into bone gaming chips but hidden dark within are the two vices of vengeance and iniquity. The "Virtues" can be rearranged according to the whims of the wearer so the dark side of ones personality can be revealed or remain hidden below the surface.

JANE DODD

Jane Dodd came to jewelry when already in her 30s, studying with Pauline Bern at Unitec in Auckland, New Zealand and then joining Workshop 6, a renowned shared jewelry studio. There she developed her individual practice, taught public jewelry classes and collaborated in many group projects. In 2009 she returned to her hometown of Dunedin where she works from her home studio.

Jane's early work was fabricated in metal and almost always narrative in nature. Themes of landscape and place, natural history, human history, and storytelling dominated. Recently, a broadened material palette incorporating bone, shell, stones, pearls and, especially, recycled wood has allowed her a change of scale and color. The softer materials have provided the challenge of carving and construction that has become crucial to her craft. The virtuosity of historical jewelers and sculptors are a constant inspiration to Jane but their use, or misuse, of resources often provokes her narratives. Concerns for the natural world, and the relationship of humans to it, remain paramount in the conceptual background to the work.

Maker: Jane Dodd | **Title:** *Ghost Walrus* | **Materials:** Cow bone, sterling silver | **Size:** 35 mm × 66 mm × 18 mm | **Image credit:** Jane Dodd

Maker: Jane Dodd | **Title:** *Wing Bit* | **Materials:** Ebony, sterling silver | **Size:** 60 mm × 104 mm × 18 mm

Narrative: A bit of a bat. Not a trophy—a relic.

Narrative: We all know there's no such thing as ghosts. This creature's clumsy attempt at a frightening disguise is never going to scare off the tusk hunters. The work is an inquiry into the techniques of Rococo sculptors while referencing the natural resources that were plundered for their work.

Maker: Jane Dodd | **Title:** *Fuchsprellen* | **Materials:** Holly wood, cow bone, sterling silver, marcasites, 18k gold | **Size:** 38 mm × 108 mm × 21 mm

Narrative: At the court of Augustus II the Strong in eighteenth-century Dresden in Germany the aristocracy enjoyed the game of *fuchsprellen*. Live foxes were tossed from slings with the highest toss winning. Masks were a fashionable adornment at such festivities. On occasion the foxes turned on the human participants.

GILI DOLINER

Gili Doliner was born in Haifa, Israel, in 1983. Gili is based in Berlin, where she creates collections of jewelry, using the medium for storytelling. She freely collects memories and imaginary moments and transforms them into material.

Maker: Gili Doliner | **Title:** *Wish Tanks* | **Materials:** Sterling silver, druze quartz, garnet | **Size:** Shortest tank: 50 mm × 8 mm × 8 mm. Longest tank: 90 mm × 10 mm × 10 mm | **Image credit:** Florian Oellers

Narrative: The idea for a wish tank grew from a need of mine to find a creative way to help in a situation I couldn't fix.

I am not a religious person, but I truly believe we have the power to affect and make a change by using the power of words and energy. The wish tank was made to fulfill this need, to make a wish that stays close to the heart of the person wearing it. A jewel filled with meaning, which has the ability to change with time, just like we do.

JAN DONALDSON

Jan Donaldson's work ranges in scale from jewelry to large sculptural works and she is noted for evocative use of the figure and text. Her recent work explores the relationships between artifacts and identity, provoking us to think more deeply about the doll as a cultural artifact. Jan has explored "the doll" as not just a plaything, but as an object intimately linked to identity; considering image, form, symbol and meaning.

As well as being interested in what is perceived as different, faulty, disfigured, damaged or violated; what contributes to one being physically or emotionally paralysed or alive, Jan is also concerned with what commonly connects us, what is seen as timeless uniformity and familiarity, the purity and perfection that can be found in the emotions of human life.

Individually and collectively her pieces allude to the drama and folly of human existence and reveal something of the intimate and personal. They are imbued with both historically generic as well as autobiographical associations—reliquaries of her own contemporary existence; artifacts that are at once "canny" and "uncanny" in their creation; objects to show our existence—a trace of self.

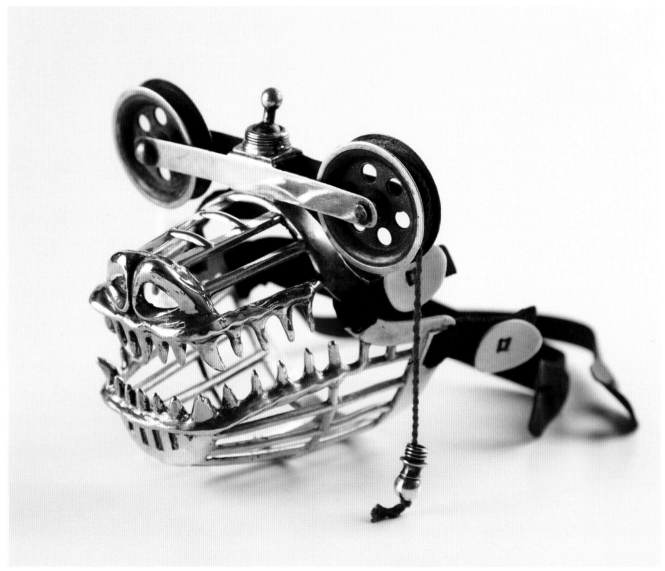

Maker: Jan Donaldson | **Title:** *"All the Better to Eat You With" Muzzle Face Mask* | **Materials:** Bronze, brass, leather, bone, elastic, embroidery cotton | **Size:** 150 mm × 120 mm × 150 mm | **Image credit:** Trevor Phillips

Narrative: Between wonder and cruel appetite; what is the nature of our desire?

Referencing the story of "Little Red Riding Hood" . . . I seek to recover a more sensual, childlike world, with all its attendant bafflement, shock, raw desire, clumsiness, illusion and disenchantment.

"Oh, but what big teeth you have . . ." "All the better to eat you with!"

Maker: Jan Donaldson | **Title:** *Infant of Prague (Brooch)* |
Materials: 925 silver, 14k gold, brass, plastic, cotton |
Size: 90 mm × 60 mm × 40 mm

Narrative: During a research journey to Prague, the discovery of a small pink plastic doll's leg wedged in the cobblestones of the street represented a significant find. The association of the "found object" with the exciting new experiences the city offered became the initial inspiration for this work. I was interested in exploring the essence of these new experiences and emotions in order to encapsulate the concepts of infant emotions; the bringing-about or capturing of the emergence of infant emotions and the subsequent development and shaping of our identities.

I chose the iconography of the "hard plastic" baby dolls of the 1940s and '50s as the ideal "infant" body to accommodate the "found" plastic leg. These particular dolls are a significant source of emotional attachment for me, connected to the memories of childhood play days.

Maker: Jan Donaldson |
Title: *The Girl with the Curl (Brooches)* |
Materials: 925 silver, nickel silver, bone, cotton fabric, cotton wool | **Size:** Each approx. 190 mm × 70 mm × 30 mm

Narrative: This series considers the effect of childhood memories and their translation through to adult life—the influence of childhood activities, nursery rhymes and fairy tales on adult perceptions.

The initial inspiration for these works was derived from childhood memories that combined a nursery rhyme, Henry Wadsworth Longfellow, "There Was a Little Girl," and a popular doll.

There was a little girl,
Who had a little curl,
right in the middle of her forehead.
When she was good,
She was very, very good,
But when she was bad,
she was horrid.

SHAYA DURBIN

Shaya Durbin is a designer and metalsmith from Northern California. Her work balances strong, sculptural forms with distinctive yet delicate compositions. At the heart of all her designs is a subtle sensibility and an appreciation of jewelry both as an object as well as an emblem of embellishment and joy.

Jewelry creates a visual expression of who we are. I enhance this relationship by creating an undeniable visual impact, either by sheer scale or implied with complex compositions of delicate forms.

Often strong and striking pieces lend themselves to greater context as well. In this case, it is the story that creates the piece, nurturing the design and stimulating the materials to a new and higher meaning.

Maker: Shaya Durbin | **Title:** *Saved* | **Materials:** Blackened silver, bright silver, porcelain | **Size:** 200 mm × 380 mm | **Image credit:** Shaya Durbin

Narrative: In the 1960s, developers planned to pave vast portions of the San Francisco Bay. This piece is made from porcelain Life Savers and a Buddha head collected from the shoreline that remains because a small group of people cared enough to fight for it. It can be viewed alternately as a memorial, a tribute, and a playful and whimsical ornament. Mosaic artist Tina Amidon found these discarded objects.

IRIS EICHENBERG

Iris Eichenberg is an artist and educator. Her work is included in several major private and public collections around the globe such as the Museum of Arts and Design in New York City, the Rijksmuseum in Amsterdam, Netherlands, the Metropolitan Museum of Art in New York City, Fondation National d'Art Contemporain in Paris, France, and the Rotasa Foundation in Mill Valley, California.

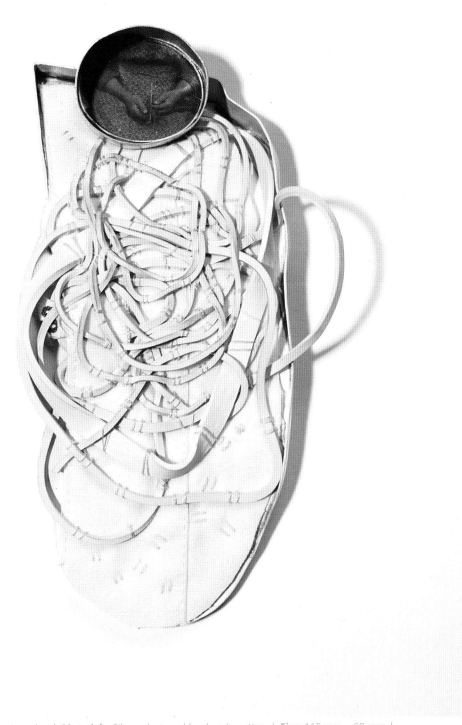

Maker: Iris Eichenberg | **Title:** *Klien-Lengden* | **Materials:** Silver, photo, rubber bands, cotton | **Size:** 115 mm × 68 mm |
Image credit: Francis Willemstijn |

Maker: Iris Eichenberg | **Title:** *Lämmer* | **Materials:** Fur, suede, cotton | **Size:** 175 mm × 125 mm | **Image credit:** Francis Willemstijn

Narrative: The Heimat series, which includes *Lämmer* and the piece *Klien-Lengden,* on page 87, evokes the German landscape. It speaks to a sense of place, an origin and a feeling of home. It is specific to the artist's childhood memories yet unbound to the artist's story as sole narrative. Heimat is everyone's story of longing and desire for his or her place.

Maker: Iris Eichenberg | **Title:** *Bombay Rubber, Delhi Thoughts* | **Materials:** Silver, enamel, rubber | **Size:** 450 mm × 300 mm

Narrative: *Bombay Rubber, Delhi Thoughts* tells the story of a body outside its known world, outside its culture, outside itself. Each of the pieces belongs to the functioning body, the instruments used to keep the body functioning, and the adornment of the body. Each of the pieces stretches and blurs the lines between those things and the bodies they engage.

MARTINA EISELEIN

Martina Eiselein is a studio jewelry designer. Her studio work is based in the style of Bauhaus and influenced by nature and her personal, emotional and mental situation. Martina is an award-winning designer based in Duesseldorf, Germany.

To me, working with the narrative means to hold a conversation with my inner self. It allows me to implement my feelings and thoughts figuratively. It helps to look on a theme and reappraise it.

Maker: Martina Eiselein | **Title:** *Cementiri Personal* | **Materials:** Bones, brass | **Size:** Approx. outer diameter 90 mm × 50 mm | **Image credit:** Juergen Pokolm

Narrative: This bracelet is the most emotional piece I've ever built.

I did it after three of my family members died shortly one after another, and it is made of bone. The three central elements are for each of my three family members; the exterior elements are the door to the cemetery. It is a bracelet because I wanted to wear the memory on the pulse of my life.

TONY ESOLA

A collage of playful memories and experience is what moves me to build and create. From the shelves of antique and comic book stores, to the thoughts of cherished moments or a found object from the street, I find direction and meaning. Fueled by the desire to construct, no matter the medium, I draw from the images and properties of childhood curiosities as a foundation for my work. I am allured by art as a means of exploration and expression of my interests. Though I develop work that is tangible, I consider the response of the viewer to be the true product of my work. Expressing myself through art is a way to explore the enjoyment of creating something that is visually and symbolically inviting to others.

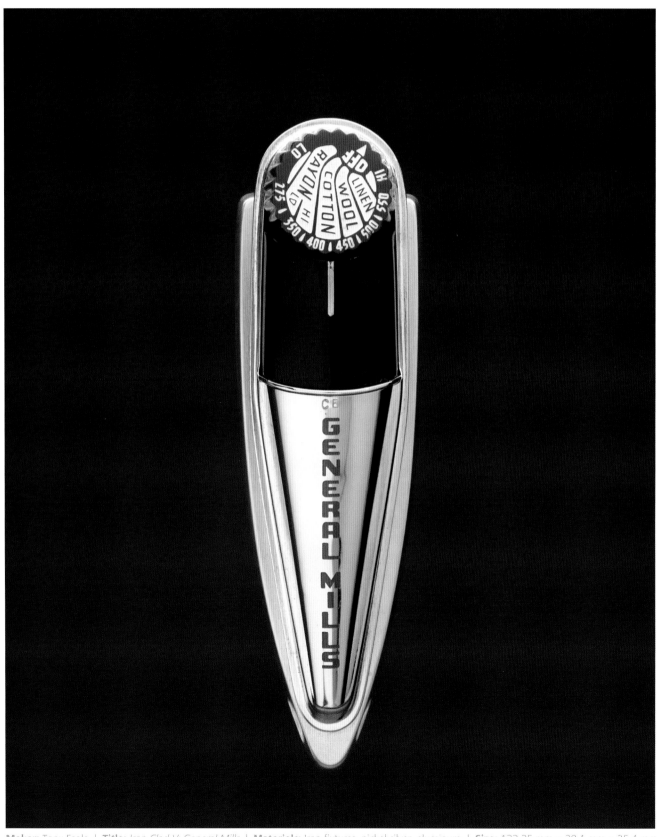

Maker: Tony Esola | **Title:** *Iron Clad V: General Mills* | **Materials:** Iron fixtures, nickel silver, aluminum | **Size:** 133.35 mm × 38.1 mm × 25.4 mm | **Image credit:** Tony Esola

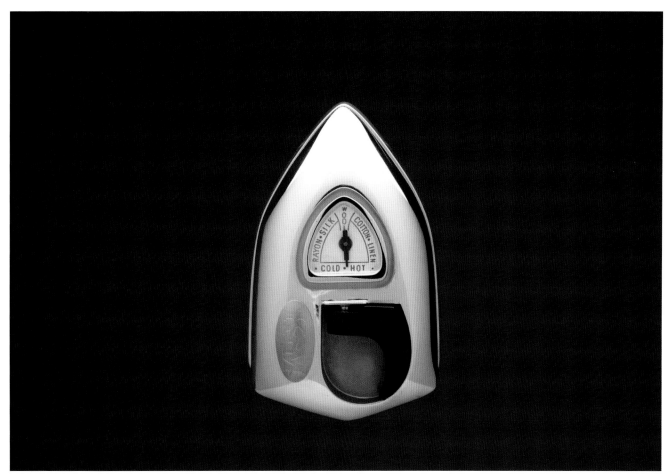

Maker: Tony Esola | **Title:** *Iron Clad IV: K+M* | **Materials:** Iron fixtures, nickel silver, aluminum | **Size:** 114.3 mm × 76.2 mm × 19.05 mm |
Image credit: Tony Esola |

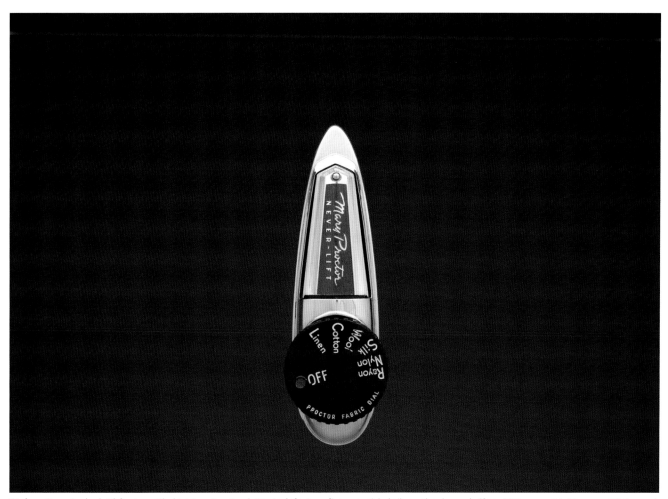

Maker: Tony Esola | **Title:** *Iron Clad I: Mary Proctor* | **Materials:** Iron fixtures, nickel silver, aluminum | **Size:** 127 mm × 44.45 mm × 25.4 mm |
Image credit: Tony Esola |

ELIZABETH EVERETT

Elizabeth is a member of the Association of Contemporary jewelry. She creates and hand makes jewelry from her workshop in Kent using precious metals and frequently features precious and semi-precious gemstones in her designs.

Elizabeth Everett's collections are often inspired by ancient tales from around the world. During her university training she became interested in how differing cultural heritage and sociological influences impact design, and found that ancient stories and narratives can often act as a window to a particular society in a particular time.

Elizabeth was struck by the importance of storytelling and keeping tales alive. For example, her Silk Road Collection was inspired by three ancient tales from along the Silk Road. The Silk Road routes not only brought precious goods from one place to another but it became the mechanism that facilitated the exchange of ideas and cultural values. It is easy to imagine traveling merchants sharing stories by campfire from the different lands they encountered.

Elizabeth enjoys sharing the narratives that have inspired the pieces of jewelry she makes with her customers who in turn take pleasure in retelling the story to others, so that the piece of jewelry becomes not only something which people love to wear but a talking point or, as it were, a catalyst for the story to be retold.

Maker: Elizabeth Everett | **Title:** *Peony Cuff* | **Materials:** Photo etched and oxidized sterling silver | **Size:** 62 mm × 30 mm × 52 mm | **Image credit:** Elizabeth Everett & Mike Pepper

Narrative: The design for this cuff is inspired by the Chinese tale of the Mandarin, one of three tales that have inspired the Silk Road Collection. In the story of the Mandarin, his daughter falls in love with his secretary and they meet in secret, often "among the huge peonies." The peony is thought to be the king of flowers and is an important and traditional Chinese design symbolizing spring. It also symbolizes nobility and value, as well as being a metaphor for female beauty.

MARK FENN

Mark Fenn is a maker and curator of narrative jewelry. He has been making for more than 30 years. Mark has recently relocated to rural Wales with his wife and two dogs. He makes commissions and small private collections. Mark runs wedding ring making days where he tutors couples to make each other's wedding rings, helping them to create an interesting story for these symbolic pieces of jewelry. The narrative and the personal inform Mark's studio work. Mark also works with the technique of *keumboo* but that is another whole story.

Within my personal practice I use the narrative as a starting point for the making process. The themes are always personal; its where I can tap into my true emotions. The pieces can help me express things that can be painful to talk of and allow me to work through them. The May *brooches are works that helped me deal with the sense of loss, the feelings of grief when death seemed to be ever present. Some of my work is very personal and I prefer that the viewer makes up his or her own story when looking at them.*

With the White Horse *brooch the starting point was a reference to my father's death and is taken from Revelation 6:8. "And I looked, and behold a pale horse: and his name that sat on him was Death, and Hell followed with him." So although my work does not explicitly reference death, the connotations are there, if the secondary subverted narrative is made known.*

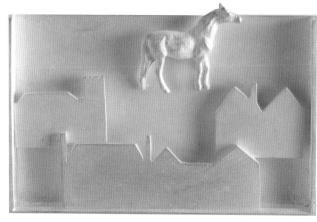

Maker: Mark Fenn | **Title:** *May Brooch Two* | **Materials:** 925 silver, cast figure 925 silver, dental steel pin | **Size:** 50 mm × 34 mm × 3 mm | **Image credit:** Mike Blissett |

Maker: Mark Fenn | **Title:** *May Brooch One* | **Materials:** 925 silver, cast figure 925 silver, 24k gold *keum-boo* detail, dental steel pin | **Size:** 34 mm × 50 mm × 3 mm | **Image credit:** Mike Blissett |

Maker: Mark Fenn | **Title:** *White Horse* | **Materials:** 925 silver, cast figure 925 silver, 24k gold, *keum-boo* detail, dental steel pin | **Size:** 34 mm × 50 mm × 3 mm | **Image credit:** Mike Blissett

TOM FERRERO

Tom Ferrero is a metal artist, painter, designer and teacher. He serves as an assistant professor of jewelry at NSCAD University in Halifax, Nova Scotia, Canada, as the department head of a metal arts program in central Maine.

Sometimes I work purely with formal design concerns in mind *while other times my work takes on a narrative approach. The direction I choose is entirely dependent on the message I'm trying to express in the work. Sometimes a work deserves to stand alone as a beautiful object while other times it has a deeper meaning requiring a more literal stance.*

Maker: Tom Ferrero | **Title:** *Dao Niger Vallis Necklace* | **Materials:** Silver, copper, gypsum, mineral pigments, coral, onyx | **Size:** 370 mm × 170 mm × 20 mm | **Image credit:** Brendan McInerney

Narrative: The *Dao Niger Vallis Necklace* is composed of three articulating, low relief, carved panels that depict the twin outflow channels of Dao Vallis and Niger Vallis respectively. Found in Mars' southern hemisphere, these canyons run approximately 750 miles in length (290 miles of which are represented in the necklace) and together are roughly 63 miles wide. Believed to be formed from melting water released by the Hadriacus Mons volcano, the two channels flow into one of the largest impact craters on the planet—1,400-mile-wide Hellas Basin.

ANNA FORNARI

Anna Fornari lives and works in Perugia, where she runs a laboratory of design jewelry.

Anna constantly applies to her work the so-called "research-action method" by which she deeply investigates the past, through a contemporary point of view and interpretation, thus finding a link between past and present.

Her most significant work in this direction is represented by her research on the complex world of seals. Seals are one of the oldest expressions of human civilization and lead back to the identity and identification of the person.

Maker: Anna Fornari | **Title:** *Viaggio, Travel* | **Materials:** Paper, sealing wax, silver | **Size:** 75 mm × 75 mm × 25 mm | **Image credit:** Anna Fornari

Narrative: This pendant preserves the multiple suggestions of a long journey.

DIMITRI GAGNON MORRIS

Dimitri Gagnon Morris is a silver and goldsmith as well as an accomplished artist with over a decade of professional experience in the media arts (including film and video, traditional animation and motion-graphics). Originally from Ottawa–Gatineau, he now lives in Montreal and dedicates most of his time to the creation of both artistic and functional objects, such as jewelry.

Movement inspires me, and I am drawn to working with metal because of its fluidity. Though the object created is rigid, the whole transformation is hidden within the hard and unyielding surface of the final piece.

By creating pieces that are inspired by my own movement through life I wish to connect with our inner narrative of sequential transformations that make up who we are and where we come from. I strive for my work to become part of that narrative, much like a wedding ring becomes part of a family's heritage.

Maker: Dimitri Gagnon Morris | **Title:** *Communion (Bracelet)* | **Materials:** Sterling silver, amber | **Size:** 70 mm × 32 mm × 27 mm | **Image credit:** Laryssa Lognay

Narrative: Be it the flickering flame of a candle, the blinding sun, or the twinkling stars, natural light draws our gaze and our consciousness. Before electricity, television and laptops, we had fire to illuminate our night and to help us share our stories, our culture, and the warmth of loved ones. It was, and still is a sacred space, a place of contemplation and communion, a place to dream up your life's story.

EILEEN GATT

Scottish jeweler and silversmith Eileen Gatt has been designing and making jewelry for more than twenty years. Based in the picturesque Black Isle in the Scottish Highlands, Eileen is fascinated by the mystical interaction between people and the sea, and often uses traditional customs and superstitions as starting points for her designs.

In her early career Eileen won a Royal Academy scholarship to work with Inuit stone carvers in Alaska, an experience that has fueled her fascination with the Arctic ever since. Eileen's work has always had a strong narrative foundation and she has collaborated with storytellers from both Scotland and North America throughout her career.

Maker: Eileen Gatt | **Title:** *Equinox (Kilt Pin)* | **Materials:** Sterling silver, 18k yellow gold | **Size:** 100 mm × 13 mm × 8 mm | **Image credit:** Ewen Weatherspoon

Narrative: A lone hare bounds across the moonlit meadow, lit by a golden moon on the dawning of the equinox.

Hares have always been closely linked with the vernal equinox; the point in the year when both day and night are of the same length—a time when opposites become equal. Hares have long since been seen as symbols of rebirth, abundance, new beginnings and good fortune. According to folklore, witnessing a solitary hare gazing at the moon is thought to bring good luck.

The *Equinox* kilt pin is a token of good fortune and an emblem of new beginnings. The shimmering white satin finish echoes the dewy springtime evenings. The warm hue of the golden moon symbolizes the dawning of the warm summer months ahead and the prosperity that they will bring. The hare leaps forward into the new dawn . . . .

ASHLEY GILREATH

My conceptual artwork explores our relationships both with family and with personal objects, and as such can best be described as artifacts of my genealogical history. I view my jewelry as abbreviations or small studies of my observations and fascination with inheritance and ancestry.

Hanging on the walls and hidden in the corners of our homes are the photographs and objects of those who came before us. These seemingly mundane and irrelevant items are the indexical records of family and human existence. Accumulating in layers and decaying through time, these remnants of our physical world provide tangible reference points for how we understand one another and our own places in history. Subtle and graceful in its passing, time is filled with ephemeral moments that we collect visually through our personal belongings. We find it hard to reconcile within ourselves the reality that we too will some day disappear, so we use heirlooms as a means of keeping our stories alive beyond our death.

Narrative: My grandmother was always known as a kind, intelligent and deeply religious person. After she died, my grandfather had a vision of her one night; a vision he swore was real and not a dream. My grandmother had appeared to him, standing tall, young and beautiful. The details of his experience and its importance in my family's narrative are enclosed within the ring itself. Rings signify promises, life cycles, secrets and are often used as heirloom objects. It is for these reasons that I chose to memorialize this story in a vessel that reflects its history.

Maker: Ashley Gilreath | **Title:** *Where She Belongs* | **Materials:** Sterling silver, gold foil, enamel, ink on sewing pattern tissue | **Size:** 25 mm diameter | **Image credit:** Ashley Gilreath

JOSEPHINE GOMERSALL

Josephine Gomersall's studio work is informed by her sense of place. Based in Sheffield, UK, the greenest city in Europe, and close to Mayfield Valley leading to the beautiful Peak District, she uses natural materials and found objects collected on nature walks in her work to evoke a sense of time, place and memory.

The theme of Josephine's work is provenance, meaning "a place or source of origin." Her focus is on the natural environment and our connectedness to it, and how to capture the essence of a locality, using craft as a vehicle and the landscape for inspiration to produce crafted objects using fragments collected from that place.

I use natural materials collected on nature walks as a means of commenting on sustainability and the preservation of the ecosystem, and our impact on the natural world, with our having already lost fifty percent of the biodiversity of the planet in the last forty years. We have lost touch with nature, and an appreciation for our natural habitat, and must learn to acknowledge the value of nature and its significance in our lives.

Walking in nature is beneficial to health and well-being, as is the art of making and owning craft objects, especially true of slow making, which acts as a counterbalance to the fast-paced lifestyle we lead today. This way of working affords time to notice and appreciate the detail and intricacies in nature, which are so often overlooked, encouraging a multisensory approach and a mindful experience.

Maker: Josephine Gomersall | **Title:** *Silver Birch Bark (Brooch)* | **Materials:** Sterling silver, copper, stainless steel brooch pin, silver birch tree bark (natural material) | **Size:** 50 mm × 40 mm | **Image credit:** Josephine Gomersall

Narrative: Using natural materials found while walking in nature, as a tangible link to the source to create wearable jewelry to evoke a sense of place, time and memory.

FRIEDERIKE GRACE

I am a German woman who has been living in Ireland for longer than I ever imagined, having learned my trade in Germany. I only now understand and appreciate the depth that jewelry making has to offer. Inspired by literature, the narrative plays a very important role in my work; it connects me with my roots and gives me space to grow. Connecting to great minds of the past and present opens more doors in the now and in how I relate to life.

Maker: Friederike Grace | **Title:** *Blue Moon (Ring Series)* | **Materials:** Sterling silver, blue agate, moss | **Size:** 30 mm × 30 mm × 10 mm | **Image credit:** Roland Pashhoff

Narrative: *Blue Moon* is inspired by Brandon Delgado's poem "Once in a Blue Moon." The illusion of time, the rare moment of meaningful events, compared to ordinary daily occurrences as shown as moss or blades of grass. Being here on earth and seeing the vastness of the universe.

DIANA GREENWOOD

Diana Greenwood is a jeweler and silversmith whose most recent work concentrates on jewelry and framed boxed pieces; her fascination with the garden and the process of gardening feeding her passion for working in metal. She is based at Farnham, Surrey, UK.

Maker: Diana Greenwood | **Title:** *The More One Gardens . . .* | **Materials:** Mantel box with a hinged glass door, containing sterling silver necklace with 18k gold detail; vitreous enamel; peridot; green tourmaline | **Size:** 420 mm × 300 mm × 50 mm | **Image credit:** Keith Leighton

Narrative: This piece was inspired by a quote from the novelist and gardener, Vita Sackville-West. "The more one gardens, the more one learns; and the more one learns, the more one realizes how little one knows. I suppose the whole of life is like that." It perfectly summed up for me how we never give up learning, whatever field we are studying.

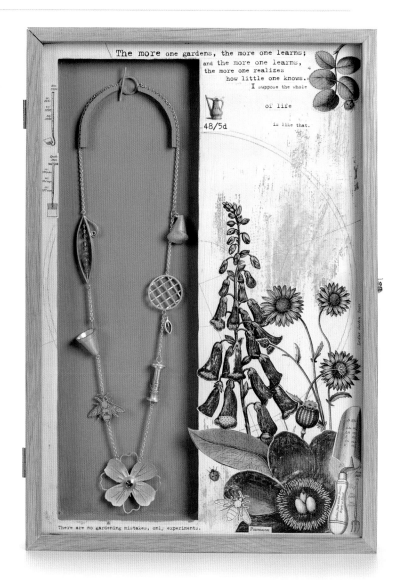

TAMARA GRÜNER

Tamara Grüner designs jewelry at the borderline between art, craft and fashion.

The transformation of the lavish ornaments of the baroque into contemporary jewelry characterizes her work. Tamara deals with the history of the Bohemian fashion jewelry-making family, Prade. From the glass stones, plastic components and metal parts she designs unique pieces. The rich ornamentation of the metal pieces and the intense colors of the glass stones do not act as ornaments in the jewelry but as essential details.

Maker: Tamara Grüner | **Title:** *Azurit Gold (Brooch)* | **Materials:** Historical metal pieces, blackened; azurite, glass, silver, paint, nylon, steel | **Size:** 140 mm × 76 mm × 40 mm | **Image credit:** Alexander König, Pforzheim

Narrative: Since my childhood I have been fascinated by antiques. Because of that I love museums. When I enter a museum and I look at the objects, I am always thinking about the artists behind the objects and how they made it. It seems that the objects can tell me a story from former times.

Maker: Tamara Grüner | **Title:** *Dark Comojet (Brooch)* | **Materials:** Historical metal pieces,blackened; glass, haematin, silver, steel | **Size:** 73 mm × 74 mm × 26 mm | **Image credit:** Alexander König, Pforzheim

Narrative: "There is no such thing as an empty space or an empty time. There is always something to see, something to hear. In fact, try as we may to make a silence, we cannot."
(from *Silence: Lectures and Writings* by John Cage)

Maker: Tamara Grüner | **Title:** *Violet Bouquet (Brooch)* | **Materials:** Historical metal pieces, blackened; glass, silver, paint, nylon, steel | **Size:** 84 mm × 58 mm × 43 mm | **Image credit:** Alexander König, Pforzheim

"I send the lilies given to me; Though long before thy hand they touch, I know that they must wither'd be . . ."
(Lord Byron, 1816)

AURÉLIE GUILLAUME

Aurélie Guillaume is a jeweler, enamelist, and illustrator residing in Montreal. She currently works as a studio artist.

The history of enameling has a longstanding tradition of storytelling dating back most notably to the Byzantine era, where it was used to depict religious icons. By engaging with these traditional techniques, my work revives the medium through a contemporary context fueled by street art, comics, pop art and counterculture. My illustrations use popular culture as a reference point, and together, these influences collide into a new narrative that is entirely my own. Ultimately the stories they tell are left for the viewer to imagine on their own. I like to believe that my characters are exploring and experiencing our environment as a departure from their own. In being worn, my characters are traveling in a foreign land, one that may seem ordinary for us but is, in reality, more extraordinary than we will ever know.

My jewelry, and my illustrations manifest themselves as part of how I observe the world around me. They are my own translation of what I see, a sort of representation of what surrounds me, and it is largely informed by my own personal experience. These characters can be inspired by a person on the bus, or a story I have heard or read, a show that I have seen or a friend that I know. And yet, that is only the starting point. Ultimately the character comes to take on a life and a story of his or her own. I think that by presenting my characters without any real context or story, the end result creates all sorts of room for ambiguity in regards to narrative that you don't necessarily get with cartoons. For me, there is something very interesting there in that experience of the ambiguous.

 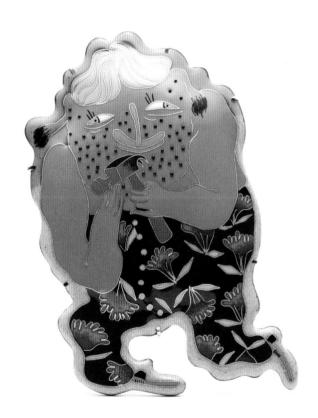

Maker: Aurélie Guillaume | **Title:** *When I Crush Ants, I Feel Happy* | **Materials:** Enamel on copper, fine silver, sterling silver, powder coat, stainless steel, micro glass beads | **Size:** 75 mm × 130 mm × 22 mm | **Image credit:** Anthony McLean

Narrative: I spent my childhood in Martinique. My family and I lived on top of a hill overlooking the Caribbean Sea, surrounded by tropical forest. I would often be by myself and play in the garden with plants and insects. There were so many ants, in all sorts of sizes and colors. I would eat the smallest and blackest ants; they were the sweetest. Later in life, one of my illustration teachers told me a story about how, when he was a child, one of his favorite games was to wait outside his home with a hammer and crush every ant that would come his way. It made me laugh so much, and it was something I immediately identified with in my own childhood experience. This has become the basis of my work when I crush ants, I feel happy. For me, the piece is an entry point into a story for viewers to imagine as if they are looking at a single frame of a larger animation that they must fill in for themselves.

SHANNON (XIN) GUO

Shannon (Xin) Guo built the jewelry and metals studio for the College of Fine Arts of Shanghai University in 2003, and is currently the director of the master's program for the Jewelry and Metals.

She is the founder, co-owner and curator of the contemporary crafts gallery Two Cities, in Shanghai, the first gallery in China specifically devoted to promoting contemporary crafts art. She has curated numerous exhibitions in the fields of contemporary glass, ceramic, lacquer, jewelry and metals.

Maker: Shannon (Xin) Guo | **Title:** *Transformation (Pendant)* | **Material:** Silver, gold plated silver, polymer clay | **Size:** 160 mm × 40 mm |
Image credit: Shannon Guo

Narrative: Often in our lives we encounter many people who seem to be noble and nice, but when you come close you find they have very different sides. Some pretend to be angels, but have an evil heart. Some look beautiful outside but are filthy inside . . . . The combination of a godly image and an evil nature can be found in one person, as perplexing and complicated as we are. We humans are always in the struggle between reality and the ideal, good and evil.

CHRISTOPHER HARDWICK

Christopher Hardwick's practice is influenced by a qualitative narrative methodology known as autoethnography, in other words, he uses his studio practice to engage with his life story in an endeavour to make sense of it. Having been involved in narrative therapy, Christopher has come to appreciate visual language and the place it has in jewelry in our contemporary culture. Although there have been major developments in contemporary art jewelry there has not been an equivalent focus on how one's art practice may occupy a place of reflection through narrative, particularly in the realm of trauma. Christopher's studio practice is motivated by an urgency to add to an emerging conversation regarding social issues, particularly suicide and domestic violence, and the traumatic ramifications in our society. He is achieving this by chronicling his life through visual narratives.

An essential aspect of this is the ability to combine materiality, theory, process and reflection in a way that is effective and affective in the production of works of art. This process allowed Christopher to relive and confront painful memories and in doing so, not only produce a body of work, but also create a pathway to healing.

Maker: Christopher Hardwick | **Title:** *Stranger Danger (interior view)* | **Materials:** Unassayed reclaimed silver, found feather. Image property of the artist | **Size:** Locket 70 mm × 50 mm × 6 mm; Chain approx. 670 mm. | **Image credit:** Faun Photography 2015

Narrative: R. Hardwick, my male biological parent, has left little physical trace on my life; an inscription from his third grade poetry book is all that remains. Despite this, a large trace has remained from years of violence, abuse and neglect. Evidence would suggest he was a coward and a bully, hence the inclusion of a white feather. A white feather has been a traditional symbol of cowardice since the eighteenth century.

Maker: Christopher Hardwick | **Title:** *Too Young to Know (exterior view)* | **Materials:** Sterling silver, etched, ferrous nitrate, oxidized, liver of sulphur. Image property of the artist | **Size:** Locket 70 × 50 × 6 mm; Chain approx. 670 mm | **Image credit:** Faun Photography 2015

Narrative: The uncut aquamarine signifies a raw natural state and the jigsaw is a metaphor for a fragmented life stemming from disassociation.

Maker: Christopher Hardwick | **Title:** *Too Young to Know (interior view)* | **Materials:** Sterling silver, etched, ferrous nitrate, oxidized, liver of sulphur. Image property of the artist | **Size:** Locket 70 × 50 × 6 mm; Chain approx. 670 mm. | **Image credit:** Faun Photography 2015

LEAH HARDY

Leah Hardy's intimately scaled mixed media sculptural works have won numerous awards and have been included in books and periodicals. Leah lives in Laramie, Wyoming with her artist husband, Mark Ritchie, and son, Ky, along with two horses, three cats, and six fish.

I have explored body ornamentation or jewelry as a vehicle for personal, wearable "shrines" or "reliquaries" imbued with *autobiographical narratives to illustrate personal relationships in a poetically distilled manner. Fragments of the human body, flora/fauna and symbolic iconography are often integrated as metaphors for family connections and spirituality. Text serves to emphasize the importance of the narrative by providing crucial clues to interpret these often surreal and mysterious life experiences.*

Maker: Leah Hardy | **Title:** *Flower: Fruit* | **Materials:** Fine silver, sterling silver, pearls, milkweed silk, cloth | **Size:** 457 mm × 102 mm × 13 mm | **Image credit:** Hap Sakwa

Narrative: "Flower" and "Fruit" are written in Hindi referring to the fruition of insight in a Buddhist context. The pendant box form is inspired by a Tibetan *gau/gao*—an amuletic prayer box imbued with the ability to protect the wearer.

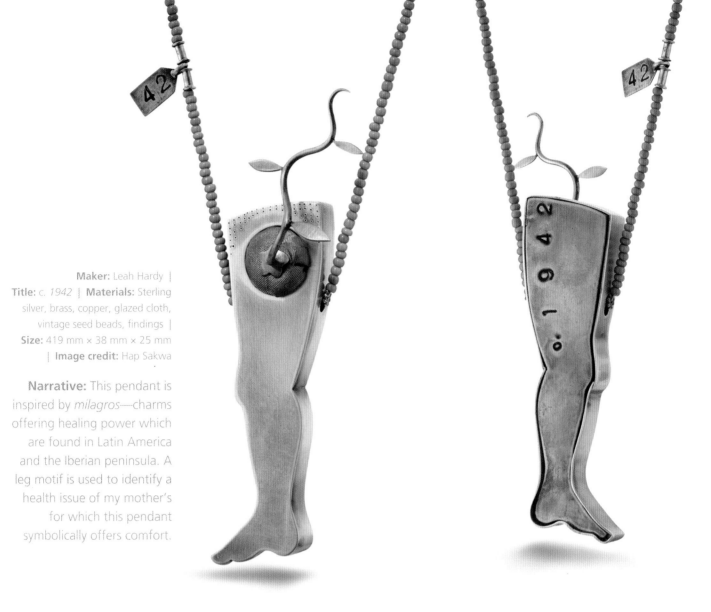

Maker: Leah Hardy |
Title: *c. 1942* | **Materials:** Sterling silver, brass, copper, glazed cloth, vintage seed beads, findings |
Size: 419 mm × 38 mm × 25 mm | **Image credit:** Hap Sakwa

Narrative: This pendant is inspired by *milagros*—charms offering healing power which are found in Latin America and the Iberian peninsula. A leg motif is used to identify a health issue of my mother's for which this pendant symbolically offers comfort.

Maker: Leah Hardy |
Title: *Reconciliation* |
Materials: Stoneware, glaze, gold luster, brass, nu gold, patina |
Size: 121 mm × 19 mm × 19 mm (amulet), 527 mm total hanging length with chain |
Image credit: Grant Hancock

Narrative: This pendant employs a heavier cable chain which in combination with the stoneware arm becomes a metaphor for the heavy burden and fragility of relationships—specifically, the challenge of reconciliation.

NOGA HAREL

Noga Harel is a jeweler and silversmith.

In my work I combine traditional silversmithing and craft techniques and materials with a wide variety of non-traditional materials such as organic materials (fish scales, salt, insects, small animals skulls, egg shells, seaweed), glass, fabrics and paper, to name just a few. All my pieces are made by hand with no use of laser or three dimensional printing . . . I consider myself as an analogical creature in a digital world in general.

Since I can remember, I have always been drawn to stories and narratives. As a child I used to wait every night in bed for my mother or father to come and read me a story, and then, with our beloved dog sitting on the carpet also listening, we would sail in our imagination to faraway places.

Growing up I continued to dwell in the realms of the unreal. My visual and aesthetic perception derive from my rich imagination, stories and tales I tell myself, create, and wish to share with others. My pieces are tales of inner worlds, fragments of biographies and realities, whether invented or authentic.

I see jewelry as miniature narratives, inscribed on the body once they are worn, pieces of memories, dreams, thoughts all brought up together to create the personal story.

Maker: Noga Harel | **Title:** *Doppelganger* | **Materials:** Copper, brass, artificial eyelashes, enamel | **Size:** 60 mm × 70 mm × 20 mm | **Image credit:** Lena Gomon

Narrative: The work is part of a two-object series with the theme of identity and metamorphosis.

The object represents a self-endeavor to find corporeal ways that express ethereal experiences of identity loss. I created this piece as part of an enamel course I was participating in. We were all asked to describe our memories from the first three years at the academy . . . here I chose to describe some uneasy territories. Memories that are painful, complicated to deal with, archaic fears of losing myself, losing my image, my personality, what defines me as a human being. The piece suggests a hidden face on the surface, hidden by an external image of a face, which in itself is hidden and enigmatic. A mask over a mask over a mask. The personal collides into the impersonal, the familiar into the unknown. The term *doppelganger* is a German term for a look-alike or double of a living person, sometimes portrayed as a paranormal phenomenon, and in some traditions as an evil twin or bad luck.

Maker: Noga Harel | **Title:** *The Legend about the Woman Who Got Too Close to Books* | **Materials:** Brass, paper, paint, thread, garlic skins |
Size: 100 mm × 37 mm × 25 mm | **Image credit:** Lena Gomon

Narrative: Those objects are inspired by a short story by the writer Alex Epstein, titled "The Legend about the Woman Who Got Too Close to Books."

It is the story of a woman who gets too emotionally attached to books others have thrown off to the street. She has books all over her house, even in the fridge. Her children are ashamed of her, and stop visiting. The writer describes her heart as an ever-growing bulb . . . one that will never rot. The beautiful yet sad description of her lonely heart inspired me to create these odd looking bulbs . . .as if they were lonely hearts scattered on the table, all fragile and exposed. The bulbs are made of an old book gone through a painstaking process of transformation.

Maker: Noga Harel | **Title:** *A Very Short Legend of the Library of Alexandria's Lost Catalog* | **Materials:** Fish bones, altered book pages, silver |
Size: 274 mm × 150 mm × 26 mm | **Image credit:** Lena Gomon

Narrative: This piece is inspired by a very short story by Alex Epstein titled, "A Very Short Legend of the Library of Alexandria's Lost Catalog."

Knowing that the library would burn soon enough, he added to its catalog a book by Borges. Then the time traveler headed to the port and watched with the crowd as the flames from Caesar's ships filled the sky.

Another great source of inspiration for this piece is one of my favorite episodes from the apocalyptic book, *In the Country of Last Things* by Paul Auster which tells us the story of Ferdinand, a man whose occupation is to create ships inside bottles out of small waste materials he finds. As materials around become scarce, fewer and smaller, his ship models are becoming smaller as well, being built out of bones of tiny animals he finds around. Ferdinand then declares his longtime wish to create the smallest ship in the whole world. So small it would be invisible. I have always felt strong empathy to Ferdinand's fascination with the invisible, the intangible. Inner worlds that exist just as much as they don't.

ERIN HARRIS

My education includes a Masters Degree in Social Work. This background, couple with the unexpected loss of a special dog, Gonzo, led me to create the work I am most passionate about: memorial, bereavement and commemorative jewelry.

I am a sentimental metalsmith. I design and create meaningful jewelry to honor life's milestones and memories. My jewelry invites you to "wear your love."

Maker: Erin Harris | **Title:** *Kinnon and Milton* |
Materials: Fine silver, sterling silver, teeth, glass |
Size: 29 mm diameter | **Image credit:** Robert Diamante

Narrative: This was made for a woman to celebrate her two loves, her pups Kinnon and Milton. Milton helped her get out of bed in the morning during a dark period in her life, and she credits him as being her savior. Kinnon later became his companion and sidekick. She collected baby teeth and those precious items are contained and displayed behind glass.

LAUREN HARRIS

Lauren Harris is a qualified jeweler. Having lived by the sea for most of her life she draws a great deal of inspiration from the ocean, which comes through in her designs, colors and materials. "The ocean conjures up thoughts of treasures, tales and mystery." From her island home south of Hobart in Tasmania, Australia there is an abundance of breathtaking sea views.

Lauren's favorite gems are the rare and unusual, often having a story of their own which becomes part of the narrative of the piece she creates. The narrative may be the way the piece is created, the thought process that cultured that design, a description of her imagination. Lauren's work is shown in galleries and exhibitions in Australia and she also makes custom pieces for her clients worldwide.

Maker: Lauren Harris | **Title:** *Giant Cephalopod (Pendant)* |
Materials: Sterling silver, 9k rose gold, labradorite, blue pearl, iolite, sterling silver ship charm, handmade chain | **Size:** 85 mm × 60 mm |
Image credit: Lauren Harris

Narrative: This piece was inspired by old maritime tales of giant monsters of the sea and its mysteries. The tiny ship represents how small we are in relation the deep dark depths of the ocean and the almighty strength and power it beholds.

ARIANE HARTMANN

Ariane Hartmann is a jewelry designer who constantly develops, works and invents her work. She uses single letter tools as a main instrument in her work.

My canvas is gold and silver—my colors are letters—letters are the building blocks of words and concepts. With the words of our language we describe ourselves and our world. Words, stories, tales are clearly messages from someone to the reader. On one hand perfectly clear but also free to interpretation. Using words and mainly letters for making narrative jewelry is explaining and searching in one step. I explain to you but by looking at my work you search for your own explanation.

Maker: Ariane Hartmann | **Title:** *Im Wort Hortensie—Within Word Hydrangea* | **Materials:** 935 silver, peridot, green agate 3 mm | **Size:** 70 mm × 50 mm × 1 mm; Length 450 mm | **Image credit:** Ariane Hartmann

Narrative: Late one evening I was sitting in our garden. The hydrangea had already lost her leaves but still her fading blooms pushed on. The light of the streetlamp created a lovely shadow of the flower on our wall. I started to draw it and envied the ability of all illustrating people to create drawings and make beautiful pictures. Why shouldn't I create a drawing on metal by using letter stamp tools, following the lines of my drawing? This autumn hydrangea began a whole new part of my work—I started to draw with letters.

Maker: Ariane Hartmann | **Title:** *Im Wort Winter—Within Word Winter* | **Materials:** 935 silver aquamarine drops and slices | **Size:** 70 mm × 50 mm; Length 700 mm | **Image credit:** Ariane Hartmann

Narrative: This piece developed itself immediately when I set eyes on the four aquamarine slices my stone cutter provided me. I had just started to draw with letters. The aquamarine slices looked like snowflakes you observe looking through ice. I remember sitting at the window looking outside and humming a lullaby so the snow would fall harder. Snowflake after snowflake falling endlessly, creating this stunning white sheet that is so peaceful, pure and calm. So I let W-I-N-T-E-R fall, stamping the letters over and over again until they created this snowsheet.

Maker: Ariane Hartmann | **Title:** *Casted—Cranes* | **Materials:** 935 silver pyrite and red agate | **Size:** 30 mm × 55 mm × 750 mm | **Image credit:** Ariane Hartmann

Narrative: Fold one thousand origami cranes and a wish comes true—on the first of November 2015 we were sitting in the garden enjoying the last warm days. It was almost like a summer's day. Suddenly there were these funny noises coming from above and we looked to the sky. A large group of cranes were flying across the sky on their way to their winter quarters. This wonderful occasion got me working on cranes—the birds of luck calling out for us, stirring up a certain longing. They hold lifelong relationships and so are symbols for true love.

MIELLE HARVEY

Mielle Harvey's artwork is driven by her investigation of the human relationship to nature and it finds form in various mediums such as jewelry, sculpture and drawing. She moves often, but is currently residing in the mountains of North Carolina.

Throughout my work, I am continually exploring the theme of "momento mori," to create narratives about our relationship to nature and impermanence. The "timelessness" of jewelry, and permanence of metalwork in particular, makes it an interesting medium for exploring ideas around mortality. I see my jewelry as a visual elegy, through which I pay homage to preciousness that we often overlook, found in this endless flux of growth and decay. By depicting transience and vulnerability, I try to evoke a sense of empathy, and enliven how we see the world around us.

Maker: Mielle Harvey | **Title:** *Golden Bird* |
Materials: Lost wax cast sterling silver, gold leaf, oil paint |
Size: 50 mm × 60 mm | **Image credit:** Mielle Harvey

Narrative: I feel that the human relationship to nature is out of balance, and I use my art as a means of expressing this. My dead bird pieces reinterpret the imagery of old master paintings depicting the bounty of the hunt, in which dead birds lay scattered in heaps, or hang suspended from strings. My jewelry pieces are a critique of human destructiveness and desire for power, as well as a reminder of the fragility and preciousness of life.

In this particular piece, I was exploring thoughts about beauty and violence, with the idea that one has to stick a finger through the golden bird in order to wear the ring.

LIISA HASHIMOTO

I am a jeweler based in Osaka. I get inspiration for my jewelry works from walking outside . . . walking around the parks and around old houses and factories. I make my jewelry pieces mostly using silver, copper and brass. All my works are made one by one, by hand. I like to make pieces that can make people smile, knowing that my jewelry is dreaming as well.

Maker: Liisa Hashimoto | **Title:** *House of Stephan (Pin)* |
Material: Silver, wood, acrylic paint | **Size:** 60 mm × 30 mm |
Image credit: Atsushi Hashimoto

Narrative: Walking outside, I see many different kind of houses. Like a house popping out from a story book.

BRUNA HAUERT

For eleven years I performed on stage as a cabaret artist, playing different roles, writing texts, designing stage settings and jewelry. The latter became an ever growing interest that I eventually turned into my career. Naturally, I am heavily influenced by my work as a cabaret artist. Fortunately, the desire to entertain, provoke, tell a story and tackle subjects with a sense of humour also challenges me in my profession as a jewelry designer—probably even more so than before.

My conceptual pieces of jewelry are narrative objects that aim to do more than just adorn the person wearing them. They are very communicative; I generally use the human body as a stage and I like my jewelry pieces to become personal companions. They are created for one theme and end in a story.

I find great pleasure in experimenting and working with unusual materials and I like to question, break or play with conventions and traditions. My favorite work approach is to research a subject and translate what I have learned into a piece of jewelry. The thing I love most about being a jewelry designer is that I can and must constantly reinvent myself. This challenges me to break new ground and advance personally and it prevents me and my work from stagnating or becoming boring.

My pieces are made for people who regard jewelry as exceptional objects that may and indeed are expected to make a statement. They are made for wearers that are headstrong and have a humorous perspective on the world.

Maker: Bruna Hauert | **Title:** *FRIDA S.: On the Topic of Psychosis and Neurosis or My Innermost Is Brilliant!* | **Materials:** Frieda S. doll: Textile with filling of 99 diamonds. Chain: 18k yellow gold, dyed slices of polyurethane women | **Size:** 270 mm × 160 mm × 20 mm | **Image credit:** Bruna Hauert

Narrative: Frieda S. is the realization of my research on the social role of women during the Belle Époque. From corsets to female hysteria and penis envy I naturally stumbled across Sigmund Freud. The quotes on the necklace are from Frieda S.'s therapy sessions with Sigmund Freud. Although the patient Frieda S. comes at a price, it is a pittance compared to her inner value and the cost of a serious psychotherapy with a good analyst.

Overheard quotes from the therapy sessions with Sigmund Freud:

"Sometimes my jewel case is also a cigar box . . ."

"Well, at least my unconscious mind is much more moral than you think!"

"I always say shilly woman instead of witty showman."

"Oh doctor, I think the couch is on fire!"

"Well, what do you mean by 'hysterical'? I simply don't have much else to laugh about."

"My innermost is brilliant!"

"Did you say something?"

Maker: Bruna Hauert | **Title:** *Annabelle S.: 2006 Haiti (Part One of the Trilogy Annabelle S.)* | **Materials:** Voodoo necklace with voodoo box: 18k yellow gold, ebony, yarn, hemp string, paint. | **Size:** 300 mm × 160 mm | **Image credit:** Bruna Hauert

Narrative: "No hay mal que por bien no venga." (Every cloud has a silver lining.) Contrary to her grandmother Frieda S.'s advice, Annabelle does seek help from an esteemed psychiatrist in Zurich, but looks for salvation in Haiti, from the voodoo priestess Mama Marie: "No hay mal que por bien no venga."

Maker: Bruna Hauert | Title: *Oscar* |
Materials: Sterling silver, enamel | Size:
120 mm × 70 mm (without necklace) |
Image credit: Bruna Hauert

Narrative: After midnight, Oscar
is on the road as super rabbit.

JOANNE HAYWOOD

Joanne Haywood is a leading studio jeweler, writer and educator. She has worked and exhibited in the UK and internationally. She is recognized for her individual voice and skill in mixed media making.

I am inspired by everything in the world around me. Many things filter into my thinking and working, including the properties of materials, museum artifacts, folklore, archaeological finds, flora and fauna, fossils, folk art, old textiles and costumes, female pioneers and trailblazers. I am also inspired by nonvisual sources such as stories and music.

I would consider all my jewelry works "narrative" pieces. Sometimes there is a literal narrative, which is easily read, or perhaps the title gives enough away to reveal the full story. Other times it may be more ambiguous and the viewer is invited to project their own thoughts onto the piece. I think there would be an argument that most jewelry is in fact narrative. As humans we all have stories and experiences which filter into our making whether this is intentional or not.

Maker: Joanne Haywood | Title: *Silvia's Brooch* |
Materials: Copper, silver, felt, silks, shell |
Size: 750 mm × 30 mm × 20 mm | Image credit: Joanne Haywood

Narrative: "As rich in having such a jewel, / As twenty seas, if all their sands were pearl."

A brooch made for Silvia, a character from Shakespeare's *Two Gentlemen of Verona*. The brooch is influenced by Victorian painters' representations of Shakespeare's Verona plays.

Valentine Rescuing Silvia from Proteus is painted by Holman Hunt, a pre-Raphaelite artist. He captures the scene from a real life woodland. The painting is set in the grounds of Knole House in Kent. He meticulously paints individual blades of grass and leaves, capturing the Kent forest of Victorian times to represent Italy in Shakespeare's time. This idea of hybrid imagery has been translated into a brooch made in present day Kent. The brooch will then make the journey to Italy, to be presented in an exhibition that captures the essence of Verona.

The shell references a painting of Silvia by Frank Dicksee, in which Silvia wears a shell necklace. The vessel represents the symbolism of objects in Victorian paintings. The daffodil flowers represent the Kentish forest flowers which the Victorian painters would have observed as primary sources.

This body of work is a narrative journey through my family tree using jewelry and found objects to convey and tell individual tales.

Many objects are recognizable within my work, and on first viewing it may seem they are merely antique pieces. But closer inspection reveals a unique and personal nature to each item through

the use of photography and artifacts, alongside a mixture of precious and non-precious metals and enamel to enhance and enrich each tale.

In visualizing my history I've aimed to help viewers to reminisce, and hopefully provoke memories of their own.

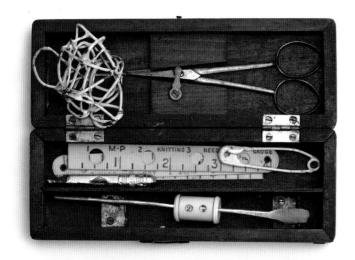

Maker: Ashley Heminway | **Title:** *Work Box* | **Materials:** Found wooden box, vitreous enameled wire, vitreous enameled safety pin, cast silver pencil, found scissors and knitting paraphernalia, vitreous enameled copper pendants with found photographs, cotton thread | **Size:** Box 180 mm × 60 mm × 40 mm; Pendants 70 mm × 35 mm and 40 mm × 45 mm | **Image credit:** Andrew Scrase

Narrative: Many of my ancestors were seamstresses, homemakers and laundry workers. The wooden box contains a commonplace collection of sewing, knitting and mending paraphernalia that one might need for this work. Through enameling and casting I have drawn attention to the beauty of these everyday objects.

Maker: Ashley Heminway | **Title:** *Friends* | **Materials:** Copper, vitreous enamel and silver leaf | **Size:** 85 mm × 30 mm and 60 mm × 40 mm | **Image credit:** Andrew Scrase

Narrative: These pieces are about me. As a shy child I was often looking down at my shoes. This depicts what I saw and how I felt.

Maker: Ashley Heminway | **Title:** *Fred* | **Materials:** Wooden handle from an etching tool, flong (material used to cast hot metal in the newspaper industry), lead type and copper | **Size:** 85 mm × 35 mm × 25 mm | **Image credit:** Andrew Scrase

Narrative: My maternal grandfather worked as an engraver and stereotyper for the newspapers. He gave me his engraving tools and a number of flongs and when he passed away I made this brooch for him. I felt connected to him through the tools of his trade and the wording on the flong suggested the item I created.

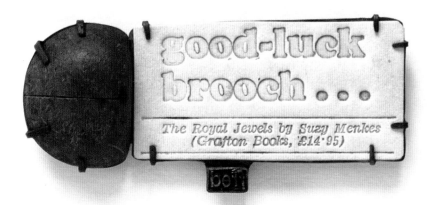

HEIDEMARIE HERB

My creations are inspired by thoughts on the relationship between man and nature in all its expressive possibilities: colors evoking feelings and thoughts, sounds, the life cycle from birth to death, mysteries and secrets concealed by nature. Movements, forms, lightness and colors in harmony with each other are important in each work. I like to awaken the senses and the mind, to conjure feelings, and destroy the superficiality and individualism prevailing in modern life. My works are therefore to look at, to experience, to make you think and to share.

Precision hides behind what seems to be disorder, leading to a harmonic overall picture.

Hiding innumerable possible representations, colors and forms merge into a whole.

Again and again nature becomes an indirect play and stimulation. In this case, as in many, mirroring our inner dialogue.

Maker: Heidemarie Herb | **Title:** *Pablo N.* | **Materials:** Silver, gold | **Size:** 62 × 83 mm | **Image credit:** Silvana Tili

Narrative: Many years ago a friend dedicated to me Pablo Neruda's poem "Your Smile." Last year this friend passed away and I wanted to dedicate this brooch to my friend's memory. Some words from the poem are engraved on the brooch.

ABIGAIL HEUSS

Abigail Heuss makes domestic and wearable objects with an unapologetically sentimental focus on narrative. Her work is based in the tradition of metalsmithing, but is largely multimedia.

Maker: Abigail Heuss | **Title:** *Pieces of Light* | **Materials:** Silver, enamel, photographs | **Size:** 65 mm × 50 mm × 13 mm | **Image credit:** Abigail Heuss

Narrative: This locket contains fragments of photographs. It illustrates the act of holding precious memories as they slowly slip away. Age-related memory loss and dementia take memories a piece at a time, and often sufferers have corners and edges of memories, but lose the ability to see whole events or understand context.

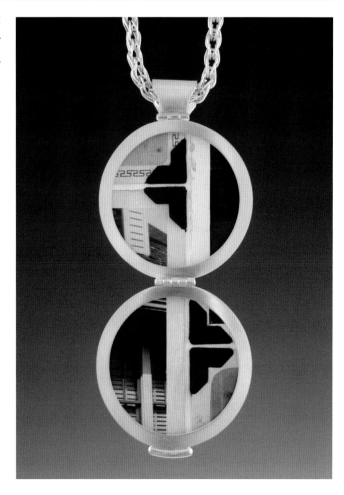

HEIDI HINDER

Heidi Hinder is an artist and maker who draws on degree studies in literature and jewelry and silversmithing to create thought-provoking stories through crafted objects and wearables. Her pieces often explore social themes, such as surveillance, memory, well-being and concepts of value.

Maker: Heidi Hinder | **Title:** *Tea O'clock* | **Materials:** Silver, rusted steel clock hand, brass wire gauze, paper, wax | **Size:** 60 mm × 20 mm | **Image credit:** Jonathan Rowley

Narrative: *Tea O'clock* celebrates the ritual of afternoon tea. It functions both as a miniature tea caddy and, when the end caps are removed, the piece can be worn as a long tubular ring, to keep the little finger straight and elevated when one is sipping tea.

EERO HINTSANEN

Eero Hintsanen is a Finnish master goldsmith. Growing up in the Finnish countryside where forest and lakeshore were his playgrounds, Eero creates works that often reflect the raw and primitive side of nature.

Maker: Eero Hintsanen | **Title:** *Winter Garden No. 1* | **Materials:** 925 o/oo silver | **Size:** 105 mm × 105 mm × 110 mm | **Image credit:** Chao-Hsien Kuo

Narrative: I wanted to create a hand ornament that expresses the strength and toughness of a woman. While not being used, this piece can live alone as a sculpture. At first glance, it might seem sharp and not easy to approach, but this is only the protective instinct. The elements of this work look like bones or something you can find from the nature. You can imagine that when the spring comes, there will be fresh green plants and colorful flowers coming out from underneath.

SOPHIA HIPPE

Sophia Hippe is a young jeweler based on Germany's largest island, Rügen. Working so close to the Baltic sea inspires her everyday to work on a lot of new pieces. Sometimes big statement necklaces, sometimes small rings with colorful gemstones are made with lots of love and fun.

I never used to work in a narrative way in my jewelry. But when *the beautiful gallery I use to work in got robbed, I became so sad, that I collected all the broken security glass and decided to make pieces out if it. And working on them felt so good, that I could feel the pleasure of getting rid of a burden. This happened in 2013, and since then I focus on narrative pieces from time to time—whether it is about a happy or sad reason.*

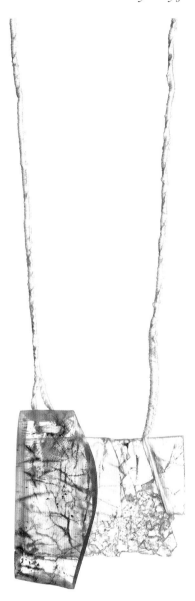

Maker: Sophia Hippe | Title: *Lichtbringer—Lightbearer* | Materials: Safety glass, wool, Baltic amber | Size: Approx. 100 mm × 140 mm × 35 mm | Image credit: Manuel Ocaña Mascaro

Maker: Sophia Hippe | Title: *Broken Mind* | Materials: Obsidian, rock crystal, wool, watercolors | Size: Approx. 120 mm × 80 mm × 25 mm | Image credit: Manuel Ocaña Mascaro

Narrative: I combined this broken safety glass with a beautiful piece of Baltic amber. In my tradition amber brings light and protects you. It is a real treasure. Putting these two materials together means a lot to me. Combining the broken, bad memories with hope and joy to create a strong necklace that brings strength to its wearer.

Narrative: This piece is inspired by the human heart and our society. I selected these two materials because they resemble the good and the bad in life and in human behavior. Everybody has both in their soul. We cannot get rid of one of them. Sometimes we are nice to people, but sometimes we are the reason why others have a bad day. And this piece is made to remind you that this is totally normal. To feel sorry if you treated somebody bad and to know that everybody can be frustrated from time to time, so if you get a rude comment, do not take it personal.

Maker: Sophia Hippe | Title: *Take Care* | Materials: Rock crystal, wool | Size: Approx. 200 mm × 250 mm × 50 mm | Image credit: Manuel Ocaña Mascaro

Narrative: Sometimes just wearing a piece of jewelry is not satisfying. Sometimes it is just a piece hanging around your neck for others to look at. I wanted to create a necklace that makes you feel that you are alive, to get in contact with your body. When you put it on, you start freezing, because the crystal feels so cold. But after a little while your body heat warms up the gemstones and you won't feel them anymore. But as soon as you move your body all the crystals make a beautiful, light and very bright sound. You let everybody know that you are around.

RON HO

Ron Ho is a practicing jewelry artist and a retired public school educator.

Ron's jewelry has used the assemblage of the "found object" to articulate narrative thoughts. Researching his upbringing in Hawaii enabled him to rediscover his Chinese ancestral heritage and ethnic beliefs to create a personal and multicultural expression in his work. World travels have allowed him to acquire a collection of unique artifacts and antiquities. The juxtaposition of these found objects with forged and fabricated silver has enabled him to communicate and narrate his anecdotes in his work.

Maker: Ron Ho | **Title:** *Bear's Reliquary* | **Materials:** Found objects: Tibetan reliquary, felted dog hair, Eskimo ulu knife, Eskimo snowshoe grip, antler, Afghanistan bone carving with forged and fabricated silver | **Size:** 355 mm × 482 mm × 38 mm | **Image credit:** Doug Yaple; image use by kind permission of Ron Ho

Narrative: This necklace was commissioned to honor the beloved loss of his Eskimo Malamute dog. The artifacts are in memory of his deceased companion. He had lovingly kept the dog's hair, which was felted and enclosed in a silver pierced reliquary box.

ANNELIES HOFMEYR

Annelies Hofmeyr is a conceptual artist with a background in graphic design (Cape Town, South Africa) and silversmithing (Melbourne, Australia). She was born in South Africa, has lived on five continents, and is currently based in Toronto.

Annelies's favorite themes include gender, sexuality and the modern female identity. She delivers her concepts in the form of adornment and prefers photographing them in context, believing the body is what gives meaning to jewelry. Some of her creations are driven by the objects she finds, while others dictate the material. As a maker, the first conversation starts between her and the material. She measures success by the conversations her work facilitates.

Maker: Annelies Hofmeyr | **Title:** *Choker* | **Materials:** Discarded cigarette butts, silver chain | **Size:** 360 mm × 200 mm | **Image credit:** Annelies Hofmeyr

Narrative: Exploring the temporary and self-destructive nature of beauty, this neckpiece was made from discarded cigarette butts and placed back in the same environment where the individual elements were found.

PETER HOOGEBOOM

Peter Hoogeboom lives and works in Amsterdam, Netherlands. He works in the area where art, design and crafts overlap. Since 1994 he has been using ceramics/porcelain in his jewelry and he has been working with concepts and stories that relate to these materials, which all over the world are best known for vessels, but in many different contexts.

Maker: Peter Hoogeboom | **Title:** *Finger Cot Hulu Green (Necklace)* | **Materials:** Porcelain, silver | **Size:** 260 mm × 55 mm | **Image credit:** Rob Bohle

Narrative: The Chinese bottle gourd (hulu) is an ancient symbol for health, prosperity and fertility. People give dried hulus and hulu-shaped items during the Chinese New Year and, for instance, at a wedding to wish the couple good health and many children.

Maker: Peter Hoogeboom | **Title:** *Red Lantern (Necklace)* | **Materials:** Taiwanese porcelain, silver | **Size:** 240 mm × 65 mm | **Image credit:** Conor Vella

Narrative: I made the molds in Taiwan for these bottle gourd–shaped lantern elements, slip cast in bright red, an auspicious color in Chinese culture. The rhythm and color of these small porcelain elements are like the fields of lanterns hung in rows above the temple yards. Lanterns are also hung for the Chinese New Year (Spring Festival) and other festivals, when people have happy thoughts.

Maker: Peter Hoogeboom | **Title:** *Spanish Collar (Necklace)* | **Materials:** Ceramics, silver, cork | **Size:** 230 mm × 70 mm | **Image credit:** Rob Bohle

Narrative: The ruff is a collar style that originated at the Spanish court halfway through the sixteenth century. It stayed fashionable for a long time in Dutch high society. Well into the seventeenth century, long after they fell out of fashion in the rest of Western Europe. That's why you see them in many Dutch Golden Age paintings. Only the rich could afford them, and having themselves painted. This "millstone collar" is made of breakable earthenware: being part of the high classes also meant you could fall down the social ladder.

SHIFA HU

Shifa Hu is a lecturer on jewelry and metalsmithing at the Shanghai University of Engineering Science.

Maker: Shifa Hu | **Title:** *The Fleeting Time* | **Materials:** Silver, ready-made object, photo, resin, pearl | **Size:** 15 mm × 58 mm × 88 mm | **Image credit:** Shifa Hu

Narrative: This series of jewelry was inspired by the works of the British photographer John Thompson. These pictures were taken in the late Qing period in China, and I was deeply attracted and moved by the characters in them. I used ready-made articles and new materials to explore the language of jewelry design. I used exquisite antique jewelry from the Ming and Qing dynasties and combined them with the pictures of the people of the late Qing dynasty and silver. I used artificial resin, a new material, to seal up these articles, symbolizing those beautiful but unreachable old days. The gaze of the people before the lens was frozen instantly. The work compares the old jewelry with the modern jewelry and the past with the present.

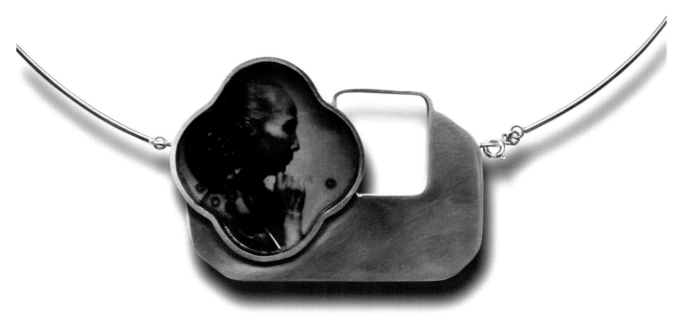

Maker: Shifa Hu | **Title:** *The Fleeting Time* | **Materials:** Silver, ready-made object, photo, resin, pearl, coral | **Size:** 15 mm × 50 mm × 72 mm | **Image credit:** Shifa Hu

Maker: Shifa Hu | **Title:** *The Fleeting Time* | **Materials:** Silver, ready-made object, photo, resin, pearl, coral | **Size:** 15 mm × 68 mm × 70 mm | **Image credit:** Shifa Hu

Maker: Shifa Hu | **Title:** *The Fleeting Time* | **Materials:** Silver, ready-made object, photo, resin, pearl, coral | **Size:** 15 mm × 55 mm × 80 mm | **Image credit:** Shifa Hu

Maker: Shifa Hu | **Title:** *The Fleeting Time* | **Materials:** Silver, ready-made object, photo, resin, pearl, coral | **Size:** 15 mm × 60 mm × 75 mm | **Image credit:** Shifa Hu

JOO HYUNG PARK

Joo Hyung Park completed a course in hotel management, only to discover her true passion for the material metal when encountering a friend's metal work a few years later. Joo Hyung made a life changing decision: to study abroad in the United States. She hopes to become an artist who does not forget her joy of making, holding, and feeling with her hands.

The works I have created are manifestations of myself. They express who I am, who I want to be, and who I will be. My primary objective has been to communicate to viewers my life, dreams and desires through my works with narratives.

Maker: Joo Hyung Park | **Title:** *Portrait of the Artist as a Young Jeweller* | **Materials:** Paper, sterling silver, gold plating | **Size:** 125 mm × 95 mm × 5 mm | **Image credit:** Joo Hyung Park

Narrative: A picture with memory is precious. So I push my finger through the picture to wear it. I cannot push through the people I care for, so my only option is to make a hole on myself.

The picture of my precious memory is on my finger. My face from the picture is gone, but my actual finger is there when I wear it. It is not about interrupting the memory but making it closer to my hands.

So, the memory becomes my jewelry.

REBECCA ILETT

Rebecca Ilett is a sculptor and jeweler whose work references stories, characters and ideas from literature. Her work often uses traditional methods and materials, chosen for their ability to illustrate a theme or story. She often uses humour and ambiguity in her work as a device to challenge.

As a maker, Rebecca is empowered by the idea that she can create an arena for her work which is not defined by reality and what is physically possible, thus working in the true spirit of a magician. For her the body is a convenient stage to tell a story; there is a narrator (jeweler), the main character (wearer) and then the audience (viewer); the jewelry is the narrative in the performance of everyday life.

Maker: Rebecca Ilett | **Title:** *Scissors, Paper, Stone* | **Materials:** Silver, paper, Carnelian | **Size:** 70 mm x 15 mm | **Image credit:** Rebecca Ilett

Narrative: This brooch is a visual representation of the childhood game rock-paper-scissors, questioning the value of each component and which one is the most powerful.

NICOLE JACQUARD

Nicole is currently an associate professor and area head at Indiana University in Bloomington, Indiana, and served as president of the Society of North American Goldsmiths from 2015 to 2017.

Within my work I am interested in exploring the narrative through the use of the souvenir, ornamentation, memory, longing, and nostalgia associated with the collection of personal objects. I am interested in how stories and the use of ordinary things transcend the mundane through the association of memory thus becoming personal and precious.

The work draws reference from objects that I've grown up with, objects that were handmade or mass-produced but due to their limited use for special occasions, they became precious and personal with meaning. In addition, by combining computer-aided design and innovative technologies, my work also explores the ideas of what it means to be made by hand in contrast to mass production and the future of mass customization.

Maker: Nicole Jacquard | **Title:** *Presence* | **Materials:** Carved felt, lace, silver, found object, embroidery thread, India ink | **Size:** 90 mm × 40 mm × 85 mm | **Image credit:** Sara Brown

Narrative: *Presence* is a brooch shaped like a mask with no holes for eyes to see. This piece is a reflection of how we can be blind to many of our actions and often not seeing what we are committing to in the first place. The only evidence can be a thing that we have accidently come into contact with along the way, which can serve as a souvenir of the entire journey.

DANIELLE JAMES

Danielle James is a native Delawarean, metalsmith, educator, curator and storyteller.

Danielle's current work celebrates American cultural narrative and the history of the American maker through re-imagining American-made objects into miniature storytelling jewelry.

Maker: Danielle James | **Title:** *New Bern, NC (Necklace)* | **Materials:** Copper, steel, brass | **Size:** 140 mm × 90 mm | **Image credit:** Danielle James

Narrative: When I was teaching at two community colleges that were one hour away from each other I drove my car a lot and saw countless dead rabbits along the way.

Maker: Danielle James |
Title: *Atlanta, GA (Necklace)* |
Materials: Copper, cloisonné enamel, brass, steel, concrete |
Size: 150 mm × 80 mm |
Image credit: Danielle James

Narrative: This sign I saw while driving over the Georgia border coming into the outskirts of Atlanta from Alabama. The store was a video rental store/gas station.

Maker: Danielle James | **Title:** *Arkansas (Necklace)* | **Materials:** Copper, steel, brass | **Size:** 145 mm × 145 mm | **Image credit:** Danielle James

Narrative: This necklace pays homage to the thousands of armadillo that are killed on the highways in Arkansas every year. The armadillo is the keyhole clasp and he pulls apart into two pieces.

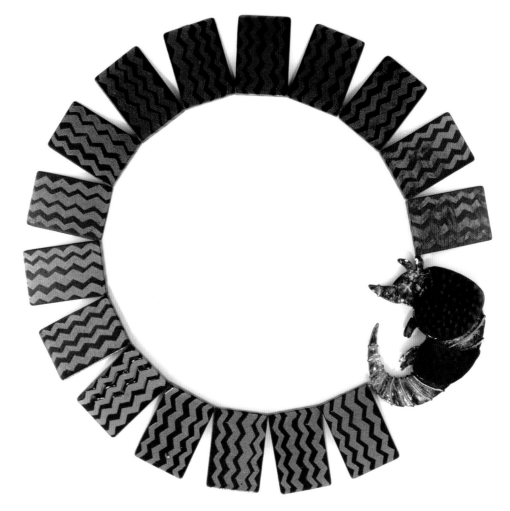

MINJI JO

Minji Jo is a studio jeweler and teacher currently based in Seoul.

This space that we are living in consists of various elements, and this idea of "living together in a relationship" is considered as the most important value of all, one that should not be neglected in our lives. However, the idea of "living together" is barely being recognized today.

Observing how living organisms in nature are continuing their lives while helping each other would provide humans with a moment to regret their loss. While taking a look at the lives of these organisms, humans recall those values forgotten in their own lives, and look back on how they have been only focusing on marching forward all alone.

Abstract jewelry was created to describe the lives of those organisms. Many different techniques, like hammering, enamel, painting, sewing and others, were applied in the process.

Maker: Minji Jo | **Title:** *Symbiosis: Living Together No. 4 (Necklace)* | **Materials:** Quail egg, egg, resin, enamel, brass and mixed media | **Size:** 90 mm × 450 mm × 45 mm | **Image credit:** Munch |

Maker: Minji Jo | **Title:** *Little Lives in a Small Space (Brooch)* | **Materials:** Quail egg, resin, enamel, copper, silver | **Size:** 30 mm × 35 mm × 20 mm, 50 mm × 40 mm × 30 mm | **Image credit:** Munch

Narrative: The theme of this project is "lifespring embracing the new life." I found sanctity and mystique in the plain but concise features of an egg.

I combined symbolic elements of eggs and plants to resemble petals absorbing nutrients from an egg. The elements that symbolize the petals make a pure sound with a swing. I feel comfortable and as if I were in nature itself as I hear the sound.

Maker: Minji Jo | **Title:** *Harmony in Nature No. 2 (Brooch)* | **Materials:** Egg, wood, enamel, copper, resin and mixed media | **Size:** 75 mm × 120 mm × 40 mm | **Image credit:** Munch

Narrative: Life, Nature, and Plant. The different elements that symbolize these are combined naturally by covering and piling on each other, and eventually they become one in harmony. This harmony brings me comfort, warmth, and stability.

MARY FRISBEE JOHNSON

Mary Frisbee Johnson is a native of Montana and spends her summers in her studio on the Oregon coast. Her work in drawing, metals/jewelry, mixed-media sculpture, and installation sculpture has been exhibited extensively.

Continuing my past explorations into humorous, mixed-media narrative imagery, the brooches in the "Cartouche" series are fabricated from sterling silver, copper, and brass combined with lithographed tin from advertising tins, product containers, and toys manufactured over the last 130 years. The sayings on the suggestively risqué 1940s

novelty pinbacks—originally sold or given as prizes at American amusement parks and arcades—are juxtaposed with the tin images to form new connotations; thus, a story is conceived.

The tin image is "sandwiched" between two layers of metal cut in the shape of an ancient Egyptian cartouche and fastened together with tiny bolts or rivets. The surface of each sterling silver cartouche is etched with hieroglyphs of my own devising, enhancing the humor of the narrative.

Maker: Mary Frisbee Johnson | **Title:** *What's Buzzin' Cuzzin? (Brooch)* | **Materials:** Sterling silver, lithographed tin, copper, 1940s novelty pinback | **Size:** 38.1 mm × 85.5 mm × 9.6 mm | **Image credit:** J. Mark McIlwain

Narrative: What a bizarre pinback! A 1940s phrase meaning "What's up?" is taken literally, bee meeting bee in this cartouche. Etched hieroglyphs depict their own wacky apian thoughts.

Maker: Mary Frisbee Johnson | **Title:** *Wild About You (Brooch)* | **Materials:** Sterling silver, copper, gold leaf, lithographed tin, 1940s novelty pinback | **Size:** 38.1 mm × 101.6 mm × 9.6 mm | **Image credit:** J. Mark McIlwain

Narrative: This cool wild panther from a 1940s lithographed tin toy is surrounded by its own cartouche. The connotations of the slightly suggestive phrase on the pinback thus has a new connotation: my panther is simply wild.

Maker: Mary Frisbee Johnson | **Title:** *You're the One (Supreme Court Same Sex Marriage Ruling June 26, 2015)* | **Materials:** Sterling silver, copper, lithographed tin, 1940s novelty pinback | **Size:** 41.4 mm × 82.5 mm × 12.7 mm | **Image credit:** J. Mark McIlwain

Narrative: The novelty button says, "You're the one." In 1940s amusement parks, this probably referred to a male-female relationship. But in this cartouche, two handsome gay men declare their love for each other, and their happiness at being able to legally marry shines through.

JUNWON JUNG

Junwon Jung is a South Korean jeweler who is now based in Munich, Germany.

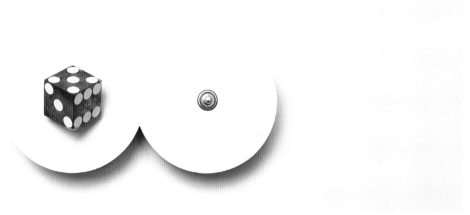

Maker: Junwon Jung | **Title:** *Dice* | **Materials:** Used dice, brass, plaster | **Size:** 20 mm × 20 mm × 20 mm (dice) | **Image credit:** Junwon Jung

Narrative: Expectations and frustrations, chance and necessity.

This work is about dice standing on edge, as if still up in the air, or it shows the possibility of landing on its corner. The dice were used in a casino and were discarded after a given period of playing time.

YOUNHA JUNG

Younha Jung was born in Busan, South Korea, and moved to the United States in 2012. Younha specializes in wearable modern jewelry. Her work expresses emotional changes that humans feel as part of a course of adaptation to the change in their surroundings. Currently, she is making jewelry made from repurposed steel and found objects collected from a particular building. She believes that these materials represent the environment and situation in which they were found, and the artwork she creates with them expresses a point of view as an insider/outsider about a particular place in time.

Maker: Younha Jung | **Title:** *VDH 104* | **Materials:** Steel, wood, rubber, brass, argentium silver, silver-plated wire | **Size:** 482 mm × 177 mm × 19 mm | **Image credit:** Younha Jung

Narrative: I am a traveler and an artist. I have questions regarding a variety of feelings that I have had while I travel to many different places. Regardless of destination, I exist as I am, but I often find myself reacting differently, both emotionally and intellectually, depending on my location.

YEONMI KANG

Yeonmi Kang was born in Seoul, Korea. Currently, she is a professor in the metalwork and jewelry department at Kookmin University Seoul, South Korea.

In my work, I like to transform personal experience, visions related to human condition, into three-dimensional objects or jewelry. I *question the inevitable fate and condition of human beings by exploiting narratives and symbolism. By trying to enter deeply into the elements of life and through the everyday journey of transforming questions into objects I want to be an observer of the unbalanced connection between the world and myself.*

Maker: Yeonmi Kang | **Title:** *Chosen Fragments 2* | **Materials:** 925 silver, copper, enamel | **Size:** 72 mm × 60 mm × 35 mm |
Image credit: Yeonmi Kang and Gwang Chun Park |

Maker: Yeonmi Kang | **Title:** *Chosen Fragments 1* | **Materials:** 925 silver, copper, enamel | **Size:** 74 mm × 73 mm × 33 mm |
Image credit: Yeonmi Kang and Gwang Chun Park

Narrative: Man's memory itself is in fact vague and obscure. Even though we try to hold real phenomenon, it becomes distorted and edited when the mechanism of our memory starts to work. Whenever we retrieve fragments from our chest of memory, they are likely adapted and/or tinted. Nevertheless, we always rely on our perceptions of these obscure fragments of memory. Thus our mind frequently edits our memories, and, in turn, the edited memories become a part of ourselves. Thousands of fragments I chose or will choose in the future from my memories offer the best and precious clues to answer the question of who I am.

In this series of work, I arranged fragmental images from photographs with parts of the human figure. For this, I used a phototransfer enameling technique. First, I took photos from everyday life around me, and modified these images using Photoshop. I then transferred these images to enamel decal and fired them onto metal. Through these processes the photo images lost their original realistic details, becoming like our memory's vague and obscure nature.

Maker: Yeonmi Kang | **Title:** *Chosen Fragments 3* | **Materials:** 925 silver, copper, enamel | **Size:** 72 mm × 58 mm × 23 mm | **Image credit:** Yeonmi Kang and Gwang Chun Park

CHIA-LIANG KAO

Chia-Liang Kao is a maker who is interested in using diverse materials in jewelry, which for her is an intermediate object that connects her to the wider world.

The major purpose of my work is to create intrigue between jewelry and its wearer. I make brooches and neckpieces in various combinations of materials to create open-ended narrative forms. The miniature human situation invites the viewer to scrutinize the pieces of jewelry.

While it is hard to measure whether or not one has succeeded in creating intrigue between the jewelry and the wearer I am not aiming to communicate any specific meaning through narrative. By using combinations of the familiar and the unfamiliar, my intention is to raise questions within the viewer and wearer. What are they looking at? What is the material? Is it wearable? I leave the viewer to ponder, allowing them to come to their own conclusion. Presenting the familiar in unfamiliar ways breaks people's expectations of what is familiar. Through doing this I aim to raise a viewer's curiosity.

Maker: Chia-Liang Kao | **Title:** *Public Scale (Neckpiece)* | **Materials:** Silver, nickel silver, brass, wood, paint and cord | **Size:** 165 mm × 19 mm × 59 mm | **Image credit:** Johannes Kuhnen

Narrative: I had an idea when I put myself on the scale at home. I thought that it would be challenging to see a group of people as well as a wild animal queuing in line for a public scale. The human figures are cast in silver and hand painted.

I want the viewer to ask questions such as, what are they doing? Why is there an elephant queuing up for a public scale? Is an elephant concerned about its own weight as well? What is the landscape? A park? A zoo? I placed the people casually and evenly spaced, naturally queuing so that the people appear to be calm and do not feel awkward with the animal in line. I want them to appear as though it's perfectly normal for an elephant to be concerned about its weight.

Maker: Chia-Liang Kao | **Title:** *High Vis (Neckpiece)* | **Materials:** Silver, wood, brass, stainless steel, found object and cord | **Size:** 146 mm × 75 mm × 44 mm | **Image credit:** Johannes Kuhnen

Narrative: Workers measuring the rabbit height on a jeweler's bench.

Maker: Chia-Liang Kao | **Title:** *U-shape (Neckpiece)* | **Materials:** Wood, silver, paint, turf and cord | **Size:** 70 mm × 50 mm × 30 mm | **Image credit:** Johannes Kuhnen

Narrative: There is one figurine at the top looking down and one at the bottom pointing up. This was to give the feeling that they are interacting quite casually with each other from different points on an impossibly warped ground plane.

NADINE KARIYA

My dad was a sergeant in the 442nd Infantry during World War II, a Japanese American unit, which meant he had to send boys into battle, and my mom was a high school student when she and her family were sent to the Minadoka, Idaho, internment prison. She had one jewelry class in school and really liked it. My family was posted to Japan after the war, shortly after I was born.

After high school my dad told me I should be an artist so I went to the University of Washington, pursued painting, and concluded with a fine art degree in metal design. I studied with John C. Marshall, a great metalsmith, and Ramona Solberg, the "Henry Ford" of the Northwest Narrative Jewelry School. I studied with master jeweler/ engraver Reinhold Eichborn for 7 years and took over his shop when

he retired. I was a manufacturing jeweler for over 20 years in downtown Seattle, also continuing my jewelry art. In 2006, I quit the shop to work on commissions and my art, and am a ring specialist at Facere Jewelry Art Gallery in Seattle.

I do not want to remain silent. I want to stand and be counted as a person with a viewpoint and a unique mode of expression to declare what is important to me. I want to celebrate, to criticize, to appeal to people's hearts, to prick their conscience about a world that needs their care and consideration. I don't care if the topics are mundane or not hip to a lot of people. In the archives of the future, our narrative art will be a historical commentary on the issues of the times, our era and our lives.

Maker: Nadine Kariya | **Title:** *Barack Obama 2009 Man of the Year Festoon Suite* | **Materials:** Sterling silver, argentium sterling silver, low oxygen sterling, fine silver, copper, brass, 18k gold, *shakudo* (5% gold, 95% copper), *shibuichi* (10% silver, 90% copper), amethyst, chrysocolla-quartz, Turbo petholatus Linnaeus 1758 operculum | **Size:** Dove: 100 mm × 75 mm; Earth: 115 mm × 65 mm; Credo: 134 mm × 95 mm; Peace: 140 mm × 116 mm | **Image credit:** Daniel Fox, Lumina Studios: Seattle and Cleveland, USA

Narrative: I was invited to represent the year 2009 with a jewel. Of course, Barack Obama was the man of the year for 2009. His 2009 Nobel Peace Prize acceptance speech, "Let us reach for the world that ought to be, that spark of the divine that still stirs within each of our souls," helped organize the ideas for this set of four brooches.

I made Obama's hands of Peace, Credo and Earth, holding these elements: War—a purple heart sits on top of a Pandora's Box; Science and Intellect—a snail operculum displays a fractile spiral; and Climate Change—the glacier-like stone is flagged

"climate refugee." Each hand has quotes that Obama has said about their topics, united by the Nobel Peace Dove, which shows the world's support of Obama. The suit sleeve denotes leadership and the robe sleeve of scholarship has a Hawaiian textile pattern of Obama's home state. The festoon idea came from my vision of the old time political dais, with rosettes and ribbons, celebrating, uniting and embracing the speaker and the moment.

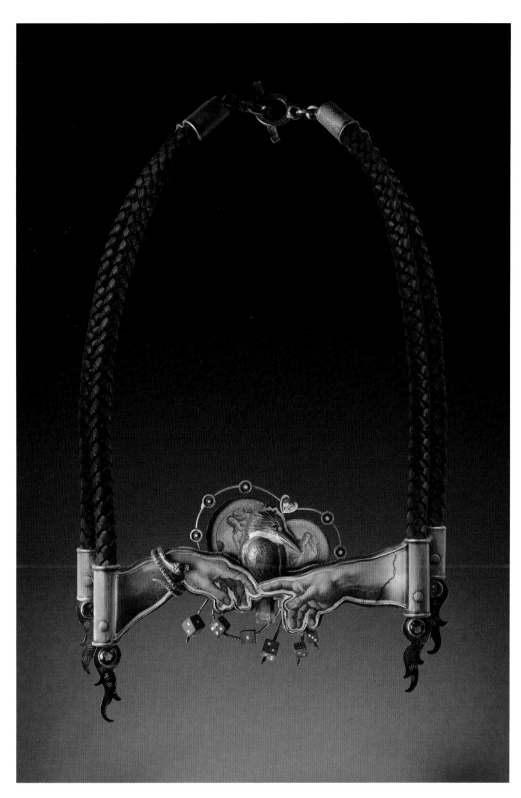

Maker: Nadine Kariya | **Title:** *The Case of the Cosmic Kingfisher* | **Materials:** Boxwood, printed melamine and vintage/antique gold snake necklace converted into a removable bracelet from mother-in-law Mildred, garnets. printed tin, sterling, *shakudo*, *shibuichi*, diamonds, aquamarine,14k gold, braided leather cord | **Size:** 310 mm × 195 mm | **Image credit:** Daniel Fox, Lumina Studios: Seattle and Cleveland, USA

Narrative: Another ecology piece: I carved a ringed kingfisher and wished to show that its fate is in our hands. I perched the kingfisher on Michelangelo's hands of God and Adam, which are throwing the die of luck and chance. The Snake of Sin on Adam's wrist indicates that he is not a clear thinker. The *Birth of Venus* with nimbus forms a lyrical ecclesiastical backdrop behind the bird. The tubing "afterburners" with flames connote the wishful thinking of space travel and escape.

Maker: Nadine Kariya | **Title:** *Obama Campaign Pin: Our Actions Matter and Bend History in the Direction of Justice* | **Materials:** Copper, sterling, 14k gold, industrial engraving | **Size:** 45 mm × 45 mm | **Image credit:** Daniel Fox, Lumina Studios: Seattle and Cleveland, USA

Narrative: The old time notion of women sitting at home embroidering is brought to consideration here. It doesn't matter how you do it, everyone can and should help justice have its rightful place in this society.

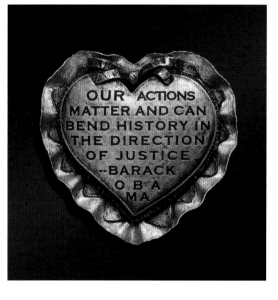

LINDA KAYE-MOSES

Linda Kaye-Moses is a studio jeweler, exhibiting in galleries and at juried craft shows.

Linda's jewels concern themselves not simply with adornment, but also with the implicit/explicit narrative capacity of adornment. The jewels are joined to enclosures (and sometimes poems and small books) that reflect the theme the jewels express. Since each of the jewels has its roots in a theme or poses a question, relating the enclosures to the form and concept expressed in the jewels is imperative.

Maker: Linda Kaye-Moses | **Title:** *Vashti Dreams (Neckpiece)* | **Materials:** Sterling and fine silver, 14k gold, cuprite, lapis lazuli, gem chrysocolla, amethyst, garnet, emerald beads | **Size:** 70.6 mm × 40.5 mm × 6 mm deep | **Image credit:** Evan J. Soldinger

Narrative: This piece reflects my interest in the Biblical character Vashti, wife of Xerxes I (Ahasuerus in the Bible). She was commanded to appear naked, but for her crown, before her husband and his friends. She refused and, although the Bible is unclear as to whether she was banished or executed, I choose to imagine that a woman with the strength of Vashti would have survived, leaving Susa (Shushan) in Persia, for regions where a strong-willed woman would be not only safe, but encouraged.

The colors of the piece echo the power of Vashti's temperament, the heat of the deserts she would have to traverse before finding refuge beyond the borders of Persia, and also the colors that might have been available for garments and other textiles (floor coverings, tapestries, saddle bags, etc.) of that region.

During the design and construction of this piece, my intention was to create a neckpiece worthy of a desert queen, a piece which she would secrete in her scant belongings as she escaped from Persia.

The symbols both on the neckpiece and the enclosure are extrapolated from cuneiform writing, using the forms that phonetically reproduce her name.

JOSHUA KOSKER

Joshua Kosker is a studio artist based in western Pennsylvania, whose practice is rooted in contemporary craft and body adornment. Driven by an underlying interest in the physical, tactile memory of material, Josh utilizes daily experiences and everyday artifacts to create one-off art jewelry and objects.

My work is informed by a sensitivity to life and the everyday. I consider objects narrators of time and place. As a maker, I am interested in how objects shape experiences and, in turn, how actions imprint meaning on the material world. Drawing from some of the most humble, discreet, and commonly found materials, my research fuses traditional craft practices and unconventional processes with questions of materiality, function, and value.

In looking to jewelry and domestic objects, to explore universal and sometimes private subject matters in daily life, my work seeks to connect viewers and wearers to their individual experiences while creating a collective dialogue through introspection.

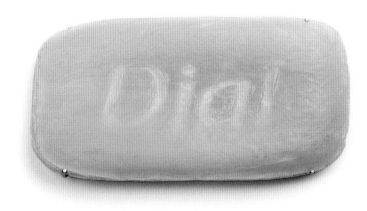

Maker: Joshua Kosker | **Title:** *Dial* | **Materials:** Soap, sterling silver, stainless steel | **Size:** 6 mm × 38 mm × 7 mm | **Image credit:** Joshua Kosker

Narrative: Separated from or existing without the body, soap serves no purpose and is generally discarded once it reaches a certain state of reduction. Transformed through the daily ritual of bathing, these forms convey a tactile, intimate relationship between owner and object. By reconnecting this material to the body as jewelry, I aim to evoke a sensual experience about the simple pleasures of bath time, with intentions of a more private dialogue.

Maker: Joshua Kosker | **Title:** *Soap Ring #2* | **Materials:** Dial, sterling silver | **Size:** 32 mm × 19 mm × 25 mm | **Image credit:** Joshua Kosker

Narrative: Moving between personal and shared spaces, this body of work is unfixed. It is likely that the soap will continue to change over time through natural wear and environmental factors, again reshaping the visual history and value of these momentary, mutable forms. Activated by and on the body, these everyday artifacts take on a precarious function as jewelry—wavering somewhere between raw and manufactured—the corporeal presence of the material to serve as a reminder of this physiological exchange.

Maker: Joshua Kosker | **Title:** *Bottom Feeder* | **Materials:** Rubber shoe sole, brass, copper, steel, thread, graphite, 23k gold | **Size:** 108 mm × 78 mm × 37 mm (630 mm chain) | **Image credit:** Joshua Kosker

Narrative: Ever since I could walk I can remember feeling the urge to constantly explore my surroundings. I have found some interesting things, most of which only exist in memory. I look back to a time when I was younger and traveling across the country for work; it feels like only a few years ago. I was a nomad of sorts, wandering from town to town, bags in hand, sleeping in strange beds and relying on the hospitality of others. Postcards mailed home recount my experiences. I never did keep a journal. The worn shoe sole contained in this work serves as one of the only surviving physical traces of my travels. I wonder how many postcards still exist.

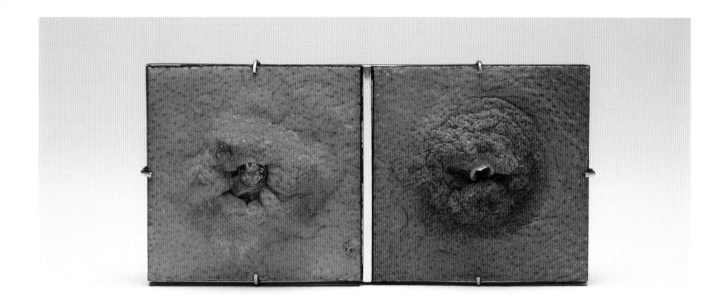

Maker: Joshua Kosker | **Title:** *Tips & Corners* | **Materials:** 4383 minneola, 925 sterling silver, 304 stainless steel, faceted stone | **Size:** 38 mm × 76 mm × 12 mm | **Image credit:** Joshua Kosker

Narrative: A piece of fruit is a thing to behold—ultimately to be eaten—and so to embody its skin would be something else. I believe there is beauty in the peel and promise found hiding in the flesh.

I can recall a former companion who became aroused every time I peeled an orange. Perhaps it was the methodical way I caressed and rubbed the fruit between my legs to loosen the skin. Maybe it was the gentle manner in which I nibbled the outer rind to separate the skin from the flesh in one meticulous strike. I only wanted to get to the center of the fruit. It developed into a bittersweet relationship. I have since moved on to tangelos.

Maker: Joshua Kosker | **Title:** *Cubic Tangelo Necklace III* | **Materials:** Tangelo peel, plywood, sterling silver | **Size:** 305 mm × 115 mm × 45 mm | **Image credit:** Joshua Kosker

Narrative: My "Cubic Tangelo" series is part of an ongoing inquiry based around connections between people and objects; the tactile allure of skin on skin, the corporeal presence of material, the touchy-feely, grab-at tendencies exhibited through want, especially that of utterly impractical objects. Japanese farmers on the island of Shikoku have been growing square watermelons. According to locals, "In matter of taste there can be no dispute here. Nobody cares what's inside of it." I created the cubic tangelo for no other reason than to hold in my hands. I had never seen one before, so I found a way to make it. Realized as a hollow block of orange rind and wood, it contains an idea made tangible. It's square, honest work; completely fabricated from hardware and produce, it is the fruit of my labor.

ALEXIS KOSTUK

Alexis Kostuk works as the manager in the cooperative studio Jewel Envy in Toronto, Canada. She maintains her own business under the name Glaciale.

My work combines the elements of painterly work using enamel and traditional goldsmithing techniques. While creating I employ the use of narrative through depicting figurative representations of the world around to make into wearable art.

Maker: Alexis Kostuk | **Title:** *You Crack Me Up* | **Materials:** Sterling silver, copper, vitreous enamel, cotton and satin cord | **Size:** 170 mm | **Image credit:** Paul Ambtman

ERATO KOULOUBI

Exploring the art of jewelry, Erato Kouloubi is interested in curating contemporary art exhibitions.

My new work addresses environmental issues. Human activities are contaminating the world's water systems and disrupting the lives of animals. From toxic chemical runoff to the accumulation of litter, miles away from land.

We alter the planet rapidly and we experience the consequences. I used tar as my main material in order to convey the threat, the fear and the crude death of all living beings that live in nature and are condemned by humanity. In my country, Greece, tar is a very common finding on our beaches. Sometimes, in collaboration with the sea, it creates unique sculptures, the content of which is a mysterious mixture of life and death.

Maker: Erato Kouloubi | **Title:** *Asphyxia* | **Materials:** Tar, bronze, pigment, wool | **Size:** 160 mm × 40 mm × 60 mm | **Image credit:** Alexis Kamitsos |

Maker: Erato Kouloubi | **Title:** *Two Bodies Cannot Occupy the Same Place (Handpiece)* | **Materials:** Tar, bronze, pigment, light bulb | **Size:** 120 mm × 50 mm × 40 mm | **Image credit:** Alexis Kamitsos

Maker: Erato Kouloubi | **Title:** *Monomolecular Neckpiece* | **Materials:** Tar, bronze, pigment, plastic bag | **Size:** 320 mm × 160 mm × 60 mm | **Image credit:** Alexis Kamitsos |

ROBIN KRANITZKY & KIM OVERSTREET

Since 1985, when serendipity brought them together, Kim Overstreet and Robin Kranitzky have always thought of their collaboration and artistic process as a natural one. Most days they are in their Richmond, Virginia studio working together in the world of mixed media and story telling. "Jewelry as theater," "timeless," and "surreal worlds" are often words used to describe their signature brooches.

Kim and Robin believe their desire to work in the narrative is partially influenced from their past. Both grew up in Virginia, during the 1950s and '60s, in large families with readily available playmates. Robin recalls siblings would be assigned parts in imaginative narratives, utilizing any found objects as props for their playful stories. A stick would become a fishing pole, a willow tree a house, moss was used as carpet, a curled leaf became a cup to drink from the creek. Kim has memories of sleeping outdoors and telling tall tales during long summer nights in a time when there were no technological distractions. With this background they feel it is natural for two Southern women to be drawn into the delight of stories, now told through their mixed-media brooches.

Maker: Robin Kranitzky & Kim Overstreet | **Title:** *Blemish* | **Materials:** Acrylic, paper, glass, mirror, wood, silver, brass, copper, bone, polymer clay, fabric, thorns, make-up brush, watch parts and Bakelite razor parts | **Size:** 114.3 mm × 76.2 mm × 25.4 mm | **Image credit:** photographer wishes to remain anonymous

Narrative: Why is there so much focus on physical appearance?

Young women learn to scrutinize their physicality to the point of disaster. A small natural blemish becomes overwhelming. Many women turn to surgery to change their bodies to society's "ideal." In our desire to make a statement about these ideas of body image, we chose a Bakelite deco razor as our starting point, building upon it to create the scene of a tender peach in the path of destruction.

MARIE-LOUISE KRISTENSEN

Marie-Louise Kristensen graduated from the Institute of Precious Metals in 2004, and she lives and works in Copenhagen.

My creative process and the narrative way of working enables me to connect with, reflect on and understand the world around me.

I work with impressions and moods and combine them with quotations from the art world. My works deals with how design icons, which comprise a static and recognizable form, also hold a diffused memory and surreal narrative . . . .

Maker: Marie-Louise Kristensen | **Title:** *How to Get Thin Quick?* | **Materials:** Silver, milliput, cernit | **Size:** 100 mm × 100 mm × 40 mm | **Image credit:** Dorte Krogh

Narrative: My works are created in close dialogue with what is currently taking place around me. The painting of my new apartment brought me into close contact with heating and radiator pipes and thermostatic radiator valves. Alongside this, I'm fascinated by the spam-box in my e-mail program; I hand-pick text from the subject fields, thereby collecting both titles and inspiration for my works.

Maker: Marie-Louise Kristensen | **Title:** *Hr. Schwann / CPH: Ducks by the Lake* | **Materials:** Silver, plastic, green diamonds | **Size:** 290 mm × 90 mm × 15 mm | **Image credit:** Marie-Louise Kristensen

Narrative: The lakes; at a distance snow white swans glide majestically over the surface of the water with their heads lifted high. Up close one can see the dirty water, the uneaten and soggy pieces of bread, bicycle skeletons; a mix of all the junk people throw into the water. The piece of jewelry is this story initiated by my own experience of how I skipped over things in an attempt to keep up a façade while some of the unacknowledged and uncontrolled fought its way to the surface and became evident and visible.

Maker: Marie-Louise Kristensen | **Title:** *Cph faire la fete, et après / CPH: Ducks Left Over* | **Materials:** Secondhand gold ring, painted brass | **Size:** 40 mm × 22 mm × 25 mm | **Image credit:** Marie-Louise Kristensen

Narrative: Copenhagen—a summer romance and the predictable break up—sensations and emotions turned into a kaleidoscopic and urban (self) portrait.

The litter bins, with the community logo, are placed all over town and graffiti from a light post are the basis of a tale of lost love. The engagement ring, now with the duck feet, is thrown away. Just like I was thrown away and the party was over . . . .

LISA KRÖBER

German-born jewelry artist Lisa Kröber lives in Tallinn, Estonia. She shares a workshop with other Estonian jewelers, taking part in several group and solo exhibitions and is member of the Estonian Artist Union. She has built a jewelry design brand and produces small jewelry series.

My way to create jewelry art pieces is always starting with a *story. These stories I mainly write myself. They can be short texts, little poems or just some phrases, thoughts or words, which come spontaneously or have been haunting me for a long time. Creating jewelry out of this by transforming my thoughts into material, I found a way to tell the stories.*

Maker: Lisa Kröber | **Title:** *Brief (in English: Letter)—Front View* | **Materials:** Brass, wax, resin, citrine | **Size:** 65 mm × 70 mm × 25 mm | **Image credit:** Lisa Kröber

Maker: Lisa Kröber | **Title:** *Wintertree* | **Materials:** Silver, wood, spray paint | **Size:** 150 mm × 300 mm × 10 mm | **Image credit:** Lisa Kröber

Maker: Lisa Kröber | **Title:** *Brief (in English: Letter)—Back View* | **Materials:** Brass, wax, resin, citrine | **Size:** 65 mm × 70 mm × 25 mm | **Image credit:** Lisa Kröber

ANDREW KUEBECK

Andrew Kuebeck works in a variety of formats ranging from functional jewelry to sculptural objects and vessels. He has lectured and taught workshops nationally on the incorporation of photographic images into jewelry pieces and vessels.

Maker: Andrew Kuebeck | **Title:** *Lumberjack Brooch* | **Materials:** Copper, sterling silver, enamel, image on enamel, amber | **Size:** 64 mm × 64 mm × 13 mm | **Image credit:** Andrew Kuebeck

Narrative: This work is from a series that depicted the emotional implications of my choice to have a career in jewelry design and metalsmithing. Each brooch looked at a traditionally "masculine" career path that past men in my family chose, each piece taking the form of a tool that they would have used in their careers. Within each brooch I staged a self-portrait battle, pitting an authentic self (one who is following his own path in life) against one that is trapped in the cloak of tradition and familial expectations. This piece specifically looks for inspiration from my grandfather who was employed in the lumber industry in Germany.

PANJAPOL KULPAPANGKORN

Panjapol Kulpapangkorn (Pai) was born in 1986 in Bangkok, Thailand. He has exhibited his work internationally at galleries and museums.

Maker: Panjapol Kulpapangkorn | **Title:** *Smile (Jewelry Is at My Feet 00, Memory from Myself)* | **Materials:** Mixed media | **Size:** 80 mm × 50 mm × 15 mm | **Image credit:** Panjapol Kulpapangkorn

Narrative: "On the way to somewhere in the UK, it is very special but I don't know where it is, just take some photos to remind me."

Maker: Panjapol Kulpapangkorn | **Title:** *Mind the Gap (Jewelry Is at My Feet 00, Memory from Myself)* | **Materials:** Mixed media | **Size:** 60 mm × 60 mm × 10 mm | **Image credit:** Panjapol Kulpapangkorn

Narrative: "Yesterday I was in Bangkok, and Birmingham today, in the kitchen!!! I always do the same thing but a different place, a different feeling, and a different culture."

Maker: Panjapol Kulpapangkorn | **Title:** *7 Days a Week with Assoc. Prof. Wipha* | **Materials:** My mum's personal jewelry collection, plastic, resin | **Size:** 80 mm × 50 mm × 10 mm | **Image credit:** Panjapol Kulpapangkorn

Narrative: "I really love to wear and buy Thai birthday color stuff, for example, Monday is yellow, Tuesday is pink, Wednesday is green, Thursday is orange, Friday is blue, Saturday is purple, and Sunday is red . . ."
—My Mum, Assoc. Prof. Wipha Kulpapangkorn, who has lost memories since 2012

CHAO-HSIEN KUO

Chao-Hsien Kuo is a master goldsmith. Chao-Hsien's works are her observations during everyday life. Her interpretation of nature is romantic and fairy tale-like, and her works reflect the closeness between humans and nature in Finland. She is based in Lahti, Finland.

Maker: Chao-Hsien Kuo | **Title:** *Spotty Flower with a Flying Seed* | **Materials:** 925 0/00 silver, keum-boo 24k gold foil, Akoya pearl |
Size: 37 mm × 25 mm × 40 mm | **Image credit:** Chao & Eero. Photography by Chao-Hsien Kuo

Narrative: I am fascinated by seeds, which are able to fly. I adore how they fly away from the original plants, how they dance in the wind, and how they manage to pass on their journey to the next generation. When a seed is ready and about to fly away, what happens around it could change its life. A sudden rain fall could scatter the seeds around the mother plant; a blow of strong wind would carry them far away; a curious little girl might just collect a few and keep them in glass jars on the table. But no matter what happens, these little seeds will do their best to live on. The seemingly fragile little seeds contain such strength and energy.

I created a flower ring that produces little flying seeds. The three flower petals hold the seed in place by tension. It looks like when the flower is in full bloom, the seed will spring out and fly away.

Maker: Chao-Hsien Kuo | **Title:** *Flying Seeds* | **Materials:** 925 0/00 silver, keum-boo 24k gold foil | **Size:** 155 mm × 155 mm × 17 mm |
Image credit: Chao & Eero. Photography by Chao-Hsien Kuo

Maker: Chao-Hsien Kuo | **Title:** *Silver Wind Neckpiece No.3* | **Materials:** 925 0/00 silver | **Size:** 290 mm × 230 mm × 150 mm |
Image credit: Chao & Eero. Photography by Chao-Hsien Kuo

Narrative: This unique neckpiece is inspired by a plant—fireweed, commonly seen on the roadside at the end of summer in Finland. After the seedpods open and the seeds fly away with the wind, the seedpods form beautiful curves on the plant. With this work, I want to interpret the elegant flowing lines I see in this ordinary plant.

CLAIRE LAVENDHOMME

Claire Lavendhomme is a jewelry designer based in Brussels, Belgium.

For me . . . the jewel as a vehicle of intimacy, color, poetry, void, sensuality, emotion, link, silence, sensitivity, hatred, love, cries, life, death, speech, laughter, art . . . .

My creation work encompasses issues such as birth, life and death, the visible, the veiled, being/becoming, distance, fusion; it suggests sensuality.

Searching for some kind of consistency between the internal, poetic, vibrant inner life of the jewel (what one wants to say about it) and its external life (material, form, color). With the desire to exchange, through the visible and the invisible things (memory, senses, being).

Maker: Claire Lavendhomme | **Title:** *Sithonia 1* | **Materials:** Silver, gold, photo resin | **Size:** 100 mm × 500 mm × 15 mm | **Image credit:** Claire Lavendhomme

Narrative: Sometimes we are faced with painful things . . . and we need time for introspection. We have to stand there—meet life—weightless—suspended in between, on a wire. Stop for the time of a breath . . . and then, remember—and live. Fully.

HELENA LEHTINEN

Helena Lehtinen has taken part in several individual and collective exhibitions during her career, both in Finland and abroad. Lehtinen lives and works in Lahti, where she has had her own workshop since 1980.

Maker: Helena Lehtinen | **Title:** *Garden 1 (Brooch)* | **Materials:** Silver, textile, glass beads, reconstructed stone | **Size:** 150 mm × 90 mm × 10 mm | **Image credit:** Kimmo Heikkilä

Narrative: In Finland, during the winter snow is abounding. The landscape is nearly black and white, or more like white mixed with gray shadows. Everything is blanketed in many layers of snow. One can only wonder what is under all those white hillocks?

It could be considered a bit contradictory to think of how a garden in bloom might look in winter. What was it again, the real narcissus yellow, or the darling blue shade? How does a mind produce these visions? How does our memory hold on to those colors? What feelings remain? Can't we almost smell the perfumes of the gardens that elude us?

The imaginary winter garden has a certain beauty that is different than a blooming garden in summer.

Maker: Helena Lehtinen | **Title:** *Garden 3 (Brooch)* | **Materials:** Silver, textile, reconstructed stone, ready-mades | **Size:** 140 mm × 60 mm × 50 mm | **Image credit:** Kimmo Heikkilä

Maker: Helena Lehtinen | **Title:** *Garden 4 (Brooch)* | **Materials:** Wood, yarn, glass beads, silver | **Size:** 180 mm × 50 mm × 30 mm | **Image credit:** Kimmo Heikkilä

ALISA LETSIUS

Alisa Letsius is a jeweler and a member of the Creative Artists's Union. Philologist by education, but a creator by vocation she started to create jewelry in 2009. She has studied various techniques with her main directions in jewelry making being color and conception. Alisa also takes an experimental approach to making. She believes that color gives life to everything. Alisa has participated in different exhibitions all over the world.

Maker: Alisa Letsius | **Title:** *Remember My Last Kiss* | **Materials:** Brass, nickel-silver, silver, red phianite, polymer clay, resin |
Size: 80 mm × 50 mm × 30 mm | **Image credit:** Alisa Letsius

Narrative: This brooch tells us a story about parting. You have said goodbye to your sweetheart but you want him to remember you and keep in mind the last kiss. Red is a color of passion and love thus meaning that the feelings are still alive.

KEITH A. LEWIS

Keith Lewis's jewelry deals with issues of identity, loss, memory and the notion of jewelry as a transportable polemic.

In addition to his work as an artist and teacher, he has also written for a number of publications.

He wishes that students would stop sleeping and start spending more time in the studio. He hates excuses. His favorite fruit is jabuticaba.

My work advertises my gay-man's preoccupations
with the sweet stickiness of the body,

with envy of the beautiful
and with the winding kelp of loss and memory
that laps about our ankles.
It seeks out hosts
willing to allow themselves to be hijacked
as carriers of lust and sorrow.
It invites familiars to recognize—
in miniature—
the carnival reflections of themselves.

Maker: Keith A. Lewis | Title: *Thirty-Five Dead Souls (Pendants)* |
Materials: Assorted materials | Size: Assorted sizes |
Image credit: Photographer wishes to remain anonymous.
Courtesy of Rotasa Foundation

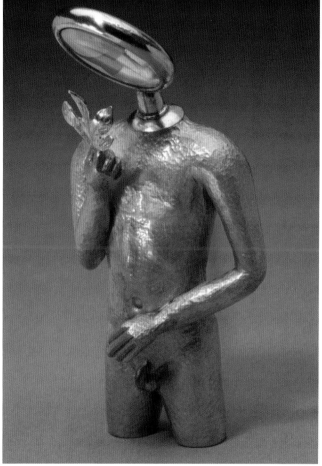

Maker: Keith A. Lewis | Title: *Figleaf Pin* | Materials: Sterling silver,
18k gold, lucite | Size: 80 mm × 50 mm × 30 mm |
Image credit: Photographer wishes to remain anonymous.
Collection of Emily Gurtman, Largo, Florida

Narrative: Jewelry has always acknowledged loss, ceremony and sentiment and there is a beauty, humanity and glory in such acts of devotion. I've tried to do the same—tried to fill gaping holes with tiny bits of metal fashioned into charms of sorts. I've made portraits that honored those fallen in my community, known to me or unknown.

"Thirty-Five Dead Souls," a series of thrity-six necklaces, attempts to give a last nod to the thirty-five friends and acquaintances gone from me at that time—some specific, some more symbolic. They assert their desire to survive while suffering decay, restriction and dementia while under viral attack.

I'm there as a thirty-sixth, watching and waiting.

Narrative: In *Figleaf* the figure removes a classical veil of modesty. He scrutinizes it with a magnifying lens. Thus he tries to gain an understanding of that leaf (and of himself) but has as a tool only the lens that he has been given.

As children, little boys (including myself) set leaves aflame with lenses, and thus such scrutiny of the self (physical or psychic) is dangerous indeed. But queer boys—not seeing ourselves in mirrors or reflected in the lives of others—feel that we must look, despite the danger. (And, as a consequence, I suppose we flame . . . .)

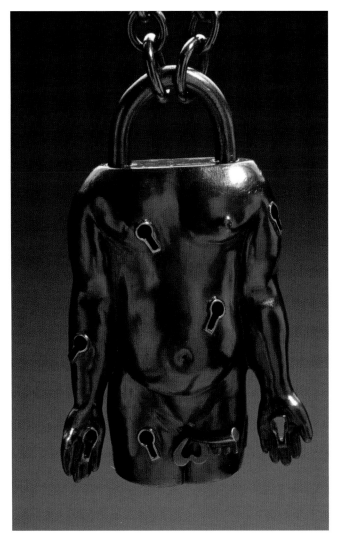

Maker: Keith A. Lewis | **Title:** *Key (Pendant and Chain)* | **Materials:** Sterling silver | **Size:** Pendant 40 mm × 80 mm × 30 mm, Chain 180 mm dia | **Image credit:** Photographer wishes to remain anonymous

Maker: Keith A. Lewis | **Title:** *Sebastian (Imaginary Self-Portrait) (Pin)* | **Materials:** Sterling silver, 18k gold | **Size:** 40 mm × 90 mm × 40 mm | **Image credit:** Photographer wishes to remain anonymous. Collection of Susan Beech, Tiburon, California

Narrative: The term "key" raises associations of inaccessibility (or the privilege of access), secrets, valuables, etc.—but also notions of capture or incarceration, illegality, theft, etc.

The story of Pandora's Box was a major consideration in making the piece as was the formulation head/heart/hand where (as in other pieces) I have in a sense substituted "crotch" for "heart." Remember, too, the expression "key to my heart."

The figure has numerous keyholes including ones at the rectum and hands, implying sexual penetration and masturbation. The various keyholes also imply the possibility of unlocking other secrets or releasing any number of ills. There is, of course, a specific connection to HIV as a "secret" or a "criminal" that might be released. I was also thinking about the binding (locking) of the HIV virus to the cells.

The piece also comments on a solitary keeping of secrets (or of the self) intact in the fact that the penis is a key that can be "satisfied" by the holes in the hands *but* that key, of course, is also the means of connecting with (or infecting) others.

Narrative: All fags have to do a St. Sebastian, given his sexy persistence in Christian art. And western art is full of his religious bondage and ecstatic look. Sebastian, in professing Christianity, was ordered to recant, and upon refusing was martyred by arrows. He was, ironically, later healed and again professing his faith was (successfully I guess) stoned to death.

I've chosen to suggest collusion on Sebastian's part (it's martyrdom after all) and by distinguishing the arrow in his hands from the others suggest that the arrow is (or only seems?) different. Does the figure proffer the tool of his subsequent destruction? Passion? Illness? What does the implied reciprocity really mean? Does his tentative offer (of love? trust? disease?) suggest a different future than our immediate past?

I tried to arrive at a stance which has a kind of tentative dignity, a willingness to trust but an attendant willingness to accept what may come. He seems to look toward a kind of tentative post-AIDS future, or at least towards the notion of ample time, bought by caution and by medication, and yet fragile, like a daydream.

Classic belief was that Apollo's arrows brought plague, and thus Sebastian's sexy arrows came to symbolize plague as well. Desire is risky, to the body and the spirit, but without it humanity is diminished.

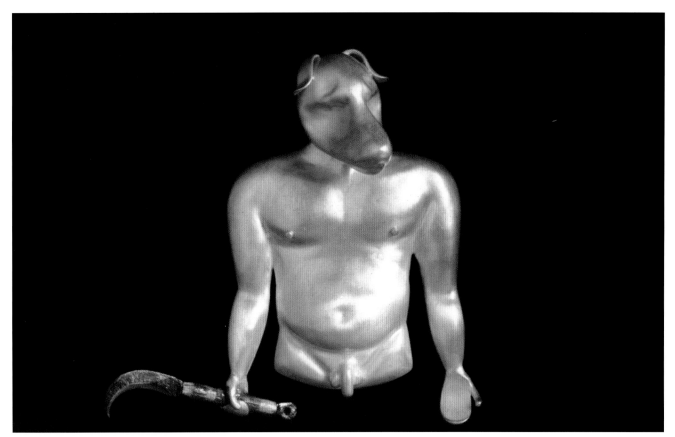

Maker: Keith A. Lewis | Title: *Well Doug, It's 36 Now . . . (Self Portrait in Memory of Doug DeSimone) (Pin)* | Materials: Sterling silver, steel, willow, pigment, epoxy resin | Size: 50 mm × 70 mm | Image credit: Photographer wishes to remain anonymous. Collection of Don and Heidi Endemann

Narrative: This is a self portrait, but commemorates Doug DeSimone who used to sniff and nuzzle like a dog as our bodies fumbled for jigsaw resolution.

Why did the virus that killed him, given every opportunity, hesitate to leap to me?

Doug DiSimone—called Big Doug for several reasons—who, when once I lamented being loved by no one, sheepishly said that maybe I just wasn't paying attention. How could I have missed that? Only to realize years later that he was offering himself heart and soul? We did fuck like dogs, though, and this self-portrait marks his place on me as the thirty-sixth death.

BELGIUM

RIA LINS

Ria Lins, a Belgian artist, is amazed by interpersonal relationships and by people's ability to adapt rather easily to the rapid changes and diversity of our society. Her jewelry is inspired by these notions, as well as by themes like contact, connection, comfort, and mending.

People can feel the stories or shared experiences behind my work, even though they may not be aware of them. Once the piece is made, the memory has found its place, and there is no need to explain it or its details. At the moment the piece is worn and shown, it will get its freedom of existence and enrichment.

Maker: Ria Lins | Title: *Holy Water* | Materials: Silver | Size: 100 mm × 20 mm × 20 mm | Image credit: Dries Van den Brande

Narrative: I made a series of brooches called "Eau Bénité," or "Holy Water." Water is a need we can't live without; it is the source of all life. Water is used for religious rituals, as a power source, a purifier, and as a sign of wealth and power. It supports, nourishes, shelters, purifies, divides, and binds. Anyone can see and feel the strength and the meaning of water.

KEITH LO BUE

The work I produce has always involved making connections between disparate phenomena: reality and surreality; preservation and decay; memory and forgetting. There is a deliberate effort to create in my artwork a fragile technology of bone and soil, exhumed from the scattered shards of lives preceding our own. In this way I can strike an empathy with those who reached for the promise of progress with one hand while shielding their fallibility with the other.

Narratives in my work, such as they are, can be thought of as "vertical" in nature, rather than horizontally linear. This vertical narrative is a slice—a moment in time, much in the way a dream is recalled upon awakening, only to have it slip from awareness a moment later.

My material process is crude and intuitive while trying to create objects of careful detail and structure. This dichotomy keeps the creative impulse coursing through me, the thrill of making married with the spontaneity of instinct.

Maker: Keith Lo Bue | **Title:** *Four, and What They Did (Neckpiece Pendant)* | **Materials:** Spigot handle, tintypes, waxed linen thread, resin, beach-worn soda can bottom, opals, sixteenth-century Ukrainian illuminated manuscript, nineteenth-century engraving and Asian text, brass wire, nineteenth-century Masonic embroidered ceremonial sash, paper, text, paint, soil | **Size:** 90 mm diameter × 25 mm; sash 70 mm | **Image credit:** Keith Lo Bue

Maker: Keith Lo Bue |
Title: *The Watcher (Brooch)* |
Materials: 1890s pinchbeck
swivel locket brooch, nineteenth-
century book cover, opals,
tourmalines, mustard seeds,
ambrotype, waxed linen thread,
early nineteenth-century
steel-point engraving, nineteenth-
century color lithograph, paint,
resin, paper, text, soil |
Size: 65 mm × 60 mm × 17 mm
| **Image credit:** Keith Lo Bue

Maker: Keith Lo Bue | **Title:** *Life's Record
(for Mira) (Neckpiece)* | **Materials:**
Victorian "pyralin ivory" serving fork,
dichroic glass beads, Mira Lo Bue's baby
teeth, resin, sea urchin spines, copper nails,
opals, carved wood from a Lo Bue baby crib,
waxed linen thread, nineteenth-century steel
keys, 1920s elastic cord, camera lens and
housing, mid-nineteenth-century steel-point
engraving and color lithograph, enamel
pocket watch face, steel and bronze wire,
paint, sixteenth- and nineteenth-century
paper, text, soil | **Size:** Pendant 14 mm ×
50 mm × 25 mm; cord/chain 444 mm |
Image credit: Keith Lo Bue

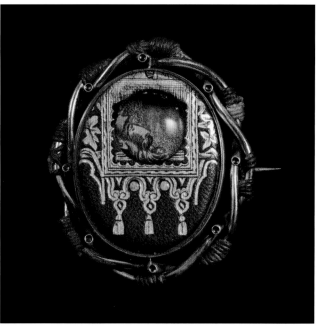

TOVA LUND

Tova Lund is a jeweler and sculptor living and working in northern California. The incorporation of found objects builds the foundation for narrative in her work. The objects themselves come to represent places and experiences and promote the potential for intimacy when engaging with objects.

Maker: Tova Lund | **Title:** *Disturbing the Sea* | **Materials:** Tin, copper, steel | **Size:** 69 mm × 40 mm × 19 mm | **Image credit:** Tova Lund

Narrative: Made after a ten-day trip around Lake Superior, the brooch reflects the industrial history of the lake, and consequently, the graveyard of ships that lies beneath its tempestuous waters. Its title, *Disturbing the Sea*, references the often absent awareness of that history and the notion of the landscape unearthing these facts when we are perceptive.

Maker: Tova Lund | **Title:** *Reciprocity* | **Materials:** Stone, tin, copper | **Size:** 38 mm × 19 mm × 12 mm | **Image credit:** Tova Lund

Narrative: This piece is made half of cut stone and half with found and altered tin. When I originally placed these two materials together I was motivated to create one solid object out of these seemingly disparate materials due to their uncanny visual relationship. The rusting tin piece on the left reflects the traces of iron in the stone. It translates the story of its material origin, its use, and its inevitable decay.

Maker: Tova Lund | **Title:** *Found* | **Materials:** Tin, shell, copper | **Size:** 76 mm × 44 mm × 12 mm | **Image credit:** Tova Lund

Narrative: I made this piece during a tumultuous life change, which included a change of location. I began to wake up early and explore the beaches of my new home on the pacific coast as a form of walking meditation. One morning I had come across a beach of washed up bull kelp, a lot of which were bound in chaotic, tangled heaps. I realized, with a touch of ironic humor, that I related to these scattered bundles. They were violently tossed in the waves, tangled into an unforgiving mess, and then strewn across the shore with their shameless, chaotic history exposed.

I added a representation of this to the back of the piece. The front represents the experiences of walking and collecting. An object collected from that morning, a piece of shell, rests in a niche inside of an altered tin.

RIKKE LUNNEMANN

Rikke Lunnemann is a jeweler born on the Faroe Islands, educated in London and now based in the seaside town of Svendborg in Denmark.

My work draws inspiration from narratives and stories. My jewelry tells something subtle or fun and there is often a personal story behind each piece. *I use the story as a tool to see things in a different light and to question certain accepted values. I wish—through their own life and experience—to make viewers and wearers wonder, feel and reflect.*

Maker: Rikke Lunnemann | **Title:** *Across Borders (An Interpretative Comment to the Danish "Jewelry Law")* |
Materials: A set of 3 rings with different numbers of pearls. 18k eco gold and 02.5 mm freshwater pearls |
Size: Ring 1, 20 mm × 30 mm × 1.5 mm; Ring 2, 20 mm × 30 mm × 7 mm; Ring 3, 20 mm × 35 mm × 20 mm |
Image credit: Iben Kaufmann Photographer

Narrative: "Across . . . Borders."
What is accepted and what may be confiscated?

PETER MACHATA

Peter Machata is a sculptor and a jewelry artist.

Maker: Peter Machata | **Title:** *Relic* | **Materials:** Silver, black corian | **Size:** 100 mm × 60 mm × 15 mm | **Image credit:** Peter Machata

Narrative: *Relic* is very personal, dealing with a couple's living together. From the jeweler's point of view the wedding ring, as a symbol, is the focus of his interest. Appearances of hands or fragments of hands, with, and specially without rings, are interpreted with digital tools and afterwards combined in compositions: objects from new materials are manufactured with traditional jeweler's methods which creates different types of reliquaries.

JANA MACHATOVÁ

Jana Machatová is a jewelry artist from Slovakia. She lives and works in her workshop together with her husband Peter Machata in the small town of Stupava.

Maker: Jana Machatová | **Title:** *Spartakiade (Brooch)* | **Materials:** Plexiglass, silver, paper in laminated plastic, gold foil | **Size:** 100 mm × 70 mm × 20 mm | **Image credit:** Peter Machata

Narrative: In my collection "Where Are You From?" I tried to show my experience with the political system and social situation from my childhood. Formal kisses between politicians without love, children in political organizations, unified living . . . this all has left imprints on our personalities. I tried to set traditional ornament, the beauty of a kiss and the cuteness of cookie cutters, in contrast to the terrible period and symbols of communism.

These jewelry pieces should not be body decorations. They are meant to be a memento, an expression of opinion.

Maker: Jana Machatová | **Title:** *Eine Unaufmerksame Lehrerin* | **Materials:** Silver, photocopy in laminated plastic, gold foil, pearls | **Size:** 10 mm × 75 mm × 70 mm | **Image credit:** Peter Machata

Narrative: In my collection "Love Is Love" I used photographs and pictures from my postcard collection. By setting them into a new context I tell new stories and bring to the fore dreams, poetry and hidden desires.

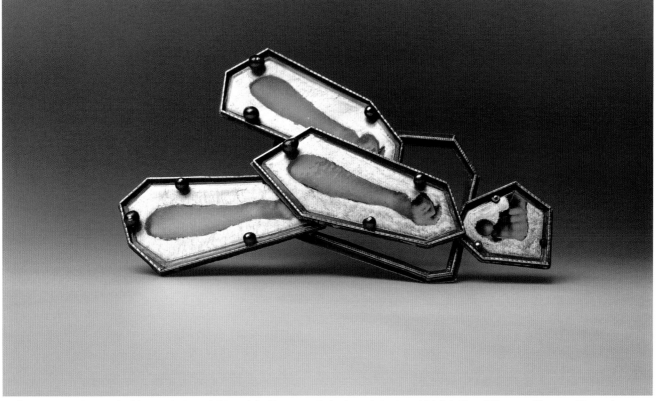

Maker: Jana Machatová | **Title:** *Apple Story* | **Materials:** Photocopy in laminated plastic, gold foil | **Size:** 110 mm × 60 mm × 20 mm | **Image credit:** Peter Machata

ELEANORE MACNISH

Eleanore Macnish is an artist working primarily in glass and silver with an interrelated practice of jewelry, sculpture and design.

For the last twenty years Eleanore has followed an independent course as a jewelry artist. Her work takes two distinct forms: candy-colored, playful yet laborious lamp-worked glass beads, and intricate, quirky, Victorian-inspired assemblages of vintage and sterling silver elements. Both jewelry lines evidence her knowledge of historical manufacturing techniques. They often include items from her personal collection of antique prints, photos, advertisements, costume jewelry, buttons and glass.

Jewelry is intimate and accessible. A tactile and visual statement, jewelry is many times a carrier of memories and is held dear through generations. I work in the narrative because I take immense satisfaction in taking old cast off things and making something new and meaningful from them—I bring them new life, give them a new story . . . and I love that.

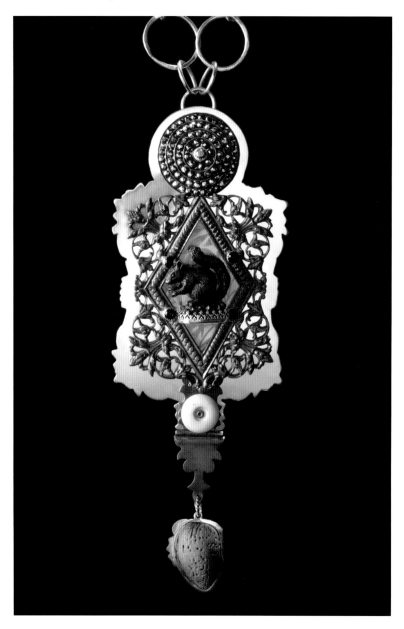

Maker: Eleanore Macnish | **Title:** *I Could Watch You Walk Away All Day* | **Materials:** Sterling silver , antique collar button, Victorian buckle, mica, bronze squirrel, onyx, furniture hinge, William Morris print, steel button, almond locket set in silver | **Size:** 75 mm × 125 mm | **Image credit:** Margot Geist

Narrative: This is about the power of words, how we interpret words and the importance of "squirreling away" a mental cache of compliments, things about yourself of which you are proud, personal milestones, etc., to see you through the low times in life. Turmoil in life can easily become all encompassing, and wearing an object with loving words against the skin can be comforting and provide a connection to one's true self. The back of this piece is inscribed with "good things" and the locket contains a slip of paper that says "I could watch you walk away all day."

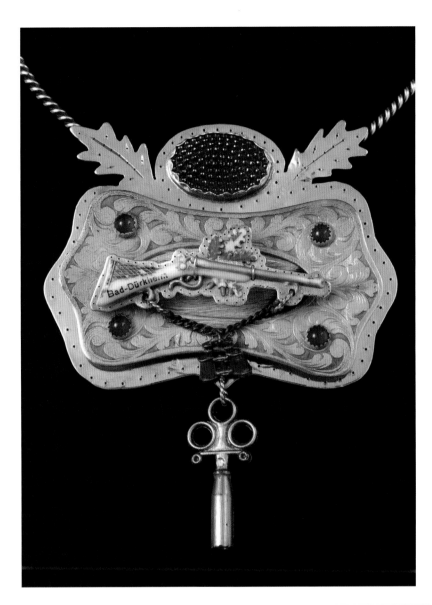

Maker: Eleanore Macnish | **Title:** *German Hunting Medal* | **Materials:** Sterling silver, vintage glass button, vintage brass buckle, cow hide, vintage travel memento pin, vintage postcard peeking through cutout window on back, mica, clock key | **Size:** 85 mm × 80 mm | **Image credit:** Margot Geist

Narrative: I love to travel and love to pick things up along the way, especially things with a history. There is something particularly special about acquiring an antique travel souvenir that someone else acquired to remember a trip. The melding of two sets of memories, one known and one unknown.

Maker: Eleanore Macnish | **Title:** *Paris Subway Station* | **Materials:** Vintage Bakelite die, vintage earring, vintage rhinestone buckle, cow fur, metal bee pin, garnet, sterling silver | **Size:** 85 mm × 100 mm | **Image credit:** Margot Geist

Narrative: I made this after returning from a trip to Paris—I had not been to the city in twenty years and loved seeing many of the same things in my forties that I had seen when I was sixteen and twenty-six, and how my appreciation for them had developed, while my love for them stayed constant.
Mixed with the influences of traditional New Mexican tin work, the lotus blossom and undulating lines of the leaves remind me of those amazing art nouveau iron subway entrances in Paris, thus the name.

ASAGI MAEDA

Asagi Maeda is a jewelry artist based in Tokyo. Some of her works are in selected collections of the Museum of Arts and Design in New York and the Museum of Fine Arts in Boston.

From an early age, I always loved making stories by using my imagination. For me, writing poems and stories is the most natural way of self-expression. Usually, words come to me first, then I start to see the vague image of work to create. Sometimes, I see some random images first. When that happens, the images end up coming together into one story. With that background behind them, my works all come with narratives.

The world is embracing you filled with a joyful heart
You descended from a rainbow
by the particles of the seven hues
Happy Birthday
to your dazzling purity vitality and heart like a cloudless sky
You were born on a truly beautiful day full of joy and motivation
with pure vision
and a noble heart
blowing clouds off in an instant
You descended from a rainbow by the articles of the seven hues
Happy Birthday to you

Maker: Asagi Maeda | **Title:** *Happy Birthday* | **Materials:** Sterling silver, 18k gold, diamond, enamel on fine silver, acrylic | **Size:** 117 mm × 138 mm × 45 mm | **Image credit:** Koichiro Shiiki

Narrative: I made this bracelet in commemoration of my son's birth. The poem above is inlayed in the acrylic part.

EVELYN MARKASKY

Evelyn lives in Santa Cruz, California, but started her life in an edgy little steel town with a large immigrant population in Youngstown, Ohio. She spent many of her college years in photo booths, creating images to use for her BFA in sculpture where she incorporated sculpture, jewelry, conceptual art, and comedy, not necessarily in that order. Evelyn works in various metals and uses vitreous enamels sometimes for their colors, but mostly as a patina adding texture and an aged effect to her pieces. She continues her love of fire by torch-firing her enamel pieces. She is always experimenting, trying to find a new way to work with metal and enamels.

In my art, I like to tell stories using the right side of my brain to express the thoughts in my head without words. I like the look of the written word and will often incorporate it in my pieces, but it is usually obscured, not meant to be read. But the essence of the story is there, absorbed into the piece through my fingertips.

Maker: Evelyn Markasky | **Title:** *Rights of Spring (Necklace)* | **Materials:** Copper, torch-fired vitreous enamels, iron oxide pigments | **Size:** 25.4 mm × 508 mm × 6.35 mm | **Image credit:** Evelyn Markasky

Narrative: This bird necklace is inspired by the story of Demeter and Persephone from the book *Lost Goddesses of Early Greece: A Collection of Pre-Hellenic Greek Myths* by Charlene Spretnak. On the front I have birds or parts of birds and on the back are the words representing the story—Leaves and Vines, Flowers and Grass, Grew into Fullness, Faded into Decay, Began Again.

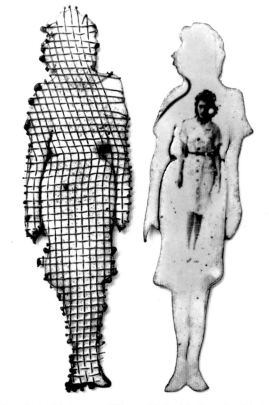

Maker: Evelyn Markasky | **Title:** *Song of Amergin (Necklace)* | **Materials:** Sterling silver, 24k gold, copper, aluminum, torch-fired vitreous enamels, iron oxide pigments | **Size:** 457.2 mm × 25.4 mm × 3.81 mm | **Image credit:** Evelyn Markasky

Narrative: The first law of thermodynamics states that energy can't be created or destroyed; it can only be converted from one type to another. Most objects that absorb visible light remit it as heat, so although an object may appear dark, it is likely that it is bright at a frequency that humans can't perceive.

Maker: Evelyn Markasky | **Title:** *Inside Sophie (from the Private Icon Series) (Two Brooches)* | **Materials:** Copper, copper mesh, torch-fired vitreous enamels, iron oxide pigments | **Size:** 76.2 mm × 25.4 mm × 3.81 mm | **Image credit:** Evelyn Markasky

Narrative: Inspired from Greek icons I had as a child. I take those memories and create new myths from modern images.

BECKA (REBECCA) MARSH

I am a sophomore student studying 3-D arts at Seton Hill University in Greensburg, Pennsylvania. I've had some great experience in the arts; I've been commissioned for murals, paintings, displays, stage fabrication, and I sell my own jewelry and purses. I'm often very drawn to taxidermy and use bones, skins, and carcasses regularly.

Narrative work, to me, is very natural. All of my works I label as conceptual and are intrinsically involved with my ideology and myself. This is where my taxidermy work sprung from; death was always interesting to me in multiple ways. I do not kill anything; I only use already dead animals. Animals die all the time, and I do not have the arrogance to take a life to make art. In fact, my work is based on the exact opposite idea. I take dead animals and make them into art to celebrate their lives. I also see my dead animals as a statement on my femininity. Playing with gross animals isn't very "ladylike," but neither am I. "Ladylike" doesn't exist and gender identity is stupid. Social justice can be found in almost all of my art. My art is sometimes subconsciously expressive of my inner political and social commentary.

Maker: Becka (Rebecca) Marsh | **Title:** *Sweet Tooth Pin Series (3 of 24)* | **Materials:** Resin, deer teeth (*Sweet Tooth Pin*)—Yarn, hemp cord, deer jaw (*Jaw-Yarn Pin*)—Deer rib (*Cunt Pin*) | **Size:** (30 mm × 25 mm × 12.5 mm *Cunt Pin*) (65 mm × 55 mm × 20 mm *Jaw-Yarn Pin*) (35 mm × 35 mm × 20 mm *Sweet Tooth Pin*) | **Image credit:** Becka Marsh

Narrative: My femininity has never been fragile; I play with dead animals for fun. I have been involved with different aspects of taxidermy for about five years now and this art form has evolved into a natural expression of not only my crude brand of art but also my fascination with death and nature. There is something magical about taking a corpse of an animal from a road and transforming it into a work of beauty. Bones are a reflection of my inner self in the most literal and abstract sense.

LIETA MARZIALI

Lieta grew up in Italy and moved to the UK at the age of twenty where she pursued diverse careers in publishing, hospitality and archaeology. Having found her true calling, she retrained as a jeweler and now practices out of her studio in Norfolk. Her current work includes teaching and mentoring young people as well as mature students and emerging makers.

Working with narrative to me has always been as immediate and instinctive as working with jewelry itself. A title is often how a new piece will first manifest itself, through just looking at an object or reflecting on a feeling or experience. And yet a story needs to be ready to be told. No matter how powerful, there is no forcing it into existence and we must remain mindful to its own rhythms.

Most of my tales are embodied in a single one-off piece or an ensemble, emerging in my creative world, like a short story or novella, with a beginning and an end. But there are times when I happen upon a narrative that just works at a slower pace, that needs to be re-examined and retold from different angles. And this is where my series are born, never finite but projects that remain open to be revisited. Re-explored. Re-experienced.

It is the narrative itself, then, that takes center stage, directing the maker through constant dialogue and play. And the objects that come to embody this process— resolutely autonomous in their will to exist but sharers of the purpose of their existence—can be a bridge, able to both carry some of the soul of the teller and to re-invent themselves through the bond with the wearer.

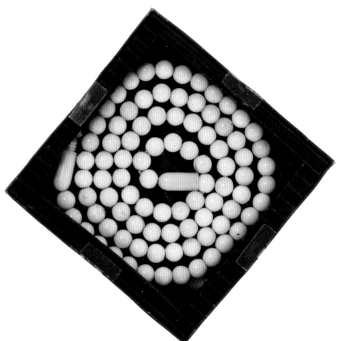

Maker: Lieta Marziali | **Title:** *De-Touch* | **Materials:** Copper, inherited ivory necklace, rubber, glass, steel pin | **Size:** 50 mm × 50 mm × 17 mm | **Image credit:** Andy Sapey

Narrative: Ivory is the perfect material to embody an emotional burden that, like this necklace, was passed down through generations bearing stories of suffering, guilt and regret. Here, archived in its own case and unable to be touched and to "touch," it loses its functionality as a necklace to acquire instead that of a badge: a severed yet inextricable part of personal identity and heritage.

Maker: Lieta Marziali | **Title:** *De-Liberate* | **Materials:** 18k gold, pebble, steel, recycled silver | **Size:** 300 mm × 220 mm × 35 mm (Chatelaine measurements 190 mm × 220 mm × 16 mm) | **Image credit:** Andy Sapey

Narrative: If the pebble wrapped in gold appears a simple metaphor for personal growth, the fundamental element in this piece is the chain. It appropriates a family heirloom and, made of steel, it provides a strong link to personal heritage. But it can also be detached and worn on the brooch, or be fully removed, its true power ultimately lying in our understanding and awareness of the availability of these choices.

MAGDALENA MAŚLERZ

Magdalena Maślerz is a jeweler journeyman (from the Krakow Chamber of Craft), a jeweler and a goldsmith. She is the founder of Xerion, the first school of traditional goldsmithing in Krakow.

In her artistic work Magdalena explores world of bones and animal origin materials, creating objects full of meaning. For her, jewelry is not only an ornament but it carries the meaning and the message that wearer wants to show to others. She finds original shapes of bones so inspiring, that she prefers to expose their natural beauty rather than to carve them. Her aim is to show people that precious materials of animal origin are not only ivory and tortoise shell.

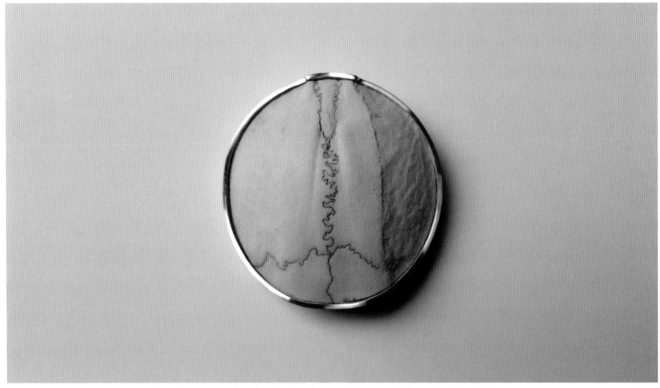

Maker: Magdalena Maślerz | **Title:** *That's Where the Shoe Pinches* | **Materials:** Dog skull, sterling silver | **Size:** 47 mm × 47 mm × 16 mm | **Image credit:** Magdalena Maślerz

Narrative: The lines on the skulls fascinate me. They look like an ancient alphabet, like a message hard to understand. Bones remind me of sculptures that are hidden under the skin. I really admire the creations of nature, which we so often tend to forget.

Maker: Magdalena Maślerz | **Title:** *Skull Bracelet* | **Materials:** Animal skull, sterling silver | **Size:** 65 mm × 65 mm × 32 mm | **Image credit:** Magdalena Maślerz

Narrative: Tribes believe that wearing a trophy from an animal gives them the power and spiritual features of the animal. The skull used in this bracelet was found in the forest. It was in pieces so it was impossible to find what animal it belonged to. What power will it give to the wearer?

Maker: Magdalena Maślerz | **Title:** *Souls of Cernunnos* | **Materials:** Deer antlers, sterling silver | **Size:** 270 mm × 120 mm × 15 mm | **Image credit:** Magdalena Maślerz

Narrative: In ancient and medieval times people used to believe that deer were able to travel from one world to the other. The inspiration behind this necklace is the Celtic god of the forests, Cernunnos, who carries the souls of the dying to the underworld. Deer antlers (an attribute of the god of the forests) are mounted with skulls and silver.

MÄRTA MATTSSON

Märta Mattsson was born in Stockholm and studied jewelry art.

Someone once told Märta: "You make jewelry for children, not for adults." Given that she draws inspiration from her childhood experiences of playing with stuffed animals and slugs, her fellow students in Tokyo were right when they described her work as "kimokawaii," which is in fact a combination of two words *kawaii* (cute) and *kimoi* (disgusting).

Sometimes I see beauty in things that other people find strange or are even repulsed by. I become fascinated when there is something you do not want to see and the feeling you get when you do not want to look at something, yet you still do. My jewelry deals with the tension that lies between attraction and repulsion. I take seemingly inappropriate materials, making ordinary and familiar objects seem extraordinary and unfamiliar.

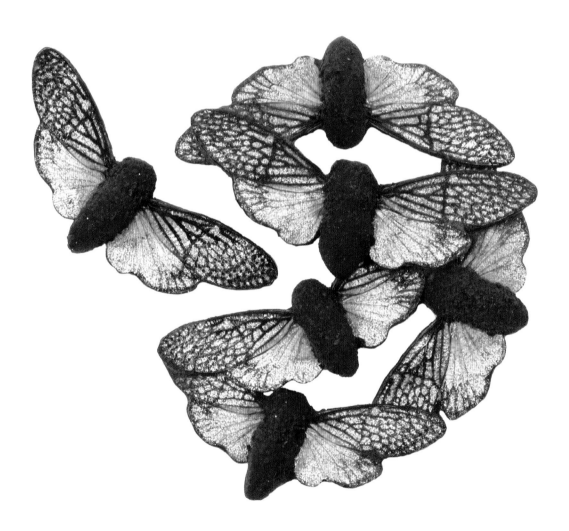

Maker: Märta Mattsson | **Title:** *Swarm* | **Materials:** Cicadas, crushed jet, resin, pigments, silver | **Size:** 100 mm × 90 mm × 20 mm | **Image credit:** Märta Mattsson

Narrative: In the eighteenth century many new breeds of animals and plants were discovered and it was the main era of cabinets of curiosities. People collected rarities because it gave them the feeling of being in the presence of something extraordinary and marvellous. The cabinets of curiosities were not meant to sympathize with the creatures on display, only marvel over their oddity.

In a world where not many new and exotic breeds are discovered I use dead creatures in my pieces to evoke wonder. The creatures are transformed and reborn; given a new life as objects of astonishment.

Maker: Märta Mattsson |
Title: *Coming Out* |
Materials: Beetle, walnut wood,
resin, wallpaper, silver, steel |
Size: 80 mm × 85 mm × 40 mm |
Image credit: Märta Mattsson |

Maker: Märta Mattsson |
Title: *Gathering* | **Materials:** Cicadas,
resin, pigments, copper, lacquer, silver |
Size: 350 mm × 200 mm × 30 mm |
Image credit: Märta Mattsson

ANNA MAZOŃ

Anna Mazoń is a full-time jewelry maker based in Krakow. Her work is mostly inspired by nature, as seen through European folklore, myths and contemporary Earth-based religions. She is an award-winning metal clay artist whose work graced covers of various magazines. She combines the sculptural quality of metal clay with traditional metalsmithing techniques.

Maker: Anna Mazoń | **Title:** *Natura Abhorret a Vacuo (Nature Abhors a Vacuum)* | **Materials:** Sterling silver | **Size:** 40 mm × 35 mm | **Image credit:** Anna Mazoń

Narrative: Vacuum/void is like the priciest jewel—so rare, with a life so short, immediately "destroyed" by nature. I wanted to catch this feeling of temporariness, constant movement, that hostility and greediness of nature. Beautiful, but blind, thus scary. And this little jewel of emptiness, in the very center, just for a blink of an eye. Emptiness/void is even more precious, because it's a reminder of something that was there. And filling this empty space, which is inevitable, is like losing something again. So why not to freeze that moment—even if only like this.

I made this piece while experiencing the terminal illness of my beloved dad, and preparing for loss.

JO McALLISTER

Since early 2015 the conceptual strand of Jo McAllister's practice is sustained by "The Ring Cycle," an ongoing series of exuberant, narrative rings based on words that end in *-ring* (flowering, feathering, powdering). New rings each year provide varied challenges not encountered in her design-led work, and the reflexive nature of the project enriches her practice and widens her audience.

The narrative element in McAllister's work began in 2011 when she was involved in "Rooms for Ideas," an exhibition based on the random allocation of a room in a museum. The Wildlife Room was full of the dark, dusty and dead. McAllister felt compelled to explore the nearby landscapes from which the inanimate creatures had originated.

She found herself walking, taking photographs and immersing herself in the sense of places in and around Hastings in the United Kingdom, sometimes accompanied by her son, and her relationship to these landscapes necessarily changed. Spaces for quiet observation became, in his presence, the hunting ground for conkers, feathers and bugs, and the scene of catapult and sword fights. A theme emerged: jewelry and objects for observation, collection and enjoyment. The collection of metaphysical jewelry and objects produced has fed back into her studio practice, thus the narrative has proved both a conduit for ideas and a platform for reflection.

Maker: Jo McAllister | Title: *Feather Collector's Box (Pendant)* | Materials: Fine silver 999, blue jay's hackle feathers, woollen felt, grosgrain ribbon | Size: 93 mm × 59 mm × 21 mm | Image credit: © Jo McAllister. Photograph by Alexander Brattell

Narrative: Tiny blue jay's hackle feathers are displayed and secretly contained in the small box with its heavy split lid and even heavier base.

Maker: Jo McAllister | **Title:** *The Ring Cycle: Coloring* | **Materials:** Fine silver 999, miniature colored pencils | **Size:** 34 mm × 32 mm × 43 mm | **Image credit:** © Jo McAllister. Photograph by Alexander Brattell

Narrative: The two-part box slides to open and to close. The coloring pencils are held securely by the act of wearing this double ring piece.

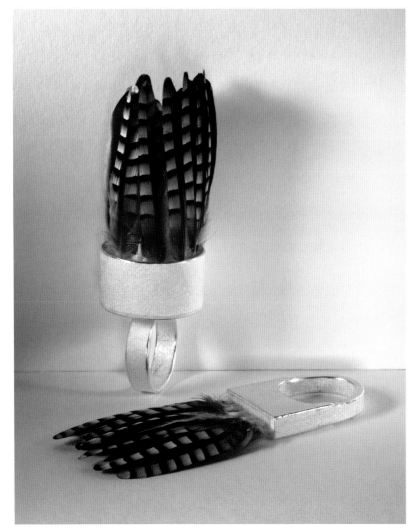

Maker: Jo McAllister | **Title:** *The Ring Cycle: Feathering No 1 and Feathering No 2* | **Materials:** Fine silver 999, woollen felt, blue jay's hackle feathers, thread | **Size:** 90 mm × 37 mm × 7 mm and 85 mm × 27 mm × 27 mm | **Image credit:** © Jo McAllister. Photograph by Alexander Brattell

Narrative: Tiny brightly colored feathers are stitched into removable woollen felt inserts.

CLAIRE McARDLE

Claire McArdle is a jewelry and object maker. She currently holds a studio in Melbourne, Australia.

Stories are how we remember, how we imagine. They communicate ideas and help place ourselves in the world. I love stories.

Worn Translations

A garment is traded and its story, told by the owner, is recorded.

Maintaining the entirety of the garment, the form is translated into a neckpiece.

From wearable to wearable, a new story begins.

The clothing has a story.
The owner shares the story.
The owner trades the clothing.
The clothing is un-made.
The material now formless.
The material re-formed.
Worn and worn.
The material is translated.
Translated, trans-formed.
The story is retold.

Maker: Claire McArdle | **Title:** *Worn Translations—Vicki* | **Materials:** Clothing with a story transformed into jewelry |
Size: 470 mm × 250 mm × 20 mm | **Image credit:** Claire McArdle |

Maker: Claire McArdle | **Title:** *Worn Translation—Edith* | **Materials:** Clothing with a story transformed into jewelry | **Size:** 480 mm × 400 mm × 80 mm | **Image credit:** Claire McArdle |

Maker: Claire McArdle | **Title:** *Worn Translations—Deb* | **Materials:** Clothing with a story transformed into jewelry | **Size:** 820 mm × 650 mm × 50 mm | **Image credit:** Claire McArdle

JUDY McCAIG

As my work has changed, so has my working process changed over the years. Previous work reflected the past, ancient cultures, history and a future unknown. I used to transform my sketches drawn from life, from traveling, during museums visits, from nature, into exact drawings for a piece and try to reproduce it in silver and different colored golds. Now a lot of the work goes on in my head beforehand. Reflections and feelings provoked by a persistent sensation of being on a permanent journey—a state of restless almost nomadic limbo.

Change, travel, journeys and time spent immersed in unknown surroundings, geographical formations, soaking up impressions, history, culture, sensations, experiences, inhabitants of the place is what inspire me. I like to let ideas filter through and hope that I manage to convey an essence of my experiences and feelings.

Maker: Judy McCaig | **Title:** *Silent Shadows* | **Materials:** Tombac, silver, 22k gold, bronze, brass, aluminum, paint, German silver, Herkimer diamond crystals, Perspex | **Size:** 105 mm × 70 mm × 12 mm | **Image credit:** Judy McCaig |

Maker: Judy McCaig | **Title:** *Winter Light* | **Materials:** German silver, steel, bronze, brass, gold, Herkimer diamond crystals, Perspex | **Size:** 87 mm × 80 mm × 10 mm | **Image credit:** Judy McCaig |

Maker: Judy McCaig | **Title:** *Sun Shower* | **Materials:** Steel, 18k gold, found material, wood, Perspex, Herkimer diamond crystals | **Size:** 85 mm × 88 mm × 15 mm | **Image credit:** Judy McCaig |

Maker: Judy McCaig | **Title:** *Towards the Light* | **Materials:** Steel, bronze, German silver, wood, paint, tombac, aquamarine | **Size:** 75 mm × 83 mm × 20 mm | **Image credit:** Julieta Anselas |

Maker: Judy McCaig | **Title:** *Between Mountains* | **Materials:** Steel, tombac, German silver, silver, wood, black Kyanite, Herkimer diamond crystals, found material | **Size:** 115 mm × 75 mm × 20 mm | **Image credit:** Xavier Ballester

CATHY McCARTHY

Cathy McCarthy is a jeweler who studied jewelry making while living in Edinburgh, Scotland. Cathy enjoys using sterling silver and 18-k gold to translate simple, everyday observations into pictorial stories which can be worn and loved. Her studio is situated in the vibrant Sorting Office studios in the town of Eastleigh in Hampshire, UK.

Cathy's passion for designing and creating narrative jewelry comes from a love of symbolism and the creation of stories through imagery. Cathy's design ideas are sparked by both outward sensory observations and internal emotions and thoughts. Using sterling silver, Cathy creates small frames which are then filled with individual component parts to tell a story through a piece of beautiful, wearable jewelry.

Maker: Cathy McCarthy | **Title:** *Coming Home* | **Materials:** Sterling silver and 18-k yellow gold | **Size:** 45 mm × 35 mm | **Image credit:** Cathy McCarthy

Narrative: This piece is inspired by living for many years away from the city where I grew up and where many of my close family and friends still live. I am originally from Southampton in England but have spent twenty years of my life in Scotland and Australia. I have enjoyed spreading my wings and sampling everything that each new place had to offer. I have recently returned to live in my home city and I have been inspired by looking at very familiar surroundings with a new perspective.

I use birds as symbols in many of my designs. In this piece the bird represents a free spirit which has come to rest in a welcoming environment, symbolized by the delicate wildflowers and soft dandelion seed heads.

IONA McCUAIG

Iona McCuaig's jewelry practice involves producing unique wearable objects that are inspired by a narrative starting point in the context of art studio jewelry. Alongside her practice as a jeweler and maker Iona has a passion for teaching her discipline and craft.

Iona's work uses jewelry as a means of communicating a narrative originating from sources in the form of letters, diaries, books, objects or places. She is inspired by human relationships or experiences that have an endearing or nostalgic quality. Her pieces aim to illustrate these moments which then act as symbols of benevolence, highlighting important human qualities which should be commemorated in our own contemporary society:

"I am fascinated with exploring our changing opinions, visions and roles through time and I have an affinity for making wearable objects that provoke questions and dialogue about contemporary life."

Her practice utilizes a range of traditional jewelry techniques including metal fabrication, printing, etching, setting, hand piercing, chasing, bead stringing and color patination. She uses a variety of base and precious metals and incorporates wood, plastic or other found objects. Iona aims to achieve an illustrative, whimsical and antiquated appearance to her work.

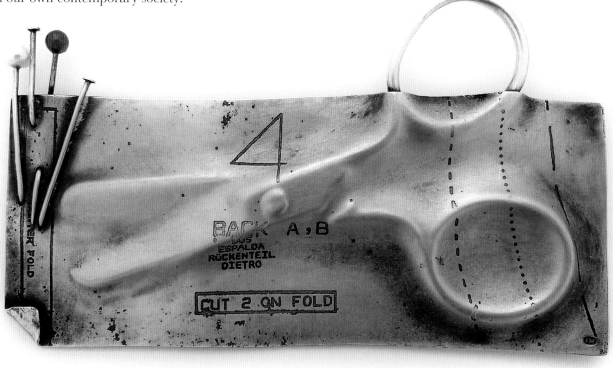

Maker: Iona McCuaig | **Title:** *Dress Making Brooch* | **Materials:** Oxidized silver, pearl, carnelian, steel | **Size:** 65 mm × 110 mm |
Image credit: Iona McCuaig

Narrative: "Whenever a repair was no longer possible, the girls would make a new article." As a teacher myself I am fascinated how education has progressed over the years. I am particularly drawn to the difference between girls' and boys' education in the eighteenth century. This brooch was made to commemorate these girls who were not given the same educational opportunities as the their male counterparts. They were expected to take on domestic duties instead of studying academic subjects.

Maker: Iona McCuaig | **Title:** *Elvis Is My Art Teacher Brooch* | **Materials:** Wood, gold leaf, Swarovski pearls, silver, badge, pencil, plastic, steel | **Size:** 105 mm × 85 mm | **Image credit:** Iona McCuaig

Narrative: I found the words "Elvis is my art teacher" inscribed onto an art room desk. Upon further research I found out that there was a former art teacher who moonlighted as an Elvis Presley impersonator. I was inspired by the image of a schoolchild thinking that their art teacher was Elvis and I wanted to tell this story through the eyes of the child. I made this brooch as though the pupil had constructed the figure of their art teacher using everyday materials found in an art room creating a naive and playful aesthetic.

Maker: Iona McCuaig | **Title:** *Writing Lines Brooch* | **Materials:** Oxidized silver, brass pen nibs, steel | **Size:** 70 mm × 70 mm | **Image credit:** Iona McCuaig

Narrative: "I often speeded up the time taken writing these by tying three pens together." I found this an endearing memory of school punishment as a student attempted to speed up his line writing by joining multiple pens together.

SANDRA McEWEN

Sandra McEwen studied classical drawing and illustration. She discovered her love of cloisonné enamels after much exploration and many adventures.

Sandra creates her enamel jewelry using both ancient techniques and modern tools. She saws and fuses each silver base by hand, inlays the intricate wirework, and painstakingly layers many coats of brilliant powdered glass enamel between the wires before grinding and polishing to a jewel-like finish.

History, and the history of personal adornment fascinates and inspires Sandra. The jewelry that one chooses to wear tells the story of who they are, or who they would like to be. Narrative art in jewelry goes even deeper—what on the surfaces seems merely decorative, on further inspection reveals a story that can be very illuminating.

She currently has a studio at Artspace in Raleigh, North Carolina.

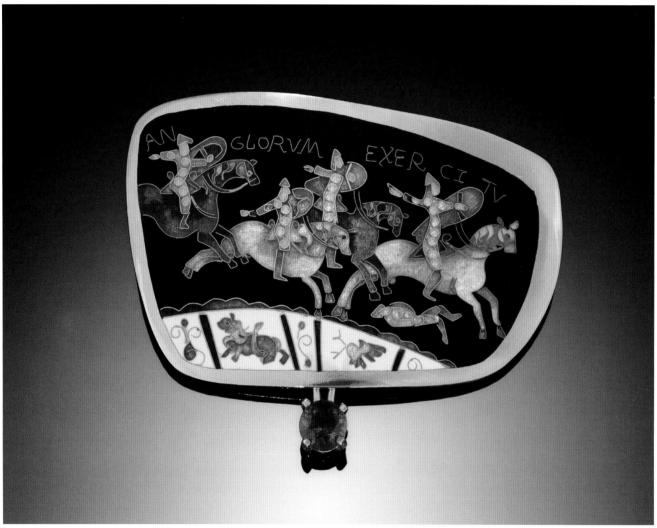

Maker: Sandra McEwen | **Title:** *A Glorious Battle* | **Materials:** Vitreous enamel, fine silver, 24k gold, garnet | **Size:** 43 mm × 55 mm | **Image credit:** Jason Dowdle

Narrative: The Bayeux Tapestry is both history and a wonderful visual story, and I've always been fascinated with it as both a narrative medium and as a great work of art. A lot of what we know about the battle of Hastings comes to us directly from the stitches and knots of this fabulous tapestry. I wanted to create a series of vignettes in cloisonné enamels that would capture the spirit of some key moments in the story.

The battle is long and bloody, lasting well into the evening. Many great men have fallen, and the tide is about to turn for the English Army.

GINGER MEEK ALLEN

Ginger Meek Allen is a master metalsmith and studio jeweler—a full-time maker. In her work Ginger blends the genius of her outer artist and her inner engineer to create an expressive body of work that is powerful and beautiful while also being exquisitely well made.

Ginger says that her work is about helping her clients to honor their relationships and themselves by giving and wearing pieces that are unique, narrative and (in the case of her custom work) exist only for them.

Her clients will tell you that, while her jewelry is really wonderful, what she really does is help them remain connected to a legacy and express their love for each other, and for themselves. Ginger believes that jewelry is above all an intimate art form that captures personal narrative and empowers a legacy. She cites literature, film and true life stories that give us countless examples of people placing high intrinsic value on jewelry—running back into burning houses or searching through the garbage to retrieve a grandmother's locket or a wedding ring.

Ginger is a primarily self-taught maker, with the exception of some carefully selected focused workshops in specific techniques such as mechanism building, hydraulic die forming, enameling, and forging. Her home is in North Carolina, on the east coast of the United States.

Maker: Ginger Meek Allen | **Title:** *A Princess among Princes* | **Materials:** Sterling silver, steel, natural gemstones, photographs, acetate | **Size:** 28 mm | **Image credit:** Ginger Meek Allen

Narrative: The first iteration of this locket was created in 2013 and given to a mother by her husband on the birth of their third son. Two years later, they returned the locket to have another panel added for their new daughter, born with three older brothers. The front panel features a "P" for the family surname and the birthstones of the parents. The next three panels feature photographs of the three sons, their birthstones, and the motif of their infant nurseries (a lion, a monkey, and an airplane). The fourth child and only daughter's panel features her photo, her emerald birthstone, and a narrative appliqué of her nursery motif, the Princess and the Pea, hence the layers of "mattresses" with the emerald "pea" beneath them, and the tiara on her head. The back panel features an inscripted quote attributed to a family library favorite by Dr. Seuss.

KONRAD MEHUS

I am not sure if I can or will answer your question, "Why narrative jewelry?"

I am not sure if it is interesting. The piece of craft should express the content of the idea and there are many possible interpretations; if not I have failed. It is not for me to explain to people what I think and mean. I do not express my ideas with words, metal is my language.

I love my craft and to work with metal is great.

I started with contemporary jewelry in 1960 and fine art was occupied with political narrative. Political statements in gold and silver strengthen the expression. Traditionally gold and silver are symbols of investment, power and wealth.

The idea of my work is closely connected to the "Norwegian national costume." Norwegian Road Silver is silver/brooches for roadies, a comment for insiders?

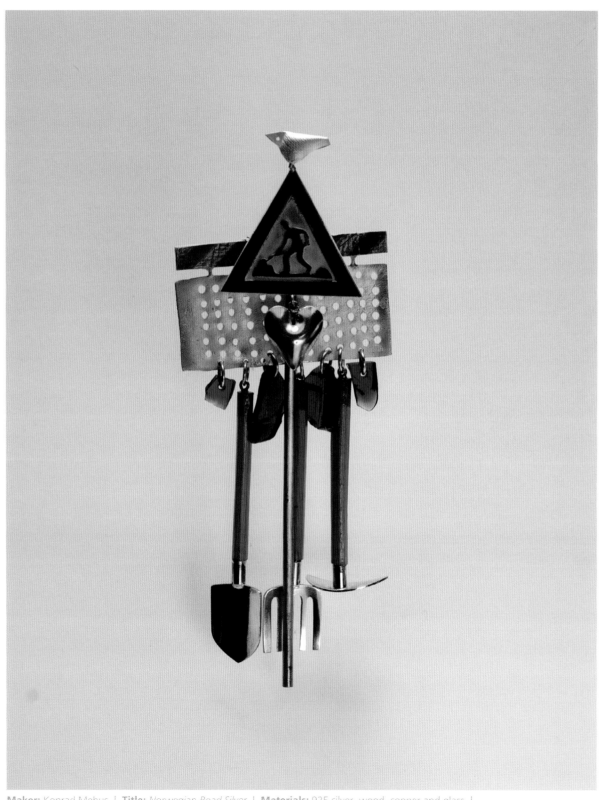

Maker: Konrad Mehus | **Title:** *Norwegian Road Silver* | **Materials:** 925 silver, wood, copper and glass | **Size:** 125 mm × 45 mm × 9 mm | **Image credit:** Konrad Mehus |

Maker: Konrad Mehus | **Title:** *Paradise Joggers* | **Materials:** Iron, wood, copper and 925 silver | **Size:** Dia.175 mm × 50 mm |
Image credit: Konrad Mehus |

Maker: Konrad Mehus | **Title:** *Ear Chairs and Grandmothers* | **Materials:** Painted wood, metal |
Size: 45 mm × 21 mm × 24 mm | **Image credit:** Konrad Mehus

IRIS MERKLE

Iris Merkle, born in 1972 in Aalen (South Germany), has lived and worked for more than ten years in Stuttgart, one of Germany's most prospering cities. She made some excursions into product design and advertisement, and after four years returned to her topic of heart: making jewelry. Since 2007, she runs her own studio.

Iris Merkle compares creating jewelry to telling stories. In her jewelry, she gives expression to themes that she really cares about. She is currently working on the themes of parting and loss, of mourning and death, using relics that she finds in nature, which are then incinerated in the casting process. Cast in metal, they convey a sense of beauty and evanescence, radiating a charm that is all their own. When the individual elements, loosely arranged on a cord, touch each other, they produce delicate sounds and melodies. Thus these creations can either be worn as jewelry, or used as wind chimes that will develop a beautiful patina.

The heavy works were developed in contrast to the light ones. Cast in massive bronze, they lie heavily and cold on the chest. You do not want to wear them around your neck for long. With this work, I trace memories and leave the interpretation to the wearer.

Maker: Iris Merkle | **Title:** *Falter I* |
Materials: Silver oxidized, iron string |
Size: 900 mm | **Image credit:**
Christoph Binder

Narrative: I am looking into the subject of parting and loss, of mourning and death. The real butterfly wings are incinerated in the casting process and transformed into metal. They are still light. When the individual elements touch each other, they produce delicate sounds and melodies.

Maker: Iris Merkle |
Title: *Falter II* |
Materials: Silver oxidized, iron string |
Size: 900 mm |
Image credit: Christoph Binder |

Maker: Iris Merkle | **Title:** *Cordis I* |
Materials: Bronze, iron, plastic | **Size:** 900 mm |
Image credit: Christoph Binder

Narrative: I am looking into the subject of parting and loss, of mourning and death. Cast in massive bronze, they lie heavily and cold on the chest. You do not want to wear them around your neck for long. With this work, I trace memories and leave the interpretation to the wearer.

BRUCE METCALF

Bruce Metcalf was an imagist from the first day he touched metal in the fall of 1970, but he made his first true narrative jewelry in 1976. At the time, J. Fred Woell was still the pioneer of narrative jewelry in the modern context. However, Metcalf was different from Woell in that his background was in cartooning, whereas Woell was informed by Pop Art. And cartooning, of course, is all about telling a story.

At first, Metcalf used images of inanimate objects—knives, pliers, generic vessels—to convey the narrative. By 1984, he changed over to making figurative jewelry,

reasoning that if he was to talk about human experience, he should represent humans. At first, his style was geometric and rather abstracted, somewhat like the old *Spy vs. Spy* cartoons by Antonio Prohias in Mad magazine. Later, the figures became more organic, and the technique changed from construction to casting. Later still, Metcalf began an extended series of carved wooden jewelry, which continued the narrative impulse.

By 2003, Metcalf felt that his exploration of both figure and narrative was played out, and he turned back to an imagist approach to jewelry making.

Maker: Bruce Metcalf | **Title:** *A Present from the Government* | **Materials:** Silver, acrylic plastic sheet, drawing on Mylar | **Size:** 90 mm × 82 mm | **Image credit:** Bruce Metcalf

Narrative: This brooch was part of an extended series that examined nuclear arms, and the complicity that all American citizens bear with their own government. Here a bundle of missiles descends upon an unsuspecting personage. The series was inspired by a former student who participated in a walk across the country to protest nuclear armament. I found his gesture courageous, and I wanted to honor his commitment in a series of brooches that addressed the same issue.

Maker: Bruce Metcalf | **Title:** *Chalice with Rubies* | **Materials:** Silver, rubies, painted wood | **Size:** 92 mm × 51 mm | **Image credit:** Bruce Metcalf

Narrative: At this time, I was thinking about the process of nurturing, and how that plays out in both parenting and teaching. I was teaching at Kent State University in Ohio at the time, and I would get fairly involved with my students' personal lives, often as a kind of moral advisor. To nurture is to offer a gift, and that gift is not always appreciated. Here, a small figure offers a chalice to an unseen party. Apparently, she is somewhat uncertain how her gift will be received.

Maker: Bruce Metcalf | **Title:** *Wood Pin #107* | **Materials:** Painted and gold-leafed maple and brass, birch wood, silver | **Size:** 127 mm × 63 mm | **Image credit:** Bruce Metcalf

Narrative: This brooch is from a long series of brooches that were based on woodcarving. Here, only the torso is carved. The arms, legs, and head are all made of metal. This particular brooch was based on the nature photography of Karl Blossfeldt. I used one of his images to develop the head, and then invented a posture that commented on the complex relationship between nature (the head) and culture (what the figure is doing).

MARISA MOLIN

Marisa Molin is a jeweler and artist. Her practice focuses on the appropriation and translation of textures and fragments, collected from walks along remote island shorelines. Marisa has recently relocated from Tasmania to Norway where she has undertaken a number of Scandinavian-based artist residency programs to further develop her fragment series, which now includes "Fragments of Iceland" (as well as "Fragments of Flinders" and "Fragments of King"). Alongside being an artist, Molin is also an arts professional.

Maker: Marisa Molin | **Title:** *Kelp Track Wandering* | **Materials:** Sterling silver, kelp, stainless steel | **Size:** 53 mm × 50 mm × 21 mm | **Image credit:** Michael Comninus

Narrative: Along the shorelines, where I focus my research, I stumbled across the island's industry kelp tracks. The locals are only permitted to collect what has been washed ashore from tide or storm. The locals then drag the washed up kelp into piles to dry, cutting off the stems and roots which are discarded along the trail. They use only the blades for their export industry (for fertilizer, dye and cordial mostly), and leave the rest of the kelp behind. Ironically much like me, this kelp is exported to Norway, where I have since relocated after my stay in King Island.

Collected from these piles of discarded kelp butts, I focused on this particular fragment. I mirrored the texture into silver and then set it with the original kelp fragment to complete the story of found object through to translation.

LILI MURPHY-JOHNSON

Lili Murphy-Johnson's work is inspired by the awkwardness of the human body; exploring aspects of being human that are shied away from or sometimes considered taboo. She is based in London.

I work with the narrative to help me decide on what object to make next. My jewelry is closely inspired by my own experiences and reflective of my surroundings. My menstrual-inspired pieces depict my experience of PMS and menstruation. Creating a narrative fueled my process on how I would turn my experiences into jewelry objects.

Maker: Lili Murphy-Johnson | **Title:** *Stained Shirt* | **Materials:** Cotton shirt, glass beads, cotton thread | **Size:** 700 mm × 450 mm | **Image credit:** Lili Murphy-Johnson

Narrative: Inspired by when you wake up and you have bled onto your pyjamas in your sleep.

JANE NEAD

Jane Nead is a jewelry designer-maker working predominantly in sterling silver. Her work is inspired by William Shakespeare, his words, plays, characters and life. Fretwork is the primary technique and the focus of her making, but she also loves working with wire and creating boxes and hollow forms.

Unlike many of her peers, she has no real interest in designing from nature or architecture and used to wonder why she was confining her source of inspiration to the physical world. Why not start with concepts, ideas, words and feelings? When she realized that she could make this the focus for her design work, she began to explore Shakespeare for her inspiration.

Jane spends a great deal of her time in Stratford-upon-Avon, especially in the early developmental stages of her work, using the Shakespeare Institute Library resources and the archives curated by the Shakespeare Birthplace Trust.

Shakespeare's words play an important part in her designs—often becoming the focal point of a piece, sometimes literally but more often figuratively, as the influence behind a collection of work. She begins by exploring a play—its themes, characters, setting and language—and then uses visual research such as costume and set designs, patterns, embroidery, or other shapes to inform her designs.

Maker: Jane Nead | **Title:** *Stolen Kisses* | **Materials:** Sterling silver | **Size:** 58 mm × 18 mm | **Image credit:** Joanne Haywood

Narrative: "A pair of star-crossed lovers." *Romeo and Juliet*, prologue, William Shakespeare

Stolen Kisses was inspired by the portrayal of romantic love in Shakespeare's plays, particularly *Romeo and Juliet*.

I drew my visual inspiration from Italian architecture, roses and rose windows, and the beautifully romantic statue of *Romeo and Juliet* by Milton Hebald (1977) that is situated outside the Delacorte Theatre in Central Park, New York City.

A quote, which appears in fretwork around the edges, was also inspired by Shakespeare. It is the perfect expression of the love Romeo and Juliet share: "When I saw you I fell in love and you smiled because you knew." Although this quote is often attributed to Shakespeare's *Romeo and Juliet*, it is in fact believed to be from the libretto of Arrigo Boito's Italian opera, *Falstaff*, which was based on *The Merry Wives of Windsor*.

The "star-crossed lovers" are partially hidden behind a rose window to suggest the forbidden love that they share.

HELEN NOAKES

Award-winning jewelry designer Helen Noakes has come a long way since her upbringing in rural New Zealand—whilst working in the corporate world in London she found her passion of silversmithing through courses at the Kensington and Chelsea College. After a chance discovery of a single set of scale models and the quandary of how she could make them into lasting keepsakes she was given a book on resin and began teaching herself resin techniques. The career switch was inevitable. The miniature scale models (commonly used on model railways) quickly became the surprising focal point for Helen's beautifully executed work, all of which is handcrafted from precious metals and resin. Intriguingly tucked into each infinitely wearable piece is an element of humor making a second look a must for this exciting collection. Now selling and exhibiting worldwide and featured in several books Helen incorporates everything from penguins to circus performers.

The very nature of the figures lends itself to narrative work—I feel I have the easy part of the deal and that I am the choreographer for my audience, placing the figures in little resin and silver scenarios. With some pieces the narrative is literal, with a stamped "message" in the silver or included subtly within the resin whilst others are open to interpretation which are often personal to the individual. My objective is to make pieces that bring joy and happiness to the wearer, and I feel privileged that this collection achieves this.

Maker: Helen Noakes | **Title:** *Solo Voyager Bangle* | **Materials:** Sterling silver, resin, miniature plastic scale model | **Size:** Inner bangle diameter 65 mm, outer bangle diameter maximum 110 mm, max depth 50 mm | **Image credit:** Toby Bennett, TJB Media

Narrative: A homage to the plight of the polar bear—a gentle reminder of the declining numbers of these beautiful beasts in their melting environment.

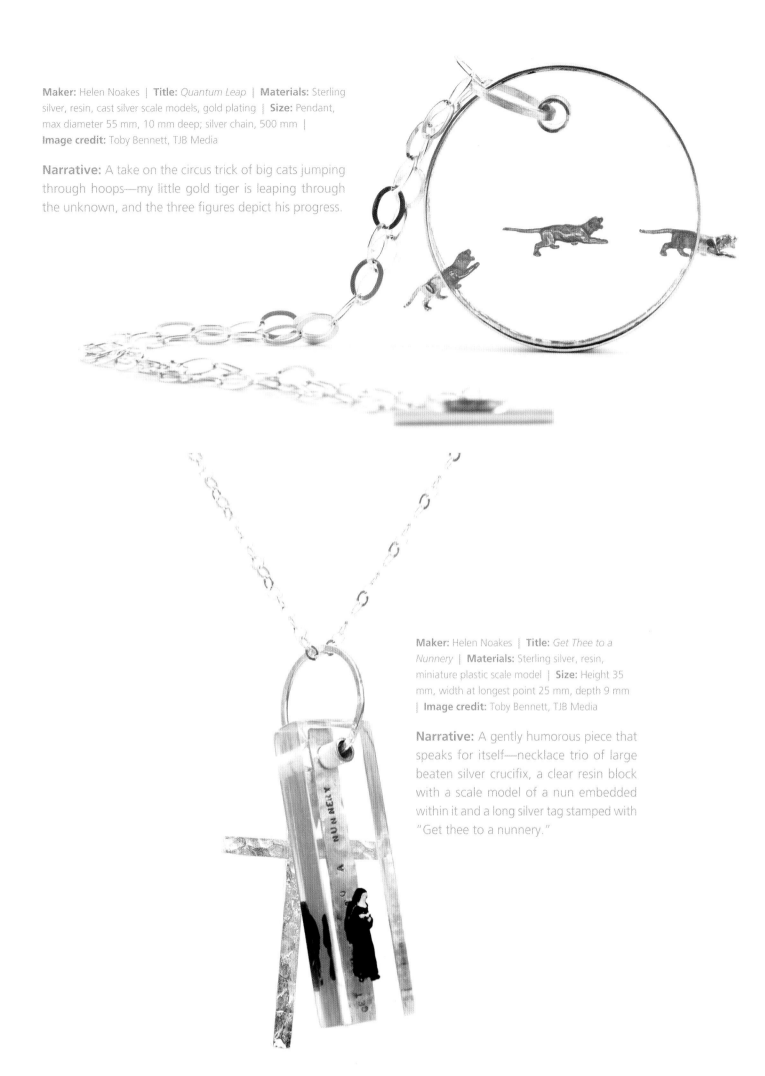

Maker: Helen Noakes | **Title:** *Quantum Leap* | **Materials:** Sterling silver, resin, cast silver scale models, gold plating | **Size:** Pendant, max diameter 55 mm, 10 mm deep; silver chain, 500 mm | **Image credit:** Toby Bennett, TJB Media

Narrative: A take on the circus trick of big cats jumping through hoops—my little gold tiger is leaping through the unknown, and the three figures depict his progress.

Maker: Helen Noakes | **Title:** *Get Thee to a Nunnery* | **Materials:** Sterling silver, resin, miniature plastic scale model | **Size:** Height 35 mm, width at longest point 25 mm, depth 9 mm | **Image credit:** Toby Bennett, TJB Media

Narrative: A gently humorous piece that speaks for itself—necklace trio of large beaten silver crucifix, a clear resin block with a scale model of a nun embedded within it and a long silver tag stamped with "Get thee to a nunnery."

KIM NOGUEIRA

Kim Nogueira is an automaton maker and award-winning jeweler who learned the goldsmithing trade on the job as a production goldsmith, and has taken intensive workshops with reknowned American enamelists and metalsmiths. She is based on the tiny island of St. John, in the US Virgin Islands. Her work combines the mechanics and wearer interaction of automata with the narrative power of text, found objects and three dimensional figures to create multi-dimensional and wearable stories in metal and vitreous enamel.

The nexus of my work is its narrative component. For over a decade I have collected early- to mid-twentieth century vending machine toys and gumball charms, antique mechanical toys and Lilliputian Victorian curiosities. I work directly with these diminutive oddments, making molds of them for use in my work, deconstructing them to make the mechanical figures and details in my wearable automata. I construct complex narratives in metal and vitreous enamel that speak to the curiosities, challenges and marvels of our time, while questioning the status quo and examining how the past has influenced our present and future. Layers of imagery and text, peppering small theatre-like frameworks, draw the wearer into my story. By incorporating movement and wearer interaction into my three dimensional narratives, with tiny automata that are activated by turning a crank, I also hope to explore and keep alive the enigma that is childhood wonder as well as draw attention to the preciousness of the extraordinary journey that we are all on together.

Maker: Kim Nogueira | **Title:** *Tales of Saints and Magicians* | **Materials:** Copper, silver, 24k gold, vitreous enamel, Herkimer diamond | **Size:** 77 mm × 32 mm × 17 mm | **Image credit:** Kim Nogueira

Narrative: This enameled pendant explores my personal journey from church-goer to atheist to spiritual/creative being. Because I think that boundaries are so fluid, a magician welcomes you to the great show that is "divinorum neglectus" or divine neglect. Look below this spectacle to find what is really important, the foundation of our humanity—a clear Herkimer diamond crystal is held in a silver hand, modeled from an antique toy, to symbolize personal and collective Truth.

Maker: Kim Nogueira | **Title:** *Lost Point of Origin* | **Materials:** Silver, copper, bronze, vitreous enamel, found object, tourmaline, paper, mica, pearl and thread | **Size:** 76 mm × 78 mm × 32 mm | **Image credit:** William Stelzer

Narrative: I made this automaton pendant in response to societal changes in child-rearing that include embracing early exposure to technology and helicopter parenting. Shown through the carnival colors of enameled text and signage, monkeys, fortune-telling and a mechanical good luck charm that extends its eyes, is my hope that childhood can still contain a sense of wonder and magic and connection to nature in this ultra-disposable and consumer-driven society. If they are encouraged to follow their inner compass, like the bezel-set antique compass below the title, this will be possible.

Children play with simple toys when you turn one crank and a fortune teller, hidden from the front behind dusty mica windows, looks into his crystal tourmaline ball and then up at you when you turn the second crank, evoking questions about the future. A monkey's mouth holds a removable paper fortune, and there are extra rolls of fortunes stored in the fortune teller's compartment, a nod to how capitalism encourages disposability in objects and people. A hidden door opens below the children playing, revealing text emphasizing the joy of imagination and daydreaming in childhood, echoing the imagination necessary to enjoy playing with simple toys above.

Maker: Kim Nogueira | **Title:** *Peepshow* | **Materials:** Copper, silver, brass, stainless steel, vitreous enamel | **Size:** 70 mm × 73 mm × 16 mm | **Image credit:** Kim Nogueira

Narrative: I recreated imagery from an 1800s children's book and animated it with a triple crankshaft to explore how new paradigms, such as a world without war, can come into being. We often forget that simple toys that children play with, such as the little mechanical boat here, and the bayonet and sword, all of which the wearer activates by turning the crank, are also weapons of war. A quote from Buddhist monk Thich Nhất Hạnh is on the back to encourage private contemplation in the wearer.

LINDSAY NONHOF-FISHER

Lindsay Nonhof-Fisher is a metalsmith, jeweler, and illustrator. Her most recent artwork narrates social and political issues with a particular focus on American culture. She is an award-winning maker with work that has exhibited internationally and regionally in over nine US states. In addition, she also produces her own unique jewelry collection called Rotation. Her studio is based in the city of Sun Prairie, Wisconsin.

I work with the "narrative."

I recognize that visual culture surrounds us in powerful and influential ways. We are saturated by its cues and soaked by its authority. For many of us it is a challenge to breakdown its cryptic nature, and to understand its cultural influence. Using the imagery of my society's media, literature and history, I want to create stories that can be a lens for the wearer. By slightly modifying familiar shapes with cultural signifiers, each piece is layered with tales to reflect upon.

Maker: Lindsay Nonhof-Fisher | **Title:** *Pause II* | **Materials:** Fabricated copper, brass and amber | **Size:** 56 mm × 56 mm × 10 mm | **Image credit:** Lindsay Nonhof-Fisher

Narrative: I am interested in devices that relate to time. As technology is continually being deemed obsolete, old devices are abandoned and they become remnants left behind as science blazes onward. Defunct and obsolete, many of these artifacts have ceased to function in our modern world. The devices I create serve to challenge the presentism approach to modernity and our concept of time.

Maker: Lindsay Nonhof-Fisher | **Title:** *Yielding to the Blonde* | **Materials:** Copper, German silver and embroidery | **Size:** 38 mm × 50 mm × 19 mm | **Image credit:** Lindsay Nonhof-Fisher

Narrative: This brooch was my response to the relationship between power and beauty. Heart shaped and reversible, this pin contains images of seemingly "feminine" faces with golden yellow hair. The blonde feminine image appears as a fashion standard and beauty icon in American culture. Many iconic and successful women have sported the pale look; they were and still are standards of elegance, beauty, and feminine sexuality. Think of all those timeless white women who use blonde "beauty" standards to gain an edge in the capitalist market like Marilyn Monroe, Madonna and Jean Harlow. Why we seem to worship these "blonde bombshells" has little to do with inherent femininity but rather the devaluation of other women's beauty and more specifically women of color.

Maker: Lindsay Nonhof-Fisher | **Title:** *White Hetero Men* | **Materials:** Fabricated German silver and gold leaf | **Size:** 41 mm × 2.5 mm | **Image credit:** Lindsay Nonhof-Fisher

Narrative: This image depicts the portraits of three famous individuals: Uncle Sam, Clark Kent, and Homer Simpson. These iconic men are a biting satire on how our mainstream culture reproduces the dominant norms, values, and practices of "we the people." With his old white skin and starry hat, Uncle Sam is the personification of America. Where there is truth and justice, there is Clark Kent who is our traditional heterosexual hero. Homer Simpson is the middle-class suburbia man and is an agent for the masculine role in family life. Each of these portraits was crafted out of metal to resemble coins. After all, what does ninety-nine percent of American currency have in common? Well they each contain a portrait of a white heterosexual man.

ITALY

MARGHERITA DE MARTINO NORANTE

I live in Florence, Italy. I've always been very interested in collaborative projects and studio sharing practices so I organized exhibitions with 1x1 Collective and at Officine Nora, in Florence, Italy.

I like making single standing pieces of jewelry or small series of unique pieces. They are all different but have a common starting point: the idea that jewelry talks about the wearer.

A piece of jewelry is a powerful instrument of communication. It is worn on the body or on top of clothing so it's directly between ourselves and the world. Not only is it the first thing to be seen, but more than clothes, it is superfluous and one makes a conscientious decision to wear it. So I make puppets, reproduce undergarments; play with fetish and icons coming from my culture, education and everyday life. My pieces are my way of ironically reflecting on human frailty and on those contrasting wishes of revealing, hiding and disguising oneself that each of us feels.

Maker: Margherita de Martino Norante | **Title:** *Camouflage* |
Materials: Natural wool, 22k gold shoes, 18k gold pin. Hand felted |
Size: 100 mm × 45 mm × 45 mm | **Image credit:** Margherita de Martino Norante

Narrative: It's their fault, after all.

"Melanie dear!" Ugh. "Didn't I tell you, not those fuchsia ones!"

Blah, blah, blah. Snide comments, sideways glances, everyone's talking, even if what comes out—needless to say—doesn't do anyone any good. I just want to be left with my things. For them, there's no difference between their pasture and yours; there's no fence in between. They should mind their own business. But they never understand.

Then it's natural that one tries to hide, don't you think? They're so set in their ways that they can't even talk with you unless they recognize you. That's the way it's done. Escape, I know, is not a solution, but for God's sake one just has to survive, and after all, none of the problems I had with them were ever serious enough to really need a solution. Sensible and superior indifference is best, I tell you.

So what's better than—voila!—a sublime disguise, which I would dare to say, suits me well and that, what's more, doesn't leave my aesthetic sense (which as you know, is quite pronounced) unsatisfied. The more I see myself, the more I like me, and in all these years I should say that even if I didn't succeed to vanish completely, I would certainly avoid a bunch of nuisance, which counts for something.

I have only one problem: after all this time I don't remember which came first, the shoes or the wool.

TED NOTEN

Ted Noten's designs act as a critique on contemporary life and on the history of jewelry, as well as on the wider context of product design. Interestingly, his work equally relates to architecture. The underlying, recurring, theme of his work is to challenge convention and processes of habituation, the familiar and the unusual.

His oeuvre gains in depth from his idiosyncratic response to the apparent familiarity of our daily surroundings, whether this be a market street in Amsterdam, the explosion of building construction in Shanghai, or a gang of road sweepers at work in a provincial town in Russia. By lifting symbols from their everyday surroundings and placing them in a new context, he doesn't so much query the symbol itself as our perception of it. Ted Noten looks for fixed meanings in the banal and the cultivated. He debunks their essence, then reinvents them back into reality. In affecting and infecting symbolic values he actually reveals their unmistakable intangibility.

Many of his most recent works are parts of larger projects in which Ted investigates familiar themes like violence, mortality, greed, love and aging. But he also turned his attention to the means of production that are not only influencing contemporary notions of mass production, but also the domain of craftsmanship. The attempt to include reproductions (and even reproductions of reproductions) into his body of work seems to point to a new direction in his designs, and in contemporary culture as a whole.

Maker: Ted Noten | **Title:** *Ageeth's Dowry* | **Materials:** 56 gold rings and other paraphernalia cast in acrylic, pearl/PC | **Size:** 180 mm × 250 mm × 80 mm | **Image credit:** Atelier Ted Noten. Private collection, the Netherlands

Narrative: A bridegroom wanted a unique wedding gift for his bride-to-be. Ted started out with nothing in mind but the budget. He drew inspiration from an old custom, according to which all the people close to the bride and groom pitch in to buy one large gift, such as a cow. He wrote to relatives and close friends of the bride and groom, asking them each to contribute a ring accompanied by a personal recollection. The physical objects that he received—ranging from valuable heirlooms to basic rings bought off the rack at a department store—were enclosed in an acrylic handbag, which Ageeth carried on the big day. Ted collected the stories in a booklet.

Maker: Ted Noten | **Title:** *Bird Bag* | **Materials:** Bag/bird "Sturnus Burmannicus," divers bijoux cast in acrylic/leather handle with silver 18k gold-plated attachments/bird head silver 18k gold-plated/total weight 5.5 kg | **Size:** 270 mm × 300 mm × 100 mm | **Image credit:** Atelier Ted Noten. Collection of the Toledo Museum of Art, Toledo, OH (US)

Narrative: The *Bird Bag* continues an ongoing theme in my work of animals (and insects) cast within acrylic, together with jewelry and other related paraphernalia.

The bird looks beautiful and is related to other birds (starling/magpie) that have shown a love for shiny materials . . . collectors of sorts—not unlike humans. In this case it felt like the bird should come out of the bag, proud to display her findings like trophies . . . so of course her face should be golden.

Although the piece continues within my oeuvre, I find it interesting that it also works within the Zeitgeist as many artists look more and more to nature as if to compensate for the digital overrule confronting us.

ISRAEL

IDO NOY

Ido Noy is an art historian specializing in the history of jewelry, ancient Jewish head decorations, Jewish wedding jewelry, and love tokens.

Maker: Ido Noy | **Title:** *Altneuland: Brooch (Dumpster)* | **Materials:** Copper, sterling silver | **Size:** 70 mm × 35 mm × 46 mm | **Image credit:** Ido Noy

Narrative: Among the countless points of view on Tel Aviv, my view as an artist who was born in the far north of Israel can be summed up in one word: *amazement*. When I first moved to Tel Aviv in 2001, the city left its impression on me as if it was built differently and from unrecognized materials. The contrast between the urban scenery that evolved during the long years and my young childhood village is no doubt the trigger for this creation.

MICHALINA OWCZAREK

Michalina Owczarek is a jeweler whose work has been shown in competitions and exhibitions in Poland and internationally. Most of her work is based on the narrative.

Michalina's inspiration comes from history and she chooses historic themes for her narrative jewelry.

Maker: Michalina Owczarek | **Title:** *No Title Necklace* | **Materials:** Gold-plated brass, lens, hornet's nest | **Size:** 90 mm × 250 mm × 60 mm | **Image credit:** Michalina Owczarek

Narrative: The work was inspired by the society of Victorian England. When I read a book about this subject I was surprised by contrasts dividing the society. On the one hand, rich people were flowing in luxury; on the other, the poor were forced to work from an early age. The necklace represents precisely this situation, in which employees who aren't noticed by the higher spheres "build state," for a better life for all of the country.

BARBARA PAGANIN

Barbara Paganin is an internationally-recognized jeweler and a goldsmith.

Barbara perceives the world as a vast field of sensory research. She investigates the principles of universe and society by observing the simplest life-forms and the most common objects. Therefore her experiences are closely connected with her art and vice versa. Through a continuous narrative process that goes back and forth across the senses, she weaves her thick net of information on a sort of genetic algorithm in which everyone can find a reflection and a precise reference. "Open Memory's" brooches represent

a peculiar bond between past and present, between dreams and reality, said and unsaid, felt and seen. They express the Proustian poetic of the lost time that the artist adopted as a cathartic means for recalling and freeing her and other people's memories. Each observer is free to perceive a diverse story; this is why the jewels have no "name." This "creative antinomianism" was an act of faith into human empathy. Each brooch, every necklace starts a story. It's up to us to choose the plots.

Note: The narrative descriptions for Barbara Paganin's pieces were translated by Silvia Valenti.

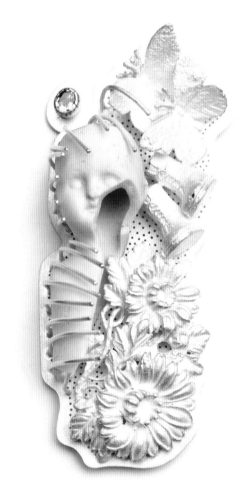

Maker: Barbara Paganin | **Title:** *Twice. Necklace* |
Materials: Oxidized silver, coral, porcelain, bone, photo, gold |
Size: 380 mm × 210 mm × 30 mm | **Image credit:** Michele Zanin

Narrative: The neckpiece represents for Barbara her twin nature. She should have had an older sister that was never born. Everything in her life became divided for two: parental love, even her name, her thoughts. She bore the responsibility of living for her never-born sister by communicating in a mirror game until this necklace came to light.

Maker: Barbara Paganin | **Title:** *Open Memory n° 7. Brooch* |
Materials: Silver, porcelain, yellow sapphire, gold |
Size: 100 mm × 45 mm × 30 mm | **Image credit:** Alice Pavesi Fiori

Narrative: A fragment of a porcelain doll seems to blossom in delicate silver flowers under a tiny sun. Could it stand for the passage from childhood to manhood?

Maker: Barbara Paganin | **Title:** *Open Memory n° 13. Brooch* | **Materials:** Oxidized silver, morganite, photo, silver, porcelain, ivory, gold | **Size:** 100 mm × 85 mm × 33 mm | **Image credit:** Alice Pavesi Fiori

Narrative: In the photo a woman, a maid perhaps. A prince near her. She took care of her prince every single day of her life, loving him secretly. She dreamed about an engagement ring and their love coming true. What happened then?

Maker: Barbara Paganin | **Title:** *Open Memory n° 25. Brooch* | **Materials:** Oxidized silver, porcelain, coral, gold | **Size:** 125 mm × 45 mm × 50 mm | **Image credit:** Alice Pavesi Fiori

Narrative: You see? The baby is so healthy! He plays, he eats, he smiles . . . . His soul is shining!

    (In his belly you can discover a secret world made of roses, mice, a doll . . . .)

Maker: Barbara Paganin | **Title:** *Open Memory no. 24. Brooch* | **Materials:** Ppatinated silver, coral, nacre, porcelain, bone, compass, gold | **Size:** 100 mm × 80 mm × 20 mm | **Image credit:** Alice Pavesi Fiori

Narrative: I was so far away from home and it was such a long time since I saw my beloved ones. Eventually would I have been able to go back home with all my precious gifts for them?

LUCY PALMER

I am fascinated by stories of all kinds, from ancient myths and legends to children's tales. I use these narratives in my work, inviting the viewer to recall a favorite story, or perhaps to make up their own. It is an escape from the mundane into a magical world of enchanted forests, mysterious creatures, and far away places.

Jewelry itself has long been surrounded by tales of magical powers and mythical wonders, from golden necklaces that enchant the wearer and bewitch others, to rings which possess great power so I find these themes particularly relevant.

The intricate designs are hand cut in precious metals and are often layered to give a three dimensional, miniature stage set effect. Decorative techniques are used to embellish the surface, including stamping, engraving and keum-boo, an ancient Korean technique of fusing 24-karat gold foil to silver.

Maker: Lucy Palmer | **Title:** *Moon Gazing Hare Pendant* | **Materials::** Silver and 24k gold foil (*keum-boo*) | **Size:** Approx. 30 mm diameter | **Image credit:** Lucy Palmer

Narrative: The hare has long been associated with the moon in folklore and mythology around the world—often symbolizing fertility, fortune and immortality. In some cultures it is also believed that the moon bears an image of the hare (much like the "man in the moon").

NICK PALMER

Nick Palmer is an artist, designer and a maker. Although a relative newcomer to precious metalwork, his diverse artistic practice spans thirty years; encompassing writing, performance and theatrical design in addition to 3-D fabrication, drawing and painting. His enduring passions are: his interest in handcrafted objects, the development of his own sculptural ideas and techniques, and collecting early twentieth century toys and ephemera.

For me, art was always about communicating complex emotional concepts through a non-verbal language of nuanced symbols, figures and constructed environments.

So why do I work with the narrative? It offers the possibility to share something personal: perhaps a point of view; something humorous, ironic or sentimental; or an expression of love or hope, in a form that escapes the constraints of spoken language, words and nationality. Demanding focus: being definite about the elements at play, clear in intent and ready to remove or adapt any component that distracts from the "truth" or message you wish to convey.

Maker: Nick Palmer | **Title:** *A Silver Brooch for Oscar Wilde* | **Materials:** Cast, press-formed and fabricated sterling silver with a double stainless-steel pin fastening | **Size:** 46 mm × 93 mm × 17 mm | **Image credit:** Nick Palmer

Narrative: This theoretical commission was inspired by research and reflection on the life and character of Oscar Wilde. Wilde exhibited a duality of nature; on the one hand an aesthete, idealistic, promoting the virtues of natural and artistic beauty. On the other: obsessive, driven by darker passions, destructive and indulgent. I wished to create a metaphor that revealed his internal struggle and conveyed the sad inevitability of his eventual undoing.

CHRISSOULA PAPAHATZI

Chrissoula Papahatzi has been designing and fabricating jewelry since 2002. She lives and works in Athens, Greece.

Surrealism, photography and the themes of childhood and memory are concepts that inspire my work. I am fascinated with the process of transformation of the intangible idea to a solid object through design and fabrication. My aim is to produce pieces that overcome their decorative use. Pieces that communicate and possibly evoke to people thoughts about their personal stories, memories or ideas.

Maker: Chrissoula Papahatzi | **Title:** *The Road* | **Materials:** Sterling silver, alpaca | **Size:** 55 mm × 60 mm × 30 mm | **Image credit:** Chrissoula Papahatzi

Narrative: In this series of works called "Inner View," I use as a starting point the figure from a childhood photo. I place it in different situations, making it an integral part of its environment, trying to explore the ways we influence and are influenced by our surroundings, experiences and the passage of time.

JULIA PARRY-JONES

A collector by nature, I draw inspiration from fragments, curiosities and hidden treasures. Fascinated by the minute and delicate, I use a variety of traditional and contemporary jewelry making techniques, combining precious, natural and vintage materials in a playful, asymmetric manner.

I enjoy exploring jewelry beyond its conventional, wearable form, but as a sculpture or artwork in its own right. It encourages the interchangeable relationship between the two, inviting the wearer to explore the hidden narrative within each piece and its environment.

My current collection is inspired by the treasure hoarding habits of the bowerbird, discovering his favorite forest gems, before meticulously arranging them in his elaborate nest. My jewelry explores the deliberate contrast of materials, forms and colors through their placement. Hardwoods, vintage elements and semi-precious stones are scattered amongst a showcase of silver and 9-karat gold, carefully arranged until a sense of harmony is achieved through their mismatching chaos.

Maker: Julia Parry-Jones | **Title:** *On Display* | **Materials:** Silver, oxidized silver, 9k gold, cherry wood, semi precious stones, pearl, mother-of-pearl, glass seed beads, antique carved amethyst, vintage glass buttons and flower | **Size:** 175 mm × 155 mm × 10 mm | **Image credit:** Ben Sturgess

Narrative: This piece is based on my studies of the treasure hoarding habits of the bowerbird. Each bird builds its own elaborate nest before collecting objects which it finds aesthetically pleasing, its treasures.

This necklace illustrates how the bowerbird meticulously arranges his foraged items until they form the perfect display. The asymmetric detail echo's the intricate nature of the bower, with its rounded form providing the perfect background for the story.

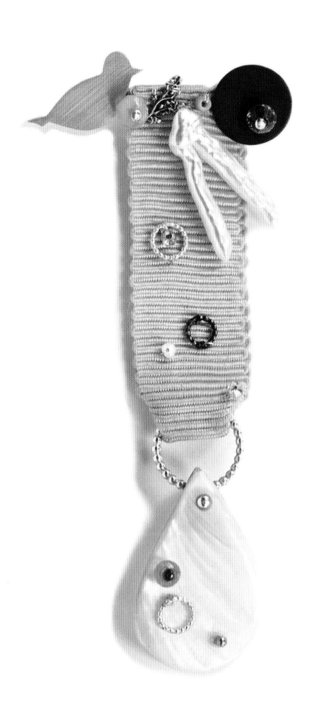

Maker: Julia Parry-Jones | **Title:** *Seek I* | **Materials:** Silver, oxidized silver, mother-of-pearl, stick pearl, pink opal, pearl, vesuvianite, glass seed bead, Swarovski crystal, vintage ribbon | **Size:** Approx 72 mm × 25 mm × 8 mm | **Image credit:** Julia Parry-Jones

Maker: Julia Parry-Jones | **Title:** *Seek II* | **Materials:** Silver, oxidized silver, 9k gold-plated silver, blue topaz, citrine, pearl, glass seed beads, antique glass seed beads, vintage bone flower, antique velvet ribbon, mother-of-pearl | **Size:** Approx. 70 mm × 28 mm × 10 mm | **Image credit:** Julia Parry-Jones

Narrative: After studying the foraging habits of the Vogelkopf bowerbird I wanted to make a brooch inspired by its adventures. It depicts the bird's flight back to the bower, carrying its cornucopia of jewels from the surrounding forest before carefully arranging them in its nest.

The form of the brooch takes inspiration from a traditional medal, an ideal design for the display of prized objects.

MARY HALLAM PEARSE

Mary Hallam Pearse's work has been exhibited both internationally and nationally and in publications such as *Ornament, Metalsmith,* and the Lark 500 books.

My ongoing work is based on conventions of eighteenth century portrait miniatures, nineteenth century portrait jewelry and classic children's dexterity games. I combine images appropriated from fashion spreads and beauty advertisements in both vintage and present-day fashion magazines. I then print the images on thin sheets of aluminum to resemble historical daguerreotypes. The framed photographs become *three-dimensional. And we become aware that the image is an object that requires our hands as well as our eyes. Like children's dexterity games the images have little impressions and glass floats above them. Precious jewels roll freely between the image and glass. This game of skill, imitating classic children's dexterity games, requires that the player complete the image by getting the jewels in the impressions. This use of the image is meant to be playful and ironic and to reflect on the game of desire.*

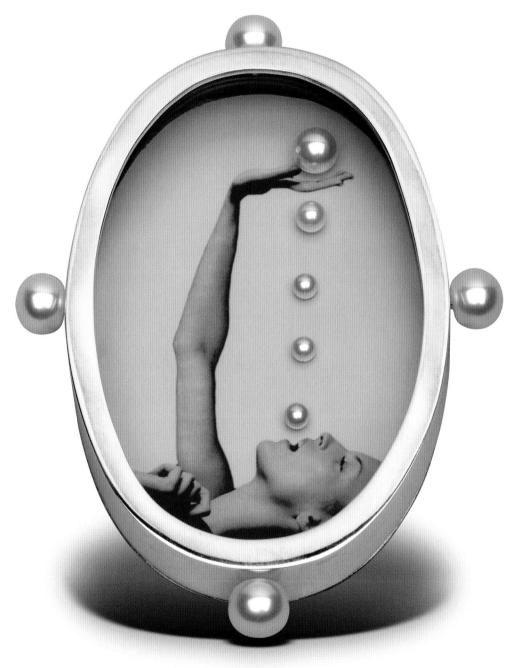

Maker: Mary Hallam Pearse | **Title:** *Feeding Desire* | **Materials:** Sterling silver, aluminum, pearls, glass |
Size: 88.9 mm × 63.5 mm × 12.7 mm | **Image credit:** Walker Montgomery

Narrative: My work is based on conventions of eighteenth century portrait miniatures, nineteenth century portrait jewelry and classic children's dexterity games. I combine images appropriated from fashion spreads and beauty advertisements in both vintage and present-day fashion magazines.

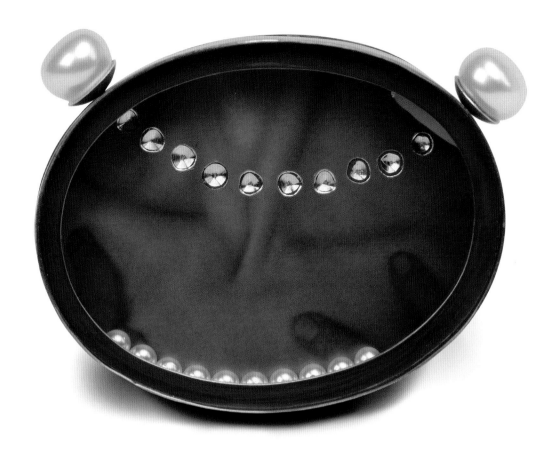

Maker: Mary Hallam Pearse | **Title:** *That Little Something* | **Materials:** Sterling silver, aluminum, pearls, glass |
Size: 57.15 mm × 66.6 mm × 12.7 mm | **Image credit:** Walker Montgomery |

Maker: Mary Hallam Pearse | **Title:** *Three Words* | **Materials:** Silver, aluminum, diamonds, glass | **Size:** 50.8 mm × 88.9 mm × 6.35 mm |
Image credit: Walker Montgomery

CHRISTINE PEDERSEN

A life-long clay sculptor, Christine Pedersen's pieces move between media exploring form and led by narrative—there is always a story—which often becomes part of her blog *Metal Is Clay*. Christine draws heavily from her early life in England through a connection to the physical mass and form of ancient buildings, and a reverence for handmade artifacts. Christine currently lives in Calgary, Canada, and is a member of the Alberta Craft Council and the Metal Arts Guild of Canada.

What I remember about things and places can often feel as rich and sensual as the thing itself: I can step inside, linger, and wander around in the story. Imagining new worlds and stories becomes a fabulous, essential, part of work that I want to make and it seems to come down to noticing—giving myself space to have even a tiny moment in which to dream, to offer a point from where something can begin . . . . The moment stretches out—looking at, thinking about, holding on to. And my very own movie-machine starts to roll, I start living in the story.

Maker: Christine Pedersen | **Title:** *Pull* | **Materials:** Yellow bronze | **Size:** 510 mm × 23 mm × 13 mm | **Image credit:** Christine Pedersen

Narrative: I caught myself—hand in mid-air—staring down at the plastic pull-tab from inside a soy-drink carton, on the way to the recycling bin, and asked myself, "What if this had a different life instead of being recycled as plastic?" So much knowledge and human technical skill already embedded in this small, beautiful, disposable part. I could join lots of them together . . . I could cast in metal . . . What if this waste plastic was the only way I had left to make jewelry? In that instant, as waste became redefined as a resource, the ReFind jewelry collection was born.

RUUDT PETERS

Ruudt Peters has exhibited his sculpture, objects and jewelry in museums and galleries in Europe and the United States.

Maker: Ruudt Peters | **Title:** *Terram "Lapansi"* | **Materials:** Hematite, silver | **Size:** 80 mm × 30 mm × 48 mm | **Image credit:** Ruudt Peters

Narrative: Terram:

We walk through the world with our feet, but we are not aware that our feet do more than merely transport us. Our feet are necessary tools, but also root us to the ground. I emphasize awareness of my place as jewelry maker in the world of body and mind. Terram helps me to connect between the micro and macro cosmos, between the upper and the underworld. Step on the ground.

BRYAN PETERSEN

Bryan Petersen makes mixed media pieces from recycled materials, from printed advertising on tin cans. The appropriation of these materials provides an encyclopedic resource of visual language allowing him to construct narratives focusing on social commentary. The text and imagery in advertising and printed packaging provide a foundation of color, pattern, and symbolism, often with a bias that plays on society's needs and desires. Petersen's work comments on politics, gender, the environment, and the plight of native people, when juxtaposing the images and text in found objects, creating irony, humor, and critical awareness.

Maker: Bryan Petersen | **Title:** *Orville Hope Brooch* | **Materials:** Tin, steel, brass and found objects | **Size:** 75 mm × 50 mm × 10 mm | **Image credit:** Bryan Petersen

Narrative: The overall shape of the brooch is of a leaf, it could be a leaf of lettuce since food production appears to be the central focus. At the top is a famous Indian chief, Crazy Horse, a Native American war leader of the Oglala Lakota. One of his famous quotes, "One does not sell the earth upon which people walk," and " Another white man's trick! Let me go! Let me die fighting!" This solemn portrait is paired with the logo of the popcorn mogul, Orville Redenbacher whose customers couldn't believe that he was real and thought he was a hired actor for the company. Orville proclaimed, "I want to make it clear that I am real."

At the bottom there is a McDonald's lapel pin in a similar fashion to a coat of arms with lettuce, tomatoes and a set of crossed silverware as spears, or weapons.

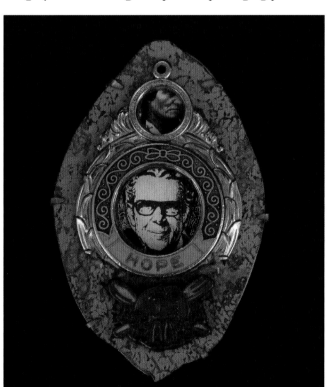

SUSAN PIETZSCH

Trained in gold and silversmithing, Susan Pietzsch started her freelance carrier in 1997, featuring wearable jewelry pieces. In parallel she started working with autonomous objects, independent from the body, presented as installations or photographs where artistic statement plays a more prominent role over the act of adornment.

Since 1997 the artist has spearheaded an international artistic collaborative project under the name Schmuck2. Within this project, Pietzsch focuses on unusual and diverse approaches to the phenomenon of jewelry, using unconventional concepts that move between fine and applied arts. Susan is based in Tokyo, Japan and the seaside town of Glashagen, Germany.

I cannot say that narrative has served as a starting point or goal for me in my work. However, thanks to Mark Fenn's request and upon reflection, I can see how my works could lend themselves quite naturally to such associations. For example, narratives are probably naturally revealed by the fact that I use the image of chocolate or sugar directly on the body. In my jewelry I focus on the idea of impermanence and indulgence, and thus my pieces tell stories of a world of cravings poised between material and human desires. It is radical in terms of traditional categories of jewelry, but in a poetic and deliciously ironic way!

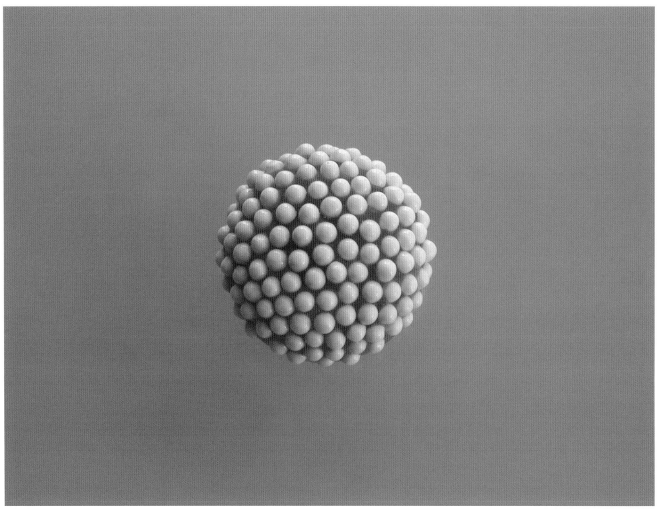

Maker: Susan Pietzsch | **Title:** *Paste di Mandorle* | **Materials:** Cast and glazed porcelain, formed acrylic, silver, stainless steel | **Size:** 50 mm | **Image credit:** Johannes Faeth

Narrative: *Paste di Mandorle* is an imitation of the traditional Italian cookie. In the jewelry work the anise pastilles are replaced by cast and glazed porcelain beads. Pink acrylic forms the "paste" using a material from dental technology. For quite some time I have been fascinated by the colors and appearances of all kinds of sweets, from the mass produced to the most sophisticated of artisinal confections. As stimulants they are linked to human desire. With my works related to this subject I have always sought to establish a very intimate relationship between the wearer and the jewelry.

WEI LAH POH

Wei Lah Poh was born in Hong Kong, but raised with a multicultural state of mind.

Wei Lah Poh's current body of work is based on found enamelware. She is deeply fascinated with the history of enamelware and investigates this subject in the context of how it can be jewelry. It is an ongoing investigation on how these found objects can become adornments. This work can be found under the Handle series.

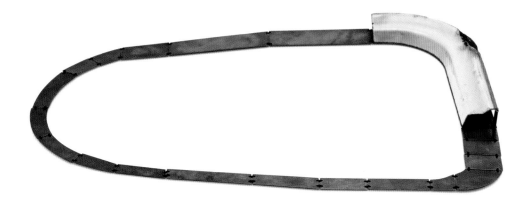

Maker: Wei Lah Poh |
Title: *Green Dish Elevated, Necklace* |
Materials: Found enamelware, silver, thread |
Size: 19.05 mm × 209.55 mm × 336.55 mm |
Image credit: Azur Mele McHugh

Maker: Wei Lah Poh |
Title: *Blue Rim Dented Edge, Necklace* | **Materials:** Found enamelware, enamel, steel, thread | **Size:** 25.4 mm × 234.95 mm × 444.5 mm |
Image credit: Azur Mele McHugh

Maker: Wei Lah Poh | **Title:** *Break-Bend, Brooch* | **Materials:** Found enamelware, silver, stainless steel | **Size:** 127 mm × 50.8 mm × 50.8 mm | **Image credit:** Azur Mele McHugh

JO POND

Jo Pond is a studio jeweler and lecturer. Jo exhibits her work on an international platform and uitilizes both modern and traditional technologies within her practice. Jo explores the potential for wearable items to become vehicles for communication; whether through sense, nostalgia, or familiarity.

My design process evolved during my master's. I identified my lifelong passion for old worn objects and the extreme contrast of their aesthetic with that of the works I was creating. The control, polish and accuracy of my works did not reflect the qualities I enjoyed and

so, tentatively, I started to incorporate these objects, so as not to imitate, but to give a true representation.

My initial ideas develop from a given theme, material or object. Each of these offers potential directions and can evoke emotion or stimulate a line of enquiry. Once a theme engages with me on some level, I research this further to inform my design process. From this point I am motivated by both lines of enquiry; firstly, the aesthetic inspiration through materials or found objects, which I may incorporate, or which may suggest form or texture; secondly, the subject, which develops from the theme or materials I use. Both lines of enquiry underpin the narrative of my works.

Maker: Jo Pond | Title: *The Reed Parure* | Materials: Repurposed Horlicks tin, leather, silver, diamonds, citrine, buttons, steel | Size: Approx. 80 mm × 60 mm × 20 mm | Image credit: Jo Pond

Narrative: Created to commission with a particular narrative, garment and gentleman in mind, the love of a small, precious and beautiful woman was suggested within this relatively tiny parure. Designed to be worn together and created from a vintage Horlicks tin to illustrate the ability to laugh at one's ailments, repurposed steel, buttons and recycled leather were bought together and given precious value, as each was set

with three diamonds, mounted in silver. Intended to commandeer a particular waistcoat, this parure bought a sense of calm to an often conflicting array of jewels, serving as a reminder of a loved one, and as a space to contain daily medicines.

Maker: Jo Pond | **Title:** *Barren. Catharsis for Consolation* | **Materials:** Repurposed watering-can rose, steel, ribbon, paper | **Size:** 111 mm × 70 mm × 10 mm | **Image credit:** Jo Pond

Narrative: Many of us are not fertile, not capable of initiating, sustaining, or supporting reproduction; instead we are labelled as unproductive; labelled as barren. We live discontent with our childlessness, bearing an undisclosed ache, a sense of emptiness; tender from the blunt questioning, presumption and surmise of others.

Through this piece, repurposing a watering-can rose, I have explored the emotional and psychological associations of what fertility means to those who are not. The watering can enables each and every one of us to feed and nurture. That which we are inherently designed for is sometimes transferrable. The challenge lies in accepting that we are enough.

Maker: Jo Pond | **Title:** *Magic City* | **Materials:** Repurposed baking tin, repurposed grater, citrine, 18k gold wire, steel | **Size:** Approx. 80 mm × 50 mm × 20 mm

Narrative: Although often considered a grey and industrial urban habitat, Birmingham is home to one of the four UK Jewelry Quarters. Utilizing this urban landscape as a starting point, I sought and repurposed kitchen equipment which presented industrial seams and pressed details; techniques employed within our industry. As with the city's preconceptions,

these pieces required the detail of finery and significance and so each was embellished with a citrine, set in 18k gold wire. My materials delivered the title for this collection "Baking Tin & Grater" which sounds rather like a firm of solicitors; quite appropriate for such a *Magic City*.

HESTER POPMA-VAN DE KOLK

Hester Popma-van de Kolk is a self-taught and award-winning visual artist. A significant part of her work takes the form of jewelry.

When I see presence
I feel absence
When I search absence
I experience presence
The tension between absence and presence is an important theme in my work.

I've been investigating all sorts of materials to capture this tension. At the moment I work with golden chips (and plastic) from used credit cards. The golden chips were once the visual part of an invisible world of communication, identity, information and money. Their function connected us to other people. At the same time we kept these symbols of communication hidden, close to our bodies, creating a form of intimacy. By transforming the used chips that were once charged with all this information, I try to reload them. Now that they have become pieces of jewelry they will be charged with new meaning by the wearer, again invisible for the viewer, shaping a new intimate context.

Looking at my work you'll find echoes of old traditions. There is usually some presence of the past, joined with present-day materials in an embracement for the future.

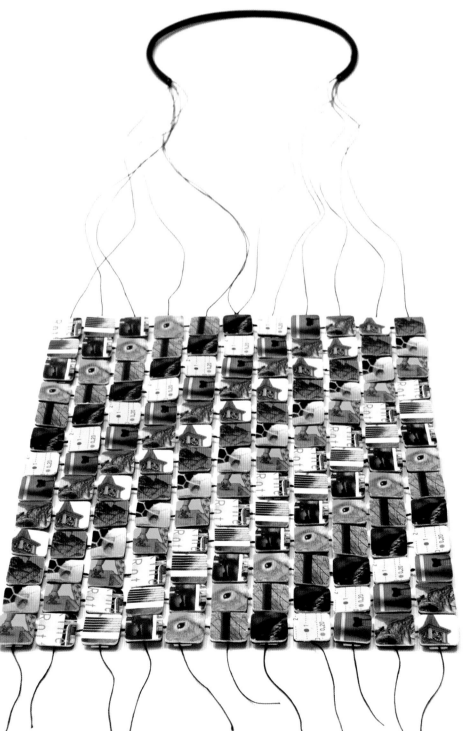

Maker: Hester Popma-van de Kolk | **Title:** *Wearable Home* ("All That Glitters Is Not Gold" Series) | **Materials:** Chips and plastic from SIM, credit-bank cards, yarn | **Size:** 140 mm × 180 mm × 4 mm | **Image credit:** ikfabriek

Narrative: This two-sided necklace was a winning design in the international biennial design contest "New Traditional Jewelry 2012." Jury report: "In several playful ways things are hidden and things are made visible and at all times only one side of the necklace is visible. The decorated side refers to the issues of the day: time, communication and money. The golden side calls up associations of illustrious civilizations, like the Egypt of the pharaohs and the Mayas. At the same time the chips contain information not visible to the naked eye. This necklace is a bridge in time."

DIANA PORTER

Acclaimed jewelry designer Diana Porter has been creating jewelry from her Bristol-based workshop since 1993. During that time, she has undertaken hundreds of commissions and been awarded UK Jewelry Designer of the Year.

Maker: Diana Porter | **Title:** *Being Ring* | **Materials:** Silver ring with oxidized etching, set with seven diamonds. Oxidized silver ball and chain with diamond detail, attached to ring | **Size:** Undulating 13-13.8 mm width of ring. 540 mm length chain. Ball diameter 8 mm | **Image credit:** Diana Porter Contemporary Jewelry

Narrative: The words used in the *Being* collection are inspired by the narrative of life's journey and all its stages. The words not only bring meaning to the ring but create a texture which adds to the design. Pieces use chains and diamonds to highlight life's twists and turns as well as its tiny precious moments.

ÁUREA PRAGA

Áurea Praga is a Portuguese jewelry designer and illustrator often crossing both areas.

As a jewelry maker and an illustrator, my work process usually enables dialogues between these two areas. I often use formal and semantic elements from my illustrations to create a piece of jewelry, using the body as a new component for what I'm trying to communicate.

The narrative character of illustration is thus carried to each piece of jewelry, implying there's a story attached to the isolated object.

And through storytelling, these personal objects that adorn the body allow us to connect with the world but mostly with who we are.

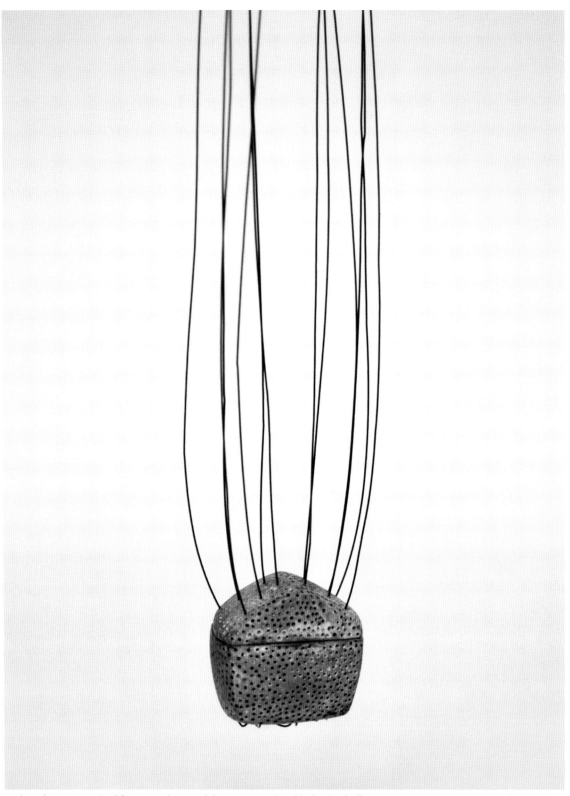

Maker: Áurea Praga | **Title:** *Home* | **Materials:** Bronze, patina, black wire | **Size:** 35 mm × 450 mm × 20 mm | **Image credit:** Áurea Praga

Narrative: What makes a house turn into a home, into this space of intimacy where things have a peculiar way of arranging themselves to roof our dreams?

ENRICA PRAZZOLI

I am ascinated by everyday life, the things we do without thinking; repetition, patterns, again and again. Connections, associations. Communication, interaction, misunderstandings. How the same things look from different points of view.

What fascinates me about jewelry is its preciousness, not about the price but the value we place on our treasures: memories. stories.

Jewelry speaks; to us, about us. The reassuring, private whisper of a medal inherited from a grandmother; worn on your skin, hidden from sight, but you know it's there. The daring tone of the badges that seem to spontaneously appear on your messenger bag. The loud voice of a big, colorful statement piece that you wear on a special occasion.

Maker: Enrica Prazzoli | **Title:** *Spare Part 1B for Device 1, or "Apparatus to Overcome the Perceived Lack of Humanity in Today's Communication"* | **Materials:** Brass, reclaimed hardwood, steel | **Size:** 100 mm × 70 mm × 20 mm | **Image credit:** Enrica Prazzoli

Narrative: Strange machines traveling through time; made a long time ago but only a few weeks old. Just because we can see their inner mechanism doesn't mean we understand what they are supposed to do, any more than we understand what's going on inside a computer chip. Someone made them, someone has to use them. By themselves they don't move; they do not solve problems, nor create them.

Device 1 is the most complex, a machine for communication. I think this is a demonstration version, composed of two stations connected by a thick bundle of cables; it wouldn't make much sense to use this machine if the person we want to communicate with is in the same room.

Each station is composed by a raised board, upon which five different humanoid figures find space. In front of each figure, a small light and a switch; if you tap the switch, the corresponding light on the other station lights up. This automata is labelled "I wish to express my affection for you in an acceptable manner despite the distance."

PAUL PRESTON, AKA RED MOLE

I do not have a philosophy regarding my work and I am very impatient with those who feel they need one. I explain myself like this: Red Mole has been adopted as a vehicle. He can be shown doing things I have done in the past or recently. Alternatively he can be sent up in a rocket ship or climb Everest, face-off a dragon with only a sticker, play an instrument I chose.

Thus is provided a never ending supply of subject matter. I am spoiled for choice. How about a series of pieces showing musicians in a more symphonic orchestra? This is playful, whimsical stuff not meant to be taken seriously.

From a personal point of view this little brooch is the most important I have ever made. It marks a significant change of direction. A firm favorite, I embarked on a series of ten over the next fourteen years, nine of which are in my private museum. It led to the spidery 3-D wire dioramas that began to occupy me, so fragile; they would have been unthinkable five years earlier.

The reason for all this is that in the late 1990s I was lost to bi-polar [disorder] and did no work for four and a half years. When I crawled out into the sunshine I found myself changed for the better and there was this fabulous fork-tailed comet hanging in the sky night after night. It seemed that I had granted myself permission not to worry any more and loosen up. That resulted in this brooch which is the first thing I made on recovery, just lashed together rather like children build rafts again; this was unthinkable five years before.

The brooch shows Red Mole with a stick and a dog marvelling at the sight with the moon, comet and Plough [Big Dipper] star system. A huge subject reduced to about the size of a postage stamp. Mock Ionic capitals from my architectural days and the whole lot supported by turtles. The latter a reference to the cosmic, divine, or world-supporting turtle myth perpetrated in China and India.

The brooch is meant to be worn on very dark fabric to mimic the black sky. The dog was called Mattie.

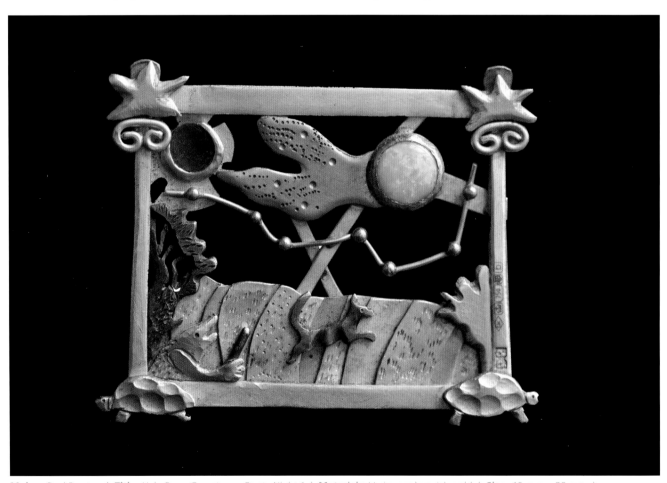

Maker: Paul Preston | **Title:** *Hale-Bopp Comet on a Frosty Night 1* | **Materials:** Various colors rich gold | **Size:** 40 mm × 32 mm |
Image credit: Jean Thomas

JO PUDELKO

Jo Pudelko is a craftsperson whose work consists of mixed-media jewelry and small scale sculptural objects with the occasional accompanying screen print. She specializes in the use of plastics and often incorporates found objects in her work. The aesthetic of her work often evokes a subtle sense of familiarity or an "echo" that is derived from the many objects she has collected and then used to inspire her work. The resulting pieces are unique and thought provoking as they seek to combine seemingly contradictory qualities; they are past and present, junk and treasure all at the same time. Jo creates works from a ramshackle caravan parked at the foot of the beautiful Ochil Hills in Scotland.

Maker: Jo Pudelko | **Title:** *Poor Aerotynamics* | **Materials:** Brass, wood, spray paint, resin, found objects | **Size:** 90 mm × 45 mm | **Image credit:** Shannon Tofts

Narrative: For me it is unusual to work in a narrative style but I think that the piece is all the more special because of that. The pendant features a small tiger that hung from a chain I wore as a child. In this new context the little tiger has become part of a much bigger "story" as a strange hybrid animal—a tiger with wings. Unfortunately for the tiger—he doesn't know how to fly; a detail referenced by the title, *Poor Aerotynamics*. He swings around rather jauntily though and to me he looks very content and happy. I think of the piece as a parable about making the best of any given situation and facing the world in a positive way.

KERIANNE QUICK

Kerianne Quick is an artist engaged in an exploration of materiality and culture through objects. Dealing with diverse subject matter–from communal sheep farming practices in the Orkney Isles to the derelict brickyards of New York's Hudson Valley, Kerianne mixes traditional and digital making processes with ethnographic research to consider how objects can be embedded with meaning.

Personal narratives play an important role in my process. While they may not reveal themselves immediately in the work, the histories and myths of my family inform how my work positions itself. I use personal heirlooms and historical industrial materials to emphasize the connection between the personal and the common, and tell my family's story of immigration and assimilation. These contrasting materials used in familiar and foreign forms evoke cultural translation and transition.

Maker: Kerianne Quick | **Title:** *Transmutations 6* | **Materials:** Brick foraged from the site of the former Hutton Brickworks, pearls—inherited from my grandmother, silk, silver, stainless steel | **Size:** 63 mm × 38 mm × 7.5 mm | **Image credit:** Kerianne Quick

Narrative: The derelict brickyards of the Hudson River Valley dot the landscape like tombstones. They are the visible detritus of invisible movement; of a land grab and subsequent displacement of native peoples, of the consumption of a finite natural resource, of the redefinition of the landscape and its ecology. Not long before, the waters of the Hudson River teamed with life—oysters, clams, sturgeon and shad. The native Algonquin speaking tribes, the Lenni Lenape, Munsee, Esopus, Mahicans and Wappingers, lived along the river and its tributaries by the tens of thousands. Beginning with the Dutch, waves of traders, colonizers, and settlers pushed the native population away from the vital waters—through wars, disease and treaties—into foreign territories. A new industrial culture took root, slowly developing into a complex system of specialized production. The Brickworks and other factories that produced the materials needed to build the growing metropolis down river slowly ate away at the ecosystem. With space and demand exhausted, the Brickworks that built New York City now lie in ruins—leaving wakes of ghostly main streets and dearth. One people are displaced by another. Cultures migrate, dissipate, blend, emerge. One fruit of the river replaces another.

In this work, material foraged out of the Hudson River and Rondout Creek or taken from dismantled parts of local historic homes in Kingston, New York are shifted in form, and used to explore histories, cultural substitutions/additions/deletions, and inheritance.

NASH QUINN

Nash Quinn is a metalsmith whose work spans a range of formats, from jewelry to vessels and mechanical objects, and has been featured in numerous national and international exhibitions and publications.

Narrative is a broad word—it is open to interpretation, and narrative artwork takes myriad forms. I choose to engage the narrative through representational images—jewelry that looks like something recognizable, often animals, bones and icons. Some of my work creates an explicit narrative, designed to send a message. Other work is open ended—the scene is set, and the tale takes the path the viewer creates.

Maker: Nash Quinn | **Title:** *Skull Ring Trio (Fish, Bird, and Reptile)* | **Materials:** Sterling silver, copper, powder coat | **Size:** Approx. 65 mm × 48 mm × 40 mm | **Image credit:** Nash Quinn

Narrative: I created these rings while working in a swampy region of rural North Carolina. They depict the skulls of a cormorant, a snapping turtle, and a perch—omnipresent aquatic fauna in the region. Their connection to death is obvious, and the powder coated white trim surrounding the skulls references an egg shell—an allusion to the perennial tale of death, decay, and rebirth present in a swamp ecosystem.

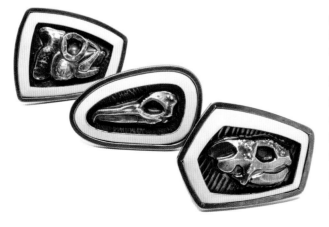

ERIN RAPPLEYE

Erin Rappleye grew up in the northwest suburbs of Chicago, Illinois. She is an interdisciplinary artist who combines wearables, installation, printmaking, and narrative performance to discuss psychological relationships between self, other and object within an immersive environment. Erin maintains her studio practice near Chicago.

More than likely, we will not experience the same events in our lives, but we will probably feel many of the same emotions. For myself, storytelling serves as a way of connecting with others emotionally through a variety of experiences. I create characters and objects that are part of a larger context exhibited in an installation environment. The objects I create are not wearer neutral, they implicate the wearer; for example, a liar's mask or a horse's bit submits the wearer directly into the role of the character. The wearer then becomes part of the story, activating an immersive environment for both the performer and the viewer. The stories expressed through my installations explore sexuality, partnership, femininity, behavior, communication, and misunderstandings in an attempt to better connect with others and understand myself.

I am interested in jewelry's ability to serve as a vehicle for revealing these narratives. The broadest objective of jewelry as an art form is to impact or complement the story of the human body. It is an objective informed by inherent material value and psychological/emotional value. The latter determined by relationships, interaction, personal history, legacy, and gesture, which I explore through performance. I believe positive and negative environments have the ability to manipulate our perception of ourselves just like something physically attached to us. My research centers on how body adornment can reflect personal psychology as influenced by a given environment and the potential for the objects within that space to respond as witnesses to further illustrate stories within an installation.

Maker: Erin Rappleye | **Title:** *Curry Comb for the Workhorse* | **Materials:** Powder-coated aluminum, brass with patina and flocking | **Size:** 215.9 mm × 101.6 mm × 63.5 mm | **Image credit:** Erin Rappleye

Narrative: *How Toys Become Real* is the alternative title to the children's book *The Velveteen Rabbit*, wherein a toy rabbit longs to be noticed and loved by a little boy. Over time the rabbit learns from the little boy that genuine love is unconditional and timeless. It is real love that transforms the stuffed animal from a toy to a living rabbit.

This installation and performance, titled *How to Become Real* was inspired by *The Velveteen Rabbit*. It approaches the search for genuine love from the context of a romantic relationship. The story is conveyed from the perspective of a partner who felt transformed into the relationship workhorse.

Workhorses are psychologically trained by partner approval. They struggle to meet the perceived expectations of their partner in hopes of enjoying a split second of affection. More often than not, the workhorse will find its efforts purposefully unappreciated. The infrequent award of affection drives the horse to perform variations on a successful routine in order to recapture a fleeting moment of love and companionship. Unfortunately, this specific horse performs a failing routine—exuding showmanship eroded by the effects of intimate and emotional neglect.

Amidst the tired routine, a moment of reflection allows the workhorse to finally acknowledge the manipulative quality of the partnership. At this moment the horse discovers, unlike *The Velveteen Rabbit*, that through an action of self-love, one can transform from a workhorse into a real person once again.

TABEA REULECKE

Tabea Reulecke is a studio jeweler and project manager. Her works can be seen in international galleries in Europe, Asia and South America. Besides her studio work Reulecke teaches at various schools and academies. She also is the founder and project manager of the International Summer Academy at Campus Idar-Oberstein.

I cannot keep still. The release valve is opened and my kettle starts to boil; imagination flowing out of my head and into the world. The next moment is a surprise. Thoughts from the past rise organically without prescription; ideas are strung to fill an infinite space, constantly changing until the materials become apparent.

These I split, saw, file and grind until a story emerges; its chapters decided intuitively. Through diversity a creature forms; to be trimmed, assembled, glued and, sometimes, part discarded. This new character, once born, is forever responsible for itself; its nature allowing it to connect, to hold, to embrace and attract.

My journeys to the north, the south, the east and the west are my inspirations. There I find exciting stories and odd materials, which I take back to my workshop, and that is were the known and the unknown meet: A cow horn and that of an antelope. Wood of a walnut tree and wood of an olive tree. Colors from pigments and colors from glass stones. I build the bridges that connect my findings.

A story provides my aim and the outcome of the final form is determined through the process of making. In a workshop, amid horns and bones, pieces of wood, stones, metals, colors, paint brushes, found objects and gifts, I set to work; trusting my imagination, my tools and the freedom around me.

There are drawings in most of my works. Animal interaction, communication and endless fantasy fascinate me. I try to capture a certain moment and make it last. I believe strongly that our subconscious being is a very powerful tool.

Each interesting moment is checked and stored in my mind.

Everything I experience, perceive, or find out—I preserve. But I would be a fool to keep these moments and thoughts just for me, because even though they have their own life inside of me, they are more now, transferred into an object or jewelry piece. They are shared, remembered, they are alive beyond me and that's the best.

Maker: Tabea Reulecke | Title: *Dos Cigueñas* | Materials: Enamel, copper, silver | Size: 320 mm × 160 mm × 50 mm | Image credit: Tabea Reulecke

Narrative: They bring the children.

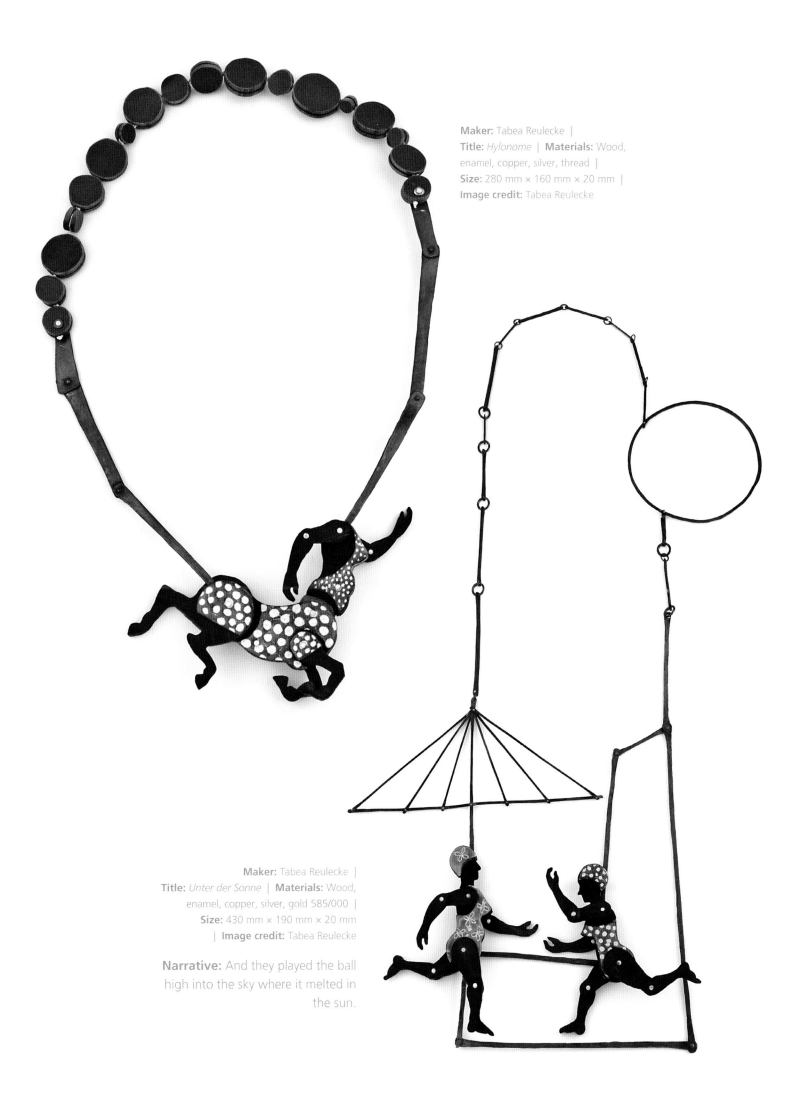

Maker: Tabea Reulecke |
Title: *Hylonome* | **Materials:** Wood,
enamel, copper, silver, thread |
Size: 280 mm × 160 mm × 20 mm |
Image credit: Tabea Reulecke

Maker: Tabea Reulecke |
Title: *Unter der Sonne* | **Materials:** Wood,
enamel, copper, silver, gold 585/000 |
Size: 430 mm × 190 mm × 20 mm
| **Image credit:** Tabea Reulecke

Narrative: And they played the ball
high into the sky where it melted in
the sun.

227

KATHERINE RICHMOND

Katherine Richmond is an award-winning jewelry Artist based in Northamptonshire.

My work is inspired by the fragility of memory and the tensions between control and disorder. I use books as a symbol of permanence and longevity to create adornment with a fragility that questions traditional notions of wearability. Every piece I make takes on its own narrative. In the same way that memories are recollected, I rearrange and pull together fragments to create ever changing, imagined compositions that hint at something they once were, or could become.

Maker: Katherine Richmond | **Title:** *Constellations (Brooch)* | **Materials:** Book pages, red book cover, linen thread, silver, gold plate | **Size:** 100 mm × 80 mm × 15 mm | **Image credit:** Katherine Richmond

Narrative: Our memories change. They meddle with each other. Pieces are added, pieces are lost, the truth gets fabricated; words change here, images change there. Threads pull together the constellations of the past; attempts to recreate the faded and fragmented. Color is added where it once did not exist; color fades into black and white. We add elements to embellish and create new, idealistic stories. Often, the recollections have been tampered with. An unconscious hybrid between new and old, falsity and fantasy; these are the Meddlesome Recollections.

Originally created for "Life Is a Bench—Meddle" exhibition, Schmuck, March 2012.

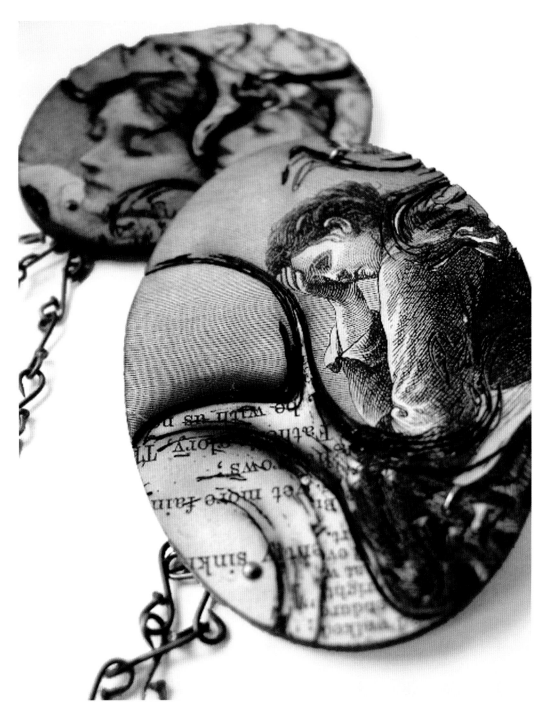

Maker: Katherine Richmond | **Title:** *Separation Anxiety (Double Brooch)* | **Materials:** Book pages, steel pins, sterling silver, gold plate, entomology pins | **Size:** Brooch 1—80 mm × 57 mm × 10 mm inc. pin. Brooch 2—70 mm × 52 mm × 9 mm inc. pin | **Image credit:** Katherine Richmond

Narrative: Our world is in a constant state of flux; we are forced to establish tangible markers of change to help shape the construction of our memories and to do so we collect objects, such as letters, photographs and souvenirs. We can control our possessions in a way that little else can be controlled, offering us a sense of stability in a world of change. For a true collector, the desire for perfection and control through the order of objects can be so strong that it develops into an obsession.

Maker: Katherine Richmond | **Title:** *Dreams (Brooch)* | **Materials:** Book pages, sterling silver | **Size:** 65 mm × 90 mm × 8 mm inc. pin | **Image credit:** Katherine Richmond

Narrative: Walter Benjamin wrote of the book collector's mysterious relationship to ownership and the "dialectical tension between the poles of disorder and order." It is, he says, a passion that "borders on the chaos of memories."

MELINDA RISK

Melinda Risk has a bachelor of arts degree in jewelry/metals. Her work is sold in galleries all over the US. She works in her studio in the state of Indiana.

My ideas come from nature and my life experiences. My subject matter varies from birds and bugs to dolls, music and lyrics, spirituality and infinitely more. I capture the beauty of each idea by selecting *outstanding characteristics to tell a story. Beauty and craft are always at the top of my agenda. My designs blur the lines between art and craft, which renders each work into a piece of sculpture that happens to be wearable. I translate my ideas into a visually pleasing story by blending archival quality with creative engineering combining gold, silver, wood, porcelain, diamonds and gemstones*

Maker: Melinda Risk | **Title:** *Osmia Avosetta Bee (Ring)* | **Materials:** Rose de France amethyst, diamonds, pink sapphires, 22k gold, sterling silver,crushed dried rose petals | **Image credit:** Melinda Risk

Narrative: This piece tells the story of the Osmia avosetta bee that was discovered in 1997. It is a solitary bee that makes a beautiful nest from flower petals. The bee is carved in the amethyst as well as on the side of the ring, and the other side has the flowers that it makes its nest from. Underneath the center stone are crushed dried flower petals.

JORGE ROJAS

Jorge Rojas lives in Hamburg. As a goldsmith he makes unique pieces, which combine traditional and non-traditional materials with the most avant-garde designs. Jorge Rojas improve his craft in New York where he collaborated with experimental sculptors and goldsmiths.

The symbolic feature of the jewelry moves in two directions: towards the outside, with a social component as it is decorated with jewels to define hierarchies and show status, but it also has more intimate, more personal meaning as talismans or amulets which establish a connection with the supernatural. In both cases the jewels are a language articulated by the particular alphabet of the goldsmith.

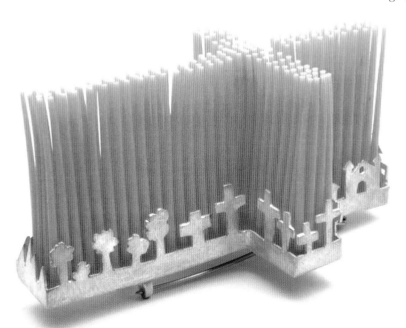

Maker: Jorge Rojas | **Title:** *Let's Go "Paco" (Pendant/Brooch)* | **Materials:** Silver 930 with orange silicone | **Size:** 83 mm × 45 mm × 40 mm | **Image credit:** Jorge Rojas

Narrative: One of the more powerful symbols; the cross with its association with life and death. I wanted to comment on the important role that the new pope is undertaking in the Christian community. With my rubber cross I express the smooth and soft revolution that he is making.

HOSANNA RUBIO

Born and raised in Southern California, Hosanna Rubio has had her work exhibited regionally and nationally, most recently at the National Ornamental Metal Museum in Memphis, Tennessee, and in Alchemy 3, the Enamelist Society's Juried Student Exhibition.

When I was first introduced to jewelry as a medium, I felt the need to explore the connection to the body, both physically and conceptually. I was raised by fundamentalist faith healers, and as an adult, I found my first encounters with modern medicine to be equally ineffective and destructive. This gave me a varied point of view on how we relate to the body, and inspired me to explore the ideas of pain, disease, medicine, and healing often in my work. My work is a reaction to the world around me; creating layered, detailed pieces allows me to find balance in the chaotic, to attempt to exert control over the uncontrollable aspects of my life.

Maker: Hosanna Rubio | **Title:** *Physician, Heal Thyself* | **Materials:** Bird skull, cast silver, cast bronze, copper, brass, silver wire, chain | **Size:** 139.7 mm × 215.9 mm | **Image credit:** Michael DeLeon

Narrative: Two-part pin with found object and environment. For this piece, I wanted to make a connection between several subjects: cabinets of curiosities, modern medicine, faith healing, and totems. I chose to use cabinets of curiosities as an inspiration because they represent the idea of reflecting on the horrors of the past, something that I feel future generations will understand when they look back on this stage in our medical history.

MARISSA SANEHOLZ

Marissa Saneholz makes narrative based jewelry and objects using humor and sarcasm to comment on gender roles in American society.

She has been published in several books, including *Art Jewelry Today II* edited by Jeffery Snyder and *Humor in Craft* by Brigitte Martin.

By referencing housewife ideals that were created in the early and mid-twentieth century and putting a modern twist on vintage graphics, my work is an attempt to converse about the loss of innocence, gender issues, and my search for identity in today's American society. The closer I get to defining my own place in the world, the less idealistic I become. In the world of comic books and fairytales, the good guy always wins and prince charming saves the damsel in distress. This work attempts to reference those ideals with cynicism and sarcasm.

I chose to use enamels in these pieces because with the unlimited color palette and the soft matte surfaces achievable, I can reproduce colors that are similar to those used in the romance comics that my mother read as a child. The found objects incorporated in these pieces were collected during a time when I was living in Europe. They reference the knickknacks that are often picked up during vacations and while traveling. The nostalgic overtone references a time of innocence and discovery, while the included text and titles intentionally disrupt this false sense of security.

Maker: Marissa Saneholz | **Title:** *The Newest Reinvention of Herself Was Her Favorite Yet* | **Materials:** Enamel, copper, pearls, silk, sterling silver, stainless steel pin wire | **Size:** 57 mm × 41 mm × 10 mm | **Image credit:** Sara Brown Studio

Narrative: This piece is a new format in an ongoing theme throughout my series: Corrupt Fairy Tales. The stories that I tell with these pieces can range from personal narratives to snippets of conversations from a coffee shop. The theme is always hinting towards gender roles and reference romance novels and dating guides from the post-World War II era in the United States. This particular piece is simple as far as the solidarity of a figure holding a single strand of pearls. It is left to the viewer to determine if the woman is picking up the pearls or placing them aside. The single strand of pearls is indicative of "the housewife persona" that was ingrained into American culture in the 1950s. The title of the piece adds to the narrative and is part of a personal story of moving past a relationship.

Maker: Marissa Saneholz |
Title: The Funny Thing Was That She Wasn't Even
Mad | **Materials:** Enamel, copper, 14k gold,
sterling silver, stainless steel pin wire, found objects,
diamond | **Size:** 86 mm × 54 mm × 10 mm |
Image credit: Sara Brown Studio

Narrative: This piece is also a commentary
on a failed relationship. The inclusion of the
found objects help to expand on the story;
the rusted nail has been rounded into a ring
with a diamond set in gold suggesting an
engagement ring and the carved coral rose
is a traditional symbol of love and devotion.
Again, the woman could either be picking
these objects up or placing them to the side.

Maker: Marissa Saneholz | **Title:** The Hits Just Kept
Coming | **Materials:** Copper, enamel, pearls, stainless
steel pin wire | **Size:** 51 mm × 89 mm × 6 mm |
Image credit: Sara Brown Studio

Narrative: With this piece I was again
exploring the connection between the figure
and a strand of pearls. The expression of the
woman could be read as serene, meditative,
or possibly somber. The title is darker and
leads the viewer to conclusions about the
narrative being told to be negative in origin.

STEPHEN F. SARACINO

Stephen Saracino is a studio metalsmith whose work relies on narrative driven by world events. He is based in Buffalo, New York.

My work embraces a wide range of subject matter and is narrative in disposition. My ideation breaks down into four basic categories: Objects created from using my own social conscience/political viewpoint; historic subject matter relating to cultural iconography from the countries where I have lived while pursuing my career in education and studio metalsmithing; humorous renditions of cultural events both historic and pop-oriented; and the making of larger objects dealing with non-objective volumetric form. Not one to be prolific, the body of work I have produced oftentimes takes me years to design and fabricate. I try not to confine myself to any one issue and like to move freely between scale related to jewelry (i.e., bracelets, rings) and one that includes larger objects like reliquaries, candlesticks, or on occasion, large non-objective volumetric forms.

For better or worse, I have tried to keep a jewelry or metalsmithing idiom as a root for the pieces, but the work (especially the social conscience/political-oriented objects) has evolved to owning only a vestige utilitarian function. I like to think that I provoke a person to resolve the utilitarian dichotomy and decide what the narrative represents. Bracelets or rings that in reality will never be worn become the platform to instigate my narration. With this said it is often hard to remind myself that my initial training in metal followed a strict traditionalist voice. One ring to each finger, all bracelets and pins must be suitable for body adornment in the pursuit of high aesthetics. I decided very early that if one finger were good, then it would follow that two, three, or even four is better, if not edgier and bracelets would be used for "weightier" ideation. Gem usage and functionality became optional as I quickly deserted my roots and never looked back.

Maker: Stephen F. Saracino | **Title:** *War Trophy. Nation Building 3rd Place. (Bracelet)* | **Materials:** Sterling silver. Cast and fabricated components | **Size:** Approx 250 mm × 100 mm × 200 mm | **Image credit:** Bruce Fox

Narrative: I thought it was well past time to design, fabricate, and distribute trophies for wars, in this case specifically for the category of Nation Building. This trophy is awarded to the United States for its "efforts" regarding nation building after its ill-conceived, ongoing, and disastrous war in Iraq.

Maker: Stephen F. Saracino | **Title:** *Pineapple of Anguish* | **Materials:** Sterling silver, mokume gane, wild boar tusk. Cast and fabricated components | **Size:** Approx. 225 mm × 88 mm × 88 mm | **Image credit:** Bruce Fox

Narrative: My particular take of a medieval torture device that has been upgraded to reflect the use of contemporary torture inflicted on enemies by the United States military during its ongoing incursions in, among other places, Iraq. Based on the Middle Age instrument of torture known as the Pear of Anguish, this operable device can be inserted into human orifices to extract information sought by the sociopaths managing these wars.

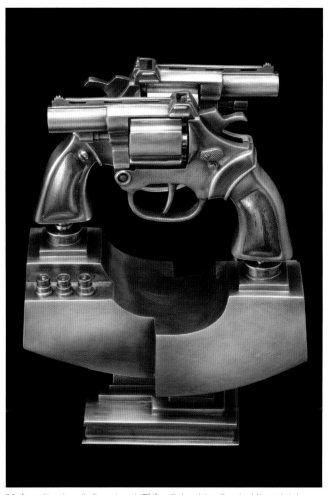

Maker: Stephen F. Saracino | **Title:** *Columbine Survival Bracelet* | **Materials:** Sterling silver, mokume gane. Cast and fabricated components | **Size:** Approx. 200 mm × 85 mm × 75 mm | **Image credit:** K.C. Kratt

Narrative: This object resulted from the actions of two American high school students who terrorized their school with violence, killing thirteen and psychologically wounding many more for the remainder of their lives. After hearing an interview with a National Rifle Association spokesperson suggesting that if everyone had been "armed" that day, that the outcome would have been very different, the idea for this bracelet was born. His statement struck me as even more insane than the act. I created a bracelet that could be worn to any school in the event a similar episode occurred so students would be prepared to fashionably endure the onslaught and retaliate in like manner.

TAMIZAN SAVILL

Tamizan Savill is an enameler and studio jeweler. She lives and works in Bristol, South-west England.

Most of Tamizan's commissioned work centres on color and pattern in enamel, but she also enjoys making story pieces, letter punched with narrative text.

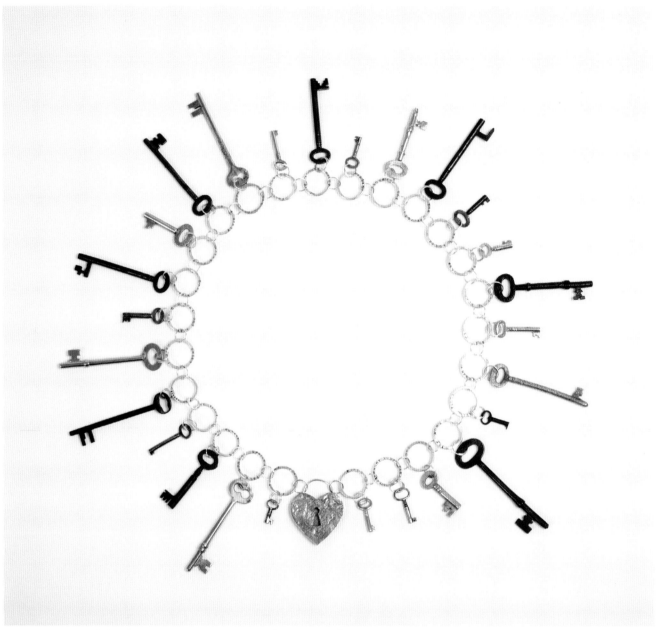

Maker: Tamizan Savill | **Title:** *Unchastity Belt—A Poem in Silver and Soundbites for My Women Friends and Their Inner Sluts* | **Materials:** Silver, brass, keys | **Size:** Belt 880 mm long, displayed 500 mm diameter | **Image credit:** Marianne Koshoni

Narrative: These keys were collected from my grandfather's house, our family home for 75 years. Rusting, bent, smoothed and worn by repeated use, these have been plated with gold, brass and copper, some with rust bubbling up through the gilding.

The phrases were gathered from women friends talking about past partners; we are of the generation where the sexual freedom our mothers struggled for was a given right (if not a duty), and most of us were serial monogamists. The clasp is in the form of the traditional padlock found on charm bracelets, and the belt sounds lovely when worn dancing.

ISABELL SCHAUPP

Isabell Schaupp lives and works in Germany. Her awarded work can be found in private and public collections.

I get inspiration from my surroundings—from nature, structures, people, everyday life . . . . If an impression touches me, it evokes stories in my mind. With my camera I'm able to "freeze" some of these ideas. Burned into enamel by a special technique, the photographs transform into tangible, narrative objects. Out of their context they start telling stories for themselves which might be endowed with entirely new meanings by the beholder.

Maker: Isabell Schaupp | **Title:** *Flying Object—Bumblebee 11* | **Materials:** Silver, copper, enamel, photo, agate, fabric | **Size:** 62 mm × 49 mm × 10 mm | **Image credit:** I. Schaupp

Narrative: This brooch is some kind of "medal" to the most faithful bumblebee I've ever known. One year from spring to autumn, from morning to night she came to feast on my lavender. It was very sad to see her fly away one day to never come back again.

GARY SCHOTT

Gary Schott is a jeweler and metalsmith who resides in Houston, Texas. For the past decade his studio practice has continually branched out to explore kinetic sculptural and wearable objects. Humor and utilitarian undertones in his work help to provide silly yet somewhat functional moments of interaction.

Maker: Gary Schott | **Title:** *Impatient Shoes (Brooch)* | **Materials:** Aluminum, brass, wood, paint, stainless steel | **Size:** 50.8 mm × 50.8 mm × 38.1 mm | **Image credit:** Gary Schott

Narrative: Most of us have experienced moments of impatience at one or another. Now, it's up to the wearer of the brooch and/or viewers to become the storyteller. In a way, my brooches are objects that ask to be given a narrative, instead of merely conveying one.

Maker: Gary Schott | **Title:** *No No (Brooch)* | **Materials:** Aluminum, brass, wood, paint, stainless steel | **Size:** 50.8 mm × 50.8 mm × 38.1 mm | **Image credit:** Gary Schott

Narrative: For the "Wearable Playthings" series of brooches, I was interested in creating works that were both playful and somewhat functional. The simple hand gesture of wagging your finger is rather universal. However, I think its perceived meaning changes per the wearer and social context. That's exciting to me!

Maker: Gary Schott | **Title:** *Polite Clapper (Brooch)* | **Materials:** Aluminum, brass, Barbie hands, paint, stainless steel | **Size:** 50.8 mm × 50.8 mm × 38.1 mm | **Image credit:** Gary Schott

Narrative: I think most people understand the gesture of clapping. I enjoy the fact that my brooches really are instigators for a narrative, and the wearer or viewer becomes the storyteller!

NICOLE SCHUSTER

Born in 1981, Nicole Schuster grew up in a town near Munich, Germany. Her childhood dream was to become an architect, but instead she was trained as a goldsmith.

After some time in Ireland she now works in her atelier in Garching, Germany since 2012.

Maker: Nicole Schuster | **Title:** *The Cycle (Necklace)* | **Materials:** Silver oxidized, acrylic plastic, nylon plastic, aluminium powder, resin, steel | **Size:** 210 mm × 220 mm × 35 mm | **Image credit:** Nicole Schuster

Narrative: I explore and play with the beauty and cruelty of growth and change: the cycle of birth, development, decay and the formation of something new, as an endless process. Fragile but powerful, inexorable and infinite. Swayed by these worlds and thoughts my wearable sculptures appear like poetic places, abstract landscapes or organisms from another time.

The necklace *The Cycle* reflects on the process of birth and its cycle. As for the universe, nature or human, some energy is gathering and gets more and more concentrated until something starts growing from a core. A very fragile and prodigious process, that when coming to its end, it might just start again . . . .

Maker: Nicole Schuster | **Title:** *Transformation II (Brooch)* | **Materials:** Oxidized silver, steel | **Size:** 81 mm × 64 mm × 17 mm | **Image credit:** Nicole Schuster

Narrative: For me, a city is a machine. Constantly transforming: itself, its elements, its inhabitants. But who is the gear wheel and who the sprout, the blossom? Is the city nurturing its residents or is it the other way around? Who is the machine?

Maker: Nicole Schuster | **Title:** *The Change (Ring)* | **Materials:** Silver ruthenium plated, turmaline | **Size:** 55 mm × 21 mm × 43 mm | **Image credit:** Nicole Schuster

Narrative: I was born in the "city of 100 fires" in the area of Ruhr, Germany, famous for its (almost former) coal and steel mines. The furnaces, gasometer, headframes, the bridges over motorways and rivers are fascinating to me, as the stories that lie within, the continuous change and the rich culture that grows out of that retired industry.

I work on the relation of nature and culture, as an opposite, as an addition, as a process.

The tension between the environment created by humans and the final recapture of nature over the structures and ruins flows into my work, creating sculptures that appear like poetic places or abstract landscapes.

INES SEIDEL

Ines Seidel is a fibre artist based near Munich, Germany. She studied linguistics and communications which reflects in her art as an investigation of language, dialogue and identity. In her autodidactic studies she explores the potential of mundane techniques such as crocheting in jewelry making. She teaches paper jewelry and paper craft workshops.

Predominantly, I work with materials that carry cultural stories, such as old books or, more recently, newspaper. By transforming them, I develop their stories further. At the same time I am constantly looking for the limits of a narrative, the point where all storytelling ends. Narrative jewelry is exciting since it potentially interferes with body language and becomes a communicator of the wearer's story.

Maker: Ines Seidel | **Title:** *Secrets, to Be Worn Openly* | **Materials:** Found objects, paper with written notes, used envelopes, yarn | **Size:** Pendant approx. 200 mm × 180 mm × 12 mm | **Image credit:** Ines Seidel

Narrative: In a play between openness and privacy protection, the necklace is allowed to adorn one's identity with personal secrets without giving them away. Wearing the necklace raises curiosity from outsiders, but the one carrying the concealed treasures may experience secrecy as something clumsy or impractical.

KVETOSLAVA FLORA SEKANOVA

Kvetoslava Flora Sekanova is a maker of objects and jewelry. She has lived in a few different cultures which has influenced her practice. The narrative aspect in her pieces is strongly connected with the use of particular materials and the story each material holds. Flora currently lives in Munich but her heart is still in New Zealand.

I make to raise awareness about the miracle of our existence . . . and because I just love it.

Maker: Kvetoslava Flora Sekanova | **Title:** *Don't Let the Cat Get You* | **Materials:** Wild birds feathers, silver | **Size:** 950 mm | **Image credit:** Kvetoslava Flora Sekanova

Narrative: Each material has its story which is connected with its history, there is my story and your story. Each can be very different and still equal and this is what is so beautiful about it.

KARIN SEUFERT

Karin Seufert went to a technical school for gold- and silversmithing in Schoonhoven in the Netherlands and after her graduation in 1995 she started an independent workshop in Amsterdam. Three years later in 1998 she went back to Germany to Berlin where she continued developing her own work. She has a preference to travel and likes to combine this passion with giving lectures, teaching or exhibiting all around the world. In her jewelry one of the recurring subjects that runs like a red thread through her work, is to use materials that contain a story from their earlier life and rebuild them to get a new story out of it.

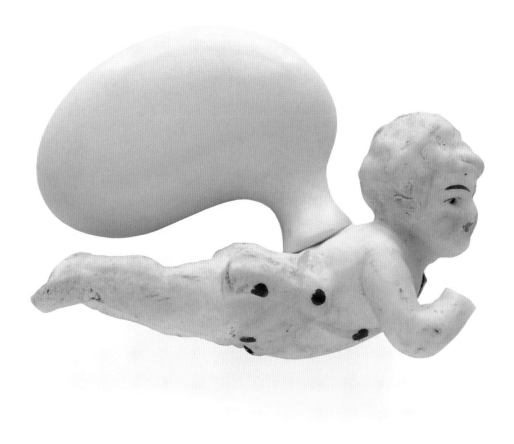

Maker: Karin Seufert | **Title:** *Untitled* | **Materials:** Porcelain, polyurethane, silver, steel |
Size: 43 mm × 59 mm × 20 mm | **Image credit:** Karin Seufert

Narrative: The origin of the porcelain figures is in a box full of material collected by the Dutch jewelry maker Marion Herbst. After her death in 1995 Berend Peter Hogen Esch, her husband offered the box to me in swap for one of my pieces of jewelry.

Inside this box were a lot of different materials like expensive stones, rarities in Bakelite, glass, plastics and also some small porcelain figures, which were all damaged.

It was around 2003 that I started working with this material, which already had an existing story and showed traces of use. When I had used all the pieces from the box, I started to buy old material at the flea market. The porcelain pieces are mainly old toys from around 1900, used, broken, thrown away and landed on garbage dumps around Berlin. Today people start digging in the ground around Berlin to find these little pieces and sell them at the flea markets.

Within my brooches I try to tell a story with my additions. I leave the basis as it is and just add little details in different material, like silver, glass, PVC, plastics, pom, etc., to give them a new expression, to let them tell a new stories.

ELIZABETH SHAW

Elizabeth Shaw is a jeweler, metalsmith and educator. Elizabeth's studio work investigates aspects of societal and cultural values and the meanings associated with objects of material culture. She exhibits regularly and has been the recipient of grants and awards. She is based in Brisbane Australia and has served on the boards of state and national crafts organizations and is an international member of the Advisory Council of Ethical Metalsmiths.

I am interested in the societal and cultural values that are reflected in the objects we surround ourselves with. I particularly like jewelry for its rich history, its portability and its close association with the wearer and its role in communicating to the viewer. I am intrigued by how quickly something that was once valued can become "valueless." A collected or found broken part of an object destined for or retrieved from landfill is quite often the starting point for my work. These "unvalued" parts bring with them a history and I construct around them to embellish their story through additions. I draw on an aesthetic of repair and value honesty in materials. Ethical and environmental concerns are central to my studio practice and these inform how I approach my work.

Maker: Elizabeth Shaw | **Title:** *Caged Arm* | **Materials:** Found broken plastic arm, recycled and reused sterling silver | **Size:** 280 mm × 155 mm | **Image credit:** Michelle Bowden

Narrative: I don't usually work with plastic, but when this fragile arm was turned up a by an earthmover, it inspired me. The constructed cage to hold it and protect is reminiscent of body parts of saints kept in reliquaries, a physical representation of a religious icon. *Caged Arm* represents a time past, of simpler childhood toys.

MARINA SHEETIKOFF

Marina Sheetikoff is a studio jeweler, with an architecture and design background. In her work she explores the tactile possibilities of jewelry to embed her pieces with subjective meaning. Employing a narrative to create some of those pieces she'll seek to find a personal and emotional connection, evoking from jewelry, the immediate connection of communicative expression between the object, wearer and the audience.

Her architecture and furniture design background, as well as an interest in drawing and nature forms, are skills that she transfers to her pieces, Although the technical construction of the pieces are a crucial part of her research, her focus is to transcend the esthetic form, and experiment with new paths of possibilities, searching results from her investigations that may communicate and lead to unexpected interpretations.

Maker: Marina Sheetikoff | **Title:** *Profile Brooch* | **Materials:** Ironwood, niobium, silver, gold | **Size:** 60 mm × 120 mm × 8 mm | **Image credit:** Marina Sheetikoff

Narrative: The *Profile* brooch permits the wearer to articulate the small parts of the body construction, in order to create different positions that suggest different actions. In our afflicted life, my personage is in movement, in that narrative, I leave space for your own interpretation. The figure might be jumping over a water puddle, or walking thru clouds, maybe searching to find its missing half. It's a tale about our days, fragments, runs, capers, searches.

SONDRA SHERMAN

Sondra Sherman's work explores the distinctive voice of jewelry in its power to both hold personal meaning and instigate social exchange. Interpretation is compelled by virtue of the overt rejection or exaggerated embrace of subjects and forms associated with traditional jewelry and the context of the body/wearer.

I have often used literary references in my jewelry to draw upon universal themes suited to the body/wearer in both the social and private realm. In this series, I have not actually read the books. The jewelry reflects the metaphors sparked in the imagination by the title and visual elements of the book within the contexts of jewelry and books. I usually prefer the book to the film of any story, because it is richer and boundless in imagination. Found subjects offers the wearer a chance to collaborate in creating a new story with every conversation engendered when wearing the work.

Maker: Sondra Sherman | **Title:** *Flowers and Still Life* | **Materials:** 925 ag, 1000 ag, altered vintage book | **Size:** Brooch: 100 mm × 10 mm × 10 mm; with book open, 250 mm × 380 mm × 20 mm | **Image credit:** Luna Perri

Narrative: The brooch is presented in a space cut into the pages of the book which inspired it. The depicted works are from an ongoing series, "Found Subjects." In this series each piece was inspired by a vintage book, which was then altered to create a presentation box for the jewelry when not being worn.

The book is *Flowers and Still Life: An Anthology in Paint* by J.B. Charles, published in 1938. The book presents sixteen color plates of cliché flower and still life paintings of every sort with varying degrees of artistic sophistication and very little text. I imagined that the book owner and possibly the author were "Sunday painters." It reminded me of my early art lessons—charcoal drawing still lives, endlessly re-drawing trying to get the perspective consistent. The brooch reflects that experience with the engraving of multiple versions of a still life drawing overlaid on each other and a silhouette of a flower bouquet emblem found on the book cover.

247

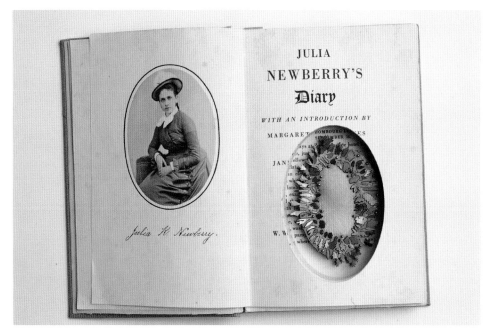

Maker: Sondra Sherman | **Title:** *Julia Newberry's Diary (Brooch)* | **Materials:** Steel, 750 au, nail polish |
Size: Brooch: 95 mm × 70 mm × 10 mm; with book open, 250 mm × 255 mm × 20 mm | **Image credit:** Luna Perri

Narrative: The brooch is presented in a space cut into the pages of the book which inspired it.

The hot pink color of the cover seems outrageous, yet the name, typeface, and gold floral border suggest a lady of certain social stature and seriousness. I used the oval form of the title border in a vertical orientation associated with portraiture/cameo, but I made the border askew to the oval; actually I decided she was a bit tipsy. I think of the brooch creating a similar ambiguity—initial viewing would be based on assumptions, presuming a classic oval with ornamental frame, but something is off, is it intentional? Upon closer viewing the hot pink nail polish interior is visible, and it becomes apparent there is no aesthetically determined order to the gold dots on the surface—they land where they are needed as support structure . . . it's sort of a promise of order which reveals a disorder that becomes more interesting to discover. I am more interested in what did not make it into Julia's diary.

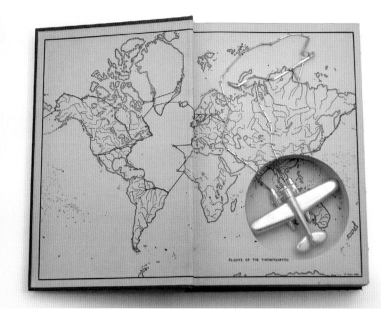

Maker: Sondra Sherman | **Title:** *Listen! The Wind (Pendant)* | **Materials:** 925 ag hollow constructed |
Size: Pendant: 57 mm × 80 mm × 20 mm; with book open, 205 mm × 310 mm × 20 mm | **Image credit:** Luna Perri

Narrative: The pendant is presented in a space cut into the pages of the book which inspired it.

Listen! The Wind. That's such a dramatic title—with its exclamation point and its appeal to have the reader imagine the circumstances that would elicit such an expression. The book is written by Anne Morrow Lindbergh, so I imagine its tales of aviation adventure. I loved the precise embossing of the airplane on the book cover; it seemed so technical in comparison to the title. For me the pendant has a similar sense of paradoxical character. Its scale, haptic experience (it is hollow and lighter than one would expect when looking at it), and precise but light-handed/reductive form send mixed messages; its presence fluctuates between toy, charm and crucifix. Everyone who handles it turns into an eight-year-old—"vroom, vroom, vroom"—but when worn, its material, scale, and quiet form make it a more poignant symbol.

CARINA SHOSHTARY

Carina Shoshtary is a maker of fine art jewelry. She is of German and Iranian descent. She has exhibited her work internationally in numerous group and solo shows.

The materials I use for my work usually already have their own story to tell as I work with reclaimed materials, e.g., the graffiti paint from the wall or the wood from the forest. While I am working in the studio, I always listen to audiobooks, so it is a combination of different stories and my own fantasy, which create a new narrative for each piece.

Maker: Carina Shoshtary | Title: *Where Blue Hides After Dark* | Materials: Graffiti, glass, silver, stainless steel | Size: 127 mm × 43 mm × 23 mm | Image credit: Mirei Takeuchi

Narrative: Blue was a cautious, thoughtful being that knew it had to take good care of itself in order not to lose any of its radiance and glow. Whenever it felt weak and turned pale, Blue retreated to a safe, well-hidden place, resting until it regained its former strength. The other colors were not that prudent. Even though they may have been stronger, bolder and more vibrant than Blue, they were blinded by their own beauty and did not grasp the peril of being present and radiant all the time. So it came that even after all other colors had faded and almost vanished from this world, Blue was still gleaming vividly on the waves of the oceans and in the currents of the sky.

GREETJE SIEDERS

Spontaneity and technique can sometimes interfere with each other. In my work I take the risk of combining them. It must appear playful but be executed with skillful workmanship.

The material to be employed is an artistic choice. It must express the narrative character of my work. I value every material from precious metal to found objects. I regard my work as wearable art with a twinkle. I am a goldsmith/designer and teacher as well, and run my own little school in Scheveningen at the edge of The Hague close to the sea.

Maker: Greetje Sieders | Title: *A Mother's Wish Come True* | Materials: Gold and silver | Size: 60 mm | Image credit: Erik Zurcher. Image used by kind permisson of Greetje Sieders

Narrative: This brooch was requested for the cover of the thesis of a gynecologist who had researched new techniques for in vitro fertilization (IVF). The brooch illustrates the fulfilment of the longing for a child. The material is gold and silver and the techniques used include rollprinting, in this case with a piece of linen.

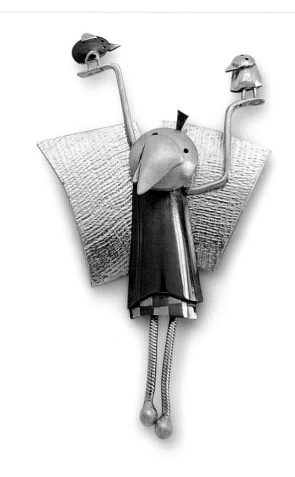

EDEN SILVER-MYER

Eden Silver-Myer is a jeweler who works within the jewelry world, as well as making from her North London studio.

Eden works with narratives she finds in Greek mythology. She finds the simultaneous wealth of idyllic and grotesque imagery, and intricate interwoven stories, a source of endless inspiration. Through her work Eden responds to this rich narrative, questioning her own understanding of the world.

Maker: Eden Silver-Myer | **Title:** *Daphne* | **Materials:** Bronze | **Size:** 110 mm × 60 mm × 70 mm | **Image credit:** Charlie Cooley

Narrative: *Daphne* captures a moment of metamorphosis. The nymph Daphne is transformed into a bay tree to escape Apollo's advances.

AMY SINOVICH

Amy Sinovich is a jewelry designer and maker based in Cape Town, South Africa. Using precious metals and semi-precious stones, she creates wearable stories inspired by poetry, illustrations and elements she encounters in her natural environment.

Jewelry provides such a wonderful platform for personal expression and storytelling—it communicates a great deal of information about both its maker and wearer. I have always been fascinated by the creative process, whereby a maker takes their ideas and inspiration, and transforms them into a tangible form with which other people can connect and identify. The concept that a piece of jewelry can have the ability to connect the maker with the wearer on a subconscious, expressive level drives my work.

Maker: Amy Sinovich | **Title:** *Wisdom Is Like a Baobab Tree . . . (Necklace)* | **Materials:** Sterling silver (oxidized), brass | **Size:** 23 mm × 1.8 mm × 500 mm | **Image credit:** Robert Frey

Narrative: There is a proverb in Africa that says, "Wisdom is like a baobab tree; no one individual can embrace it." These words beautifully encapsulate the massive scale of the ancient baobab trees as well as the vast knowledge that exists within the world. There are moments in most of our lives when we are reminded of just how vast our universe is and how much has come before us. This piece is inspired by one such moment looking at an African night sky.

KAREN SMITH

Scottish jewelry designer Karen Smith creates narrative jewelry inspired by her passion for music. Each piece is treated like a storybook where Karen buries secret meanings beneath the surface. Over the years she has worked for several jewelry companies in Scotland, Canada and Holland. Now settled back in her Native Scotland Karen is bringing her own designs to life from her Dundee workshop.

I'm passionate about music. I love the hidden stories within songs and the affect they have on us. This is where I draw my inspiration from which I then translate into my quirky storybook jewelry.

I enjoy creating jewelry which is wearable but also very individual and interesting to look at. I like to think my jewelry says something about the wearer without actually disclosing it. Almost like wearing a secret in full view without everyone being aware of it, unless you really want them to.

Of course the stories I create within my work are up for interpretation by the viewer/wearer. Perhaps the story I connect with the piece is not the story the person who wears it associates with it. After all everyone's perception is different. However, the most important thing about my work is that the wearer connects with it on a personal level making it more than just a pretty object.

Maker: Karen Smith | **Title:** *Peep Show Brooches* | **Materials:** Silver, paper, textiles, Perspex |
Size: 60 mm × 60 mm × 60 mm | **Image credit:** Karen Smith

Narrative: These brooches (three in total) sit in their own little peep show box. Therefore they can be enjoyed both on and off the body.

Inspired by the song "Through Glass" by Stone Sour, these brooches explore how things are not always how they seem/appear.

ELFI SPIEWACK

Elfi Spiewack is a jewelry designer and goldsmith. Her work is informed by her environment, nature and the search for a new "form language." Elfi's work has been widely collected and exhibited in group and solo shows throughout Germany, The Netherlands, New Zealand, USA and Australia. Elfi is based in Lyttelton, the port town of Christchurch, New Zealand.

Experiencing a massive earthquake and more than 13,000 aftershocks that destroyed a city and changed people's lives for good was the initiator for this body of work. Being surrounded by debris and broken shards led to the urge for creating something beautiful with the remains, somehow trying to make sense of something so incomprehensible.

Maker: Elfi Spiewack | **Title:** *Crindley China (Necklace)* | **Materials:** Oxidized sterling silver, broken china, peridot, old typesetting letter | **Size:** 57 mm × 59 mm | **Image credit:** Johannes van Kan

Narrative: A piece of broken china telling a story in its new context.

Maker: Elfi Spiewack | **Title:** *Beginnings (Necklace)* | **Materials:** Oxidized sterling silver, pearls, coral, old typesetting letter | **Size:** Approx. 70 mm × 73 mm | **Image credit:** Johannes van Kan

Narrative: A historical newspaper text about the first settlers and the building of Christchurch, New Zealand, imprinted in metal as a memento after the city's destruction in the 2011 earthquakes.

Maker: Elfi Spiewack | **Title:** *The Prospects of Canterbury 2 (Brooch)* | **Materials:** Sterling silver, broken china, rubber, peridot | **Size:** 42 mm × 45 mm | **Image credit:** Elfi Spiewack

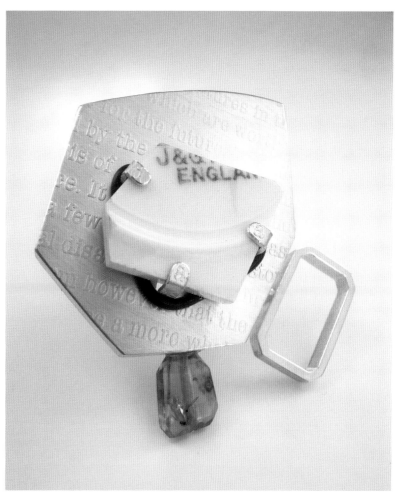

KATRIN SPRANGER

As a conceptual jewelry designer/artist, Katrin Spranger create stories that comment on consumer culture, environment and science fiction. Focusing on resources that might become depleted in the future, Katrin explores natural materials including crude oil, water and honey to develop wearable but also time-based and interactive jewelry.

Katrin Spranger's interest in immateriality in relation to jewelry such as performances, narratives and transient materials emerged from her master's studies. Using metamorphic, time-sensitive materials alongside precious metals, the primary aim is to convey a message or idea and to make the jewelry experience engaging and more memorable.

As a starting point, she often develops science fiction narratives that draw future dystopias in which important natural resources are on the verge of depletion. In this reality the last drops of crude oil are transformed into valuable jewelry material. The resultant hybrid outcome includes performance such as adornment made of oil melting on the body when being worn.

Recent works refer to the decline of the bee population and our dependency on pollination. For Collect 2015, the international art fair for contemporary objects, a 3-D-printed honey jewelry sculpture was developed, then destroyed and consumed by the audience on the last day of the exhibition. The audience's engagement and interaction played with the symbolism of the food chain, the material and immaterial, precious and temporal, and the audiences' bodies as internal as well as external sensorial sites for jewelry. The work was produced as an interdisciplinary partnership with a food scientist in the Netherlands.

Maker: Katrin Spranger | **Title:** *Best Before (Necklace)* | **Materials:** Crude oil and its products, gold | **Size:** Variable | **Image credit:** Katrin Spranger

Narrative: *Best Before* was developed as a science fiction narrative, that draws a dystopia of the future and refers to consumption and depletion of resources. It deals with questions of anticipated value perceptions. Due to crude oil exhaustion, the last drops of oil transform into precious jewelry material like that of gold. Telling a story about depletion, the work is executed the same. If a piece is worn, oil parts are slowly melting through body temperature. Stained clothes and skeleton structures remain; however they still communicate the story.

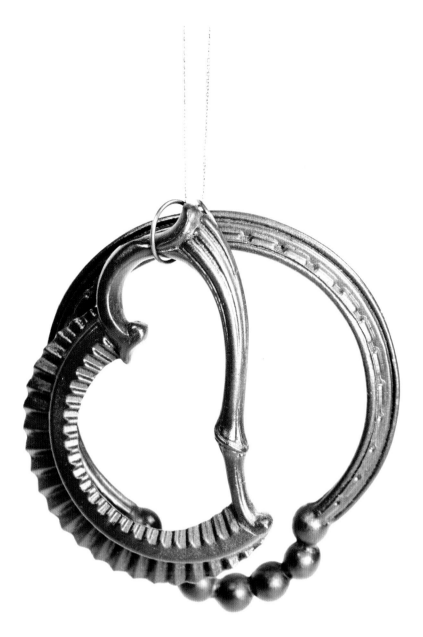

Maker: Katrin Spranger | **Title:** *Best Before Extended (Pendant)* | **Materials:** Polyurethane resin, silver oxidized | **Size:** 150 mm × 140 mm × 10 mm | **Image credit:** Katrin Spranger

Narrative: The bold, industrially styled pieces appeal to the androgyny and gender ambiguity of contemporary society. A story of unbridled consumption and the resultant reality is told through cold, oxidized silver and matte gold shaped into severe pieces with hard edges. Diamonds adorn a repurposed plastic bottle part, giving value to consumables and commenting on society's attitude of disregard and ideas surrounding value and quality. Cable ties are repurposed, chains are formed of heavy duty corrupted links and construction components are transformed into wearable jewelry.

Maker: Katrin Spranger | **Title:** *Best Before (Necklace)* | **Materials:** Crude oil and its products, silver | **Size:** Variable | **Image credit:** Katrin Spranger

DANA STENSON

I am a full-time metalsmith and jeweler. My designs are inspired by my fascination with natural and cultural history. Having been born overseas, my work explores my own personal and ancestral history as well as that of other people and cultures. The narrative quality of the jewelry I make is reflective of my desire to produce pieces that *can be interpreted on multiple levels, with layers of context from past and present, with personal as well as universal human significance. I have a particular fascination with the doorway in architecture and as a symbol of passage in the human psychological or spiritual journey.*

Maker: Dana Stenson | **Title:** *Georgia Helen Griffith* | **Materials:** Copper, sterling silver, garnet, found antique compass, resin | **Size:** Pendant approx. 95 mm × 55 mm; chain length 475 mm | **Image credit:** John Dowling

Narrative: This locket tells the story of Georgia Helen Griffith, my great-grandmother. In 1890 she traveled to Jamaica from the United States as a Quaker missionary. For her time she was an unusually educated and independent woman. On the reverse of the locket is the Quaker star.

Maker: Dana Stenson | **Title:** *Courage* | **Materials:** Antique medal, found bobcat claw, black spinel, black onyx, sterling silver | **Size:** Pendant approx. 45 mm × 70 mm; necklace length 550 mm | **Image credit:** Cindy Bell

Narrative: Inspired by Joan of Arc, this necklace symbolizes courage in battle and in life. On the reverse is a quote from Joan of Arc, "To live without belief, that is a fate more terrible than dying."

Maker: Dana Stenson | **Title:** *Bud* | **Materials:** Sterling silver, brass, found WWII military medals, amethyst, found "Forget Me Not" WWII bracelet links, family photograph, watch crystal | **Size:** Pendant 85 mm × 65 mm; chain length approx. 470 mm | **Image credit:** Cindy Bell

Narrative: This locket was made in honor of my grandfather James "Bud" Blythe who fought in WWII in France and earned a purple heart for his military service. He survived his injuries and lived into old age. The vintage bracelet links used in this piece were worn by loved ones at home and have names of soldiers written on the backs.

GABBEE STOLP

*My work involves a philosophical exploration of spirituality, my-
thology and human connectedness with the natural world, together
with a belief in the inseparability of life and death.*

*Through this exploration I have opened myself to the idea that
all animals will die and that their death has a somewhat necessary
presence in my life.*

*Using materials thoughtfully sourced from the lives of animals,
I work with jewelry and object making in order to provoke ideas of
the biological and the metaphysical and to inspire a connection with
nature through art.*

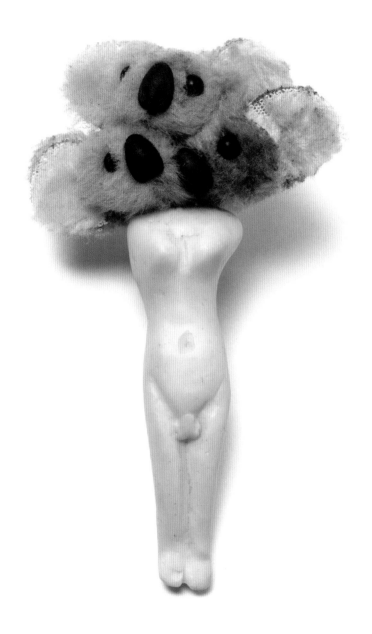

Maker: Gabbee Stolp | **Title:** *Sexually Promiscuous Marsupial* | **Materials:** Galalith (milk plastic), found objects, sterling silver |
Size: 100 mm × 65 mm × 30 mm | **Image credit:** Andrew Barcham

Narrative: The story of this piece comes from the writings
and art depicting early European encounters of Australian
native wildlife. Colonial writer George Barrington said of the
marsupials he encountered: "One would almost conclude,
from the great resemblance of the different quadrupeds
found here, that there is promiscuous intercourse between
the different sexes of all those various animals" (Olsen, *Upside

Down World: Early European Impressions of Australia's Curious
Animals*).

I wanted to create a creature that looked mythological
and mutated, one as bizarre and outrageous as those described
by Barrington yet one that also reflected my childhood love
for Australian animals through the use of humour and kitsch.

CUONG ABEL SY

Cuong Abel Sy was born in a refugee camp clinic in 1981 in Indonesia. He enlisted with the US Air Force as a weather forecaster and spent his last year of service in South Korea. Following his military career he remained living abroad and moved to England. He is a metalsmith and jewelry designer.

I work in the narrative format conceptually, as a means to distill attributes of strength, empowerment and hope. I utilize my personal history as a means to convey and remind myself of who I am and where I come from. My personal narrative is that of the immigrant refugee; it is a unique and foreign perspective.

I grew up as an avid fan of the science fiction genre because of abundant associations I found within my own life and the fictitious lives of space voyagers attempting to find a new home planet. Mysterious to most individuals, my personal narrative is represented in a science fiction aesthetic in hopes that the alluring properties found within my necklaces will allow others to see what I see within myself—an immigrant refugee with good intentions, empowered and hopeful because he has a home.

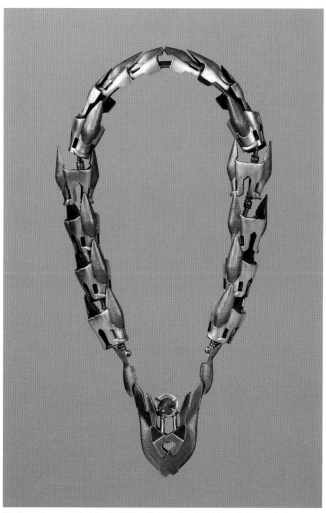

Maker: Cuong Abel Sy | **Title:** *This Is the Re-Write* | **Materials:** Bronze, sterling silver, 14k gold | **Size:** 228 mm × 140 mm × 19 mm | **Image credit:** Henry Daniel Gatlin

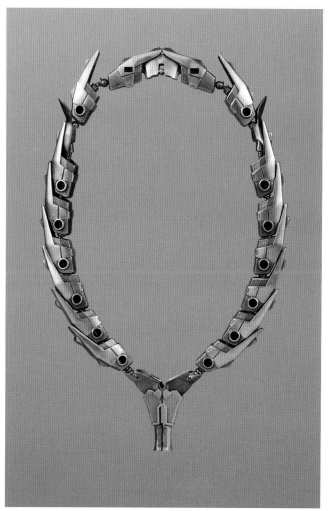

Maker: Cuong Abel Sy | **Title:** *The Gatekeeper* | **Materials:** Bronze, sterling silver, 14k gold, lab sapphire | **Size:** 304 mm × 203 mm × 38 mm | **Image credit:** Henry Daniel Gatlin

Narrative: I first visited my homeland of Cambodia when I was twelve, in 1993. I created *This is the Re-Write* after my most recent visit to Cambodia at the age of 34 in 2016. My initial reaction was one of disgust, in seeing how poorly maintained the streets were and in initially perceiving all the negatives found within the landscape of a developing country. As my revisit to my homeland concluded I was able to walk away from the experience with a newfound perspective of strength and beauty found within the struggles of a country that has come back from the dark trenches of genocide.

Narrative: I am my family's gatekeeper. I cannot tell you how many times I have volunteered to help out family and friends by translating or walking them through complex government paperwork. As one who introduces and assists others to new "territory," this thought is the reason why I have titled this piece *The Gatekeeper*.

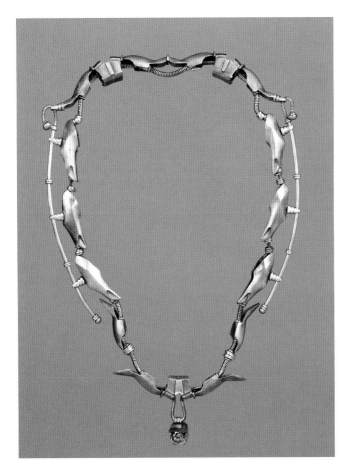

Maker: Cuong Abel Sy | **Title:** *Saving Birds* | **Materials:** Sterling silver, bronze, 14k gold, moissanite | **Size:** 228 mm × 152 mm × 13 mm | **Image credit:** Henry Daniel Gatlin

Narrative: *Saving Birds* was my final MFA thesis necklace. During the Cambodian genocides approximately eighty percent of the educated population in Cambodia was wiped out. My father and several other family members were placed in a forced labor camp simply because they were students. *Saving Birds* represents my struggle as a Cambodian-American, attempting to refill our ranks with educated individuals. I have had an overwhelming amount of support from my family and friends throughout my tumultuous life. I created *Saving Birds* as a means to represent the feeling of the unyielding support I have felt throughout my higher education endeavors.

UNITED STATES

L. SUE SZABO

L. Sue Szabo is an award-winning studio art jeweler living and working in Toledo, Ohio. Her work has appeared in numerous books and publications as well as national and international exhibitions. She often works in a narrative format using the illustrative qualities of enamel as a means of self-examination and catharsis. She also works as an internal medicine physician.

Maker: L. Sue Szabo | **Title:** *Victorian Erotica Brooches* | **Materials:** Enamel on steel, sterling silver, emeralds, rubies, peridots | **Size:** Various, approx. 50 mm × 40 mm × 6 mm | **Image credit:** Ericka Crissman

Narrative: Society can try to hide the baser aspects of human nature it's ashamed of, but it can't change them.

Maker: L. Sue Szabo | **Title:** *What Remains* | **Materials:** Enamel on copper, andalusites, trilobites, ammonites, fossilized coral, misc. fossils, python ribs and vertebrae, sterling silver | **Size:** 610 mm × 200 mm × 10.5 mm | **Image credit:** Ralph Gabriner, courtesy of the artist

Narrative: I wanted to tell a story about evolution and extinction using real and imaginary fossils and bones. I wanted the piece to have a rustic, unearthed quality, as if it were a fossil itself.

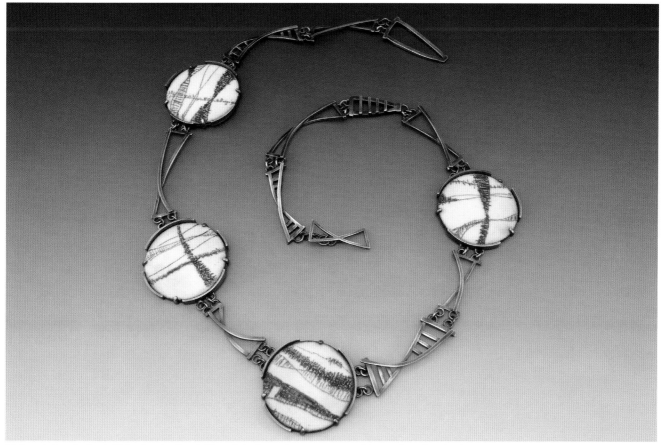

Maker: L. Sue Szabo | **Title:** *Destination* | **Materials:** Enamel on copper, graphite, sterling silver | **Size:** 400 mm × 230 mm × 10 mm | **Image credit:** Ericka Crissman

Narrative: This stark black and white piece tells of a difficult personal journey. The metalwork and enamel suggest the many paths, twists, and turns taken.

ANNA TALBOT

Anna Talbot is a British/Norwegian jewelry artistwho lives and works in Oslo, Norway.

Her jewelry is inspired by fairy tales, nursery rhymes, songs and stories. Wolves, deer, trees, forests and Little Red Riding Hood are all central elements in her universe. She works in layers to build up a three dimensional piece.

Some of her pieces are quite large, but the materials she uses are light enough to be worn. The size makes the wearer aware of the piece at all times, they demand both space and attention. Her jewelry can be hung on a wall or worn on a body.

Maker: Anna Talbot | **Title:** *Blue Moon (Necklace)* | **Materials:** Readymade box, aluminium, lacquer, brass, silver, steel and silk ribbon | **Size:** 200 mm × 200 mm × 130 mm | **Image credit:** Laila Meyrick |

Maker: Anna Talbot |
Title: *Don't Lead Me Astray
(Necklace)* | **Materials:**
Readymade box, aluminium,
lacquer, brass, silver and steel |
Size: 190 mm × 190 mm × 110
mm | **Image credit:** Laila Meyrick

Maker: Anna Talbot |
Title: *Oh My Deer! (Necklace)* |
Materials: Readymade box, aluminium,
lacquer, brass, silver and steel |
Size: 120 mm × 100 mm × 50 mm |
Image credit: Laila Meyrick

RUDEE TANCHAROEN

Rudee Tancharoen is a jeweler and a director of Atelier Rudee, an international academy of contemporary jewelry in Bangkok. Her work has been published and exhibited in several countries in Europe, America, Asia and Australia.

My jewelry pieces are not made for body decoration, but are objects to carry with the body, to remind the carrier of their existence and context. By filling the works with stories, the works not only express but also explain. They carry content within like a story waiting to be unfolded and told.

It is not about the expression of the maker, but is more about something that the wearer wants to keep in mind and perhaps leads to a certain conversation, a healthier conversation beyond object and material.

Maker: Rudee Tancharoen | **Title:** *Listen* | **Materials:** Copper, tinted freshwater pearl | **Size:** 100 mm × 240 mm × 20 mm | **Image credit:** Waroot Tangtumsatid

Narrative: Since 2013 the political situation in my country has unavoidably influenced my work. I've found that many problems and questions I have, not only political problems but also other general matters in everyday life, have led me to the same answers.

The main message of the "Tales of the Truth" series is the importance of Sati or mindfulness, which is the answer to the questions. I would like to use the jewelry pieces to recall Sati to the wearer, and as a medium to invite people into certain conversations, since that would reduce many problems we face nowadays.

Words are powerful. They could construct and they could destroy.

Words are quick. Once they are launched, they cannot be retrieved.

Let's not allow words to travel alone without companions.

Accompany them with thought and kindness. Guide them with listening and looking.

Maker: Rudee Tancharoen | **Title:** *Companions* | **Materials:** Copper, vitreous enamel | **Size:** 147 mm × 125 mm × 15 mm | **Image credit:** Waroot Tangtumsatid |

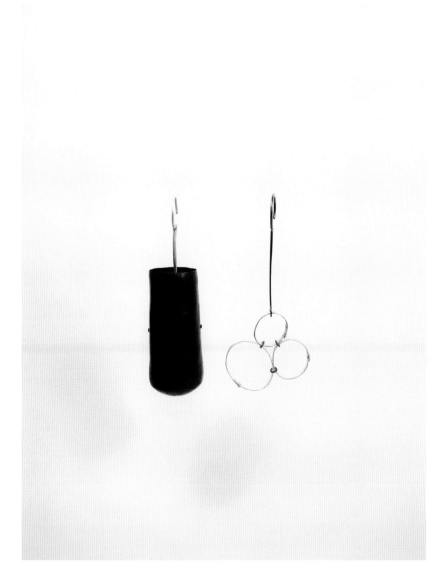

Maker: Rudee Tancharoen | **Title:** *Armonia* | **Materials:** Silver 925, copper | **Size:** 60 mm × 20 mm × 20 mm | **Image credit:** Rudee Tancharoen

Narrative: At the time I started to work on this series our political situation was very sensitive. I'm not usually active in political activities but at that time it seemed unavoidable. Political discussion became our everyday life. I saw many discussions and arguments. Friends, family, husbands and wives, employers and employees fought for red, or for yellow, even for not having color.

That year I participated in an earring show. I wanted to communicate that being a pair does not need to be identical. With harmony, two different entities can be together peacefully.

While working on this series I found that harmony is not the key but it could be a trap. Searching for harmony is not different from searching for any other identical pair.

If being together peacefully is the goal, then simply "being together peacefully," with or without harmony, is the key.

AMY TAVERN

Amy Tavern is an artist, metalsmith, instructor, and lecturer. Originally from Richfield Springs, her work is based on memory and, although autobiographical, refers to shared experience and universal themes.

I am devoted to observing the world that surrounds me and questioning the human condition through the lens of my own life experience. Through a variety of traditional and exploratory multimedia techniques, I create jewelry and sculptural objects that hint at memory, time, and loss. I intuitively select materials and forms to represent the intangible and to create abstract narratives. Using my own memory of people, places, and objects, I seek to communicate the human experience, convey emotion, and connect with others.

Maker: Amy Tavern | **Title:** *Forget Me Not* | **Materials:** Sterling silver, spray paint, picture of my father, my father's hair, acrylic | **Size:** 457 mm × 381 mm × 6.35 mm | **Image credit:** Hank Drew

Narrative: I began mourning my father when he was diagnosed with Alzheimer's disease in 2011. Based on mourning jewelry from the Victorian Era, this necklace is spray-painted black to resemble jet and includes my father's picture and a lock of his hair.

Maker: Amy Tavern | **Title:** *Wayfinder* | **Materials:** Brass, address book, compass, key to my parents' house, pencil | **Size:** 330 mm × 110 m × 10 mm | **Image credit:** Hank Drew

Narrative: This chatelaine is about the many places I have lived in the US and serves as a tool to help me find my way. The shapes of the four states I have lived in when it was made were combined to form a new state and abstract map. Hanging from this map is a pencil, an address book with the addresses of the twenty-five places I have lived listed in the "T" section, a compass, and the key to my parents' house.

Maker: Amy Tavern | **Title:** *Since 1882, Since 1976* | **Materials:** Stones from the foundation of my childhood home, sterling silver | **Size:** Necklace 457 mm × 38 mm × 19 mm; Box 152 mm × 114 mm × 25.4 mm | **Image credit:** Hank Drew

Narrative: My childhood home was built in 1882 and my family moved into it in 1975. I was a year and a half then. To make this suite of jewelry, I collected stones from the house's foundation and set them like diamonds, creating royal-like jewels that pay homage to this important place.

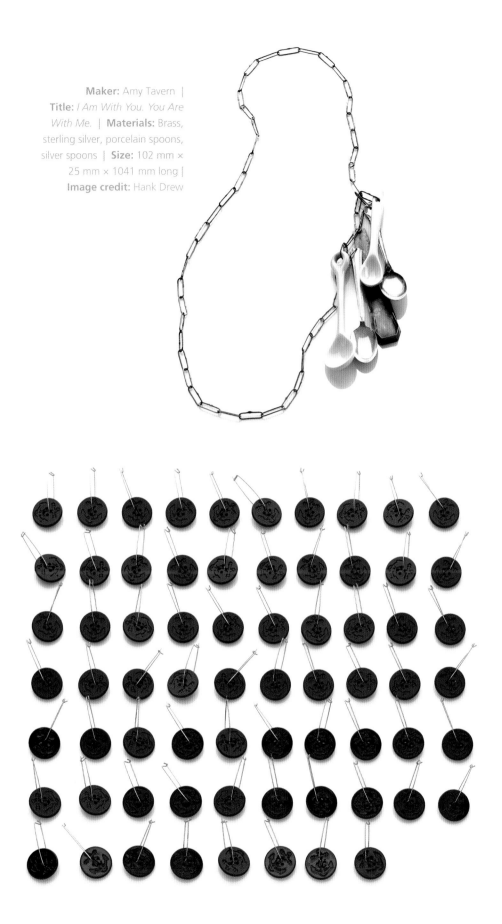

Maker: Amy Tavern | **Title:** *I Am With You. You Are With Me.* | **Materials:** Brass, sterling silver, porcelain spoons, silver spoons | **Size:** 102 mm × 25 mm × 1041 mm long | **Image credit:** Hank Drew

Maker: Amy Tavern | **Title:** *Departing Ship* | **Materials:** 68 Navy peacoat buttons, steel safety pins | **Size:** 635 mm × 254 mm × 6.35 mm | **Image credit:** Hank Drew

Narrative: My father served in the Navy during Vietnam and one of the most precious objects I have that belonged to him is a button from the peacoat he wore as a sailor. I later wore this coat as a teenager. *Departing Ship* is an installation of 68 Navy peacoat buttons turned into pins. My father was 68 when I made this work and, as the individual pins are collected by others, the piece will disappear much like his memory did as he suffered from Alzheimer's disease.

JOAN TENENBAUM

Joan Tenenbaum is academically trained as an anthropologist and linguist and holds a PhD from Columbia University but irrevocably changed her life by becoming a jeweler, embracing her heart's desire. It was in Alaska that Tenenbaum did field work for her doctoral thesis and since first setting foot in Alaska she has never truly left her spiritual home.

Because her work lies at the intersection between the study of culture and language and traditional goldsmithing Tenenbaum's jewelry tells intricate stories with multiple layers of meaning. Texts describing the symbolism and stories behind the pieces often accompany her work.

Maker: Joan Tenenbaum | **Title:** *Feasts of Tradition* | **Materials:** Sterling silver, 14k yellow, pink and palladium white gold, 18k green gold, *keum-boo* (fine gold and silver), champagne diamond and red, blue, orange, and green sapphires | **Size:** 57 mm × 60 mm × 13 mm | **Image credit:** Doug Yaple

Narrative: Ocean to tundra,

This land fed my ancestors.

Unending circle.

The idea and title for this piece were developed in collaboration with Eliza Tunuchuk of Chefornak, Alaska, where I lived and continue to visit.

This piece condenses the entire year of coastal Yup'ik Eskimo subsistence foods into one circular form divided into three sections representing the conditions on which the people hunt and gather: tundra, ice and water. The three connectors represent berries, fish and ocean. Many details of Yup'ik life are encompassed in this piece.

Starting at the top right, the first section represents tundra with an expansive feeling of openness and wind, with a pierced spiral sun, pierced flying birds, pierced and engraved sour dock plant with a *keum-boo* flower stalk representative of all tundra greens.

Continuing counter-clockwise, the top connector represents berries and mouse food. Balls of sterling, white and yellow gold on sterling stalks emerge from a wavy sterling grid beneath. Three gemstones represent salmonberries, blueberries, and lowbush cranberries.

The second section represents ice with a piercing of a hunter dragging a seal home, and the *keum-boo* of tiny fish represents winter fish: needlefish, tomcod, blackfish, smelt, pike.

The second connector is of gold fish swimming on a wavy sterling grid below, with gemstones representing the colors of salmon and herring.

The third section (bottom) represents water, with pierced flying birds, and the *keum-boo* diamond shapes represent summer fish: herring, halibut, whitefish, pike, hooligan, flounder.

The third connector represents ocean with green and yellow gold waves over a sterling spiral beneath representing sometimes dangerous ocean spirits. Gemstones represent the color of water: blue and green.

CYNTHIA TOOPS

Cynthia Toops has been an artist and jeweler in Seattle, Washington, for thirty years. She works in various materials but regards polymer clay as her main medium. In the 1990s, an interest in Roman mosaics and Huichol Indian seed beadwork led her to develop a unique micro-mosaic technique using polymer clay. Her work has been featured in numerous publications, galleries and museums.

Maker: Cynthia Toops | **Title:** *Polar Bear, Ice Floe* | **Materials:** Polymer clay, silver | **Size:** 57 mm × 47 mm × 6 mm | **Image credit:** Doug Yaple | **Additional credit:** Metalwork by Chuck Domitrovich

Narrative: Inspiration for this piece came from glaciers I saw on the Alaskan cruise I took with my husband a few years ago. I wanted to create a piece with a beast in the center surrounded by a pattern from its environment. I wonder how long either of these images can be seen in the wild.

Maker: Cynthia Toops | **Title:** *Rabbit* | **Materials:** Polymer clay, silver | **Size:** 57 mm × 50 mm × 6 mm | **Image credit:** Doug Yaple | **Additional credit:** Metalwork by Chuck Domitrovich

Narrative: My husband and I had two rabbits. This micromosaic reminds me of Wooster, our second bunny. We also made a straw bed for our first bunny, Toto, so the brooch is a reminder of both pets.

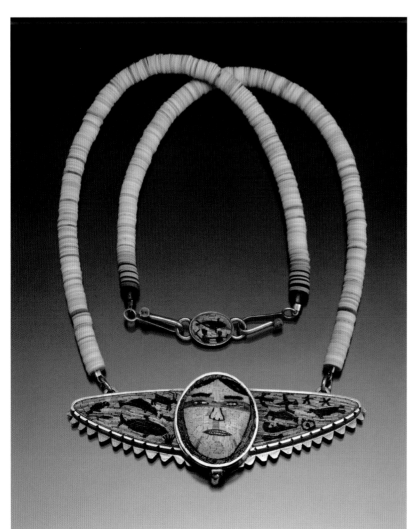

Maker: Cynthia Toops | **Title:** *Capture & Preserve* | **Materials:** Polymer clay, silver, glass | **Size:** Pendant: 92 mm × 32 mm × 10 mm; Necklace length: 633 mm | **Image credit:** Doug Yaple | **Additional credit:** Metalwork by Nancy Bonnema

Narrative: Dan and I were planning a road trip down the Pacific coast to Northern California. We were hoping to see whales, dolphins and other wildlife along the way so I created this amulet based on an Inupiak whaling mask. (We had only seen the original piece in a book but after this was finished I happened to bump into the inspiration at the NYC Natural History Museum!)

JEN TOWNSEND

Jen Townsend is a studio jeweler and an author. Her work can be seen in *Showcase: 500 Art Necklaces, 500 Gemstone Jewels* and in *Art Jewelry Today 2*. Her work is also in the permanent collection of the Imperial War Museum in London, England. Her first book, coauthored with Renee Zettle-Sterling, is called *Cast*.

As the child of an illustrator, I grew up thinking in pictures and stories. *I've always thought of art jewelry as a form of communication and, for me, images have always been the most natural way to communicate. My work has become more abstract in recent years to leave more room for the wearer and viewer to conjure their own stories, so the imagery has become more minimal, but I don't think it will ever go away entirely . . . it's just a little quieter now.*

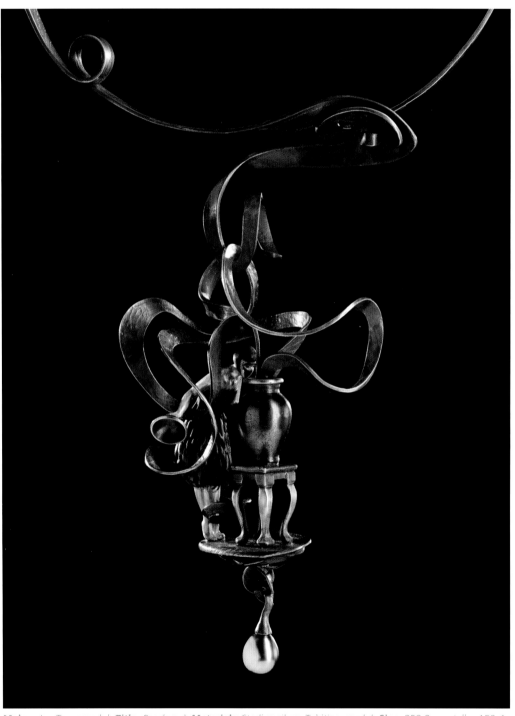

Maker: Jen Townsend | **Title:** *Pandora* | **Materials:** Sterling silver, Tahitian pearl | **Size:** 323.8 mm tall × 152.4 mm × 44.4 mm | **Image credit:** Hank Drew Photography

Narrative: This necklace is based on the myth of Pandora opening a jar that was forbidden to her. Her curiosity overpowered her better judgment and she inadvertently unleashed evil that spread throughout the world. She tried to close the jar, but most of the contents had escaped with the exception of one thing that was left in the jar . . .that thing was hope.

LUANN UDELL

Luann Udell is a mixed media artist and writer now living in Santa Rosa, California. Her work is inspired by prehistoric cave art, especially the Lascaux Cave in France. She uses faux ivory and scrimshaw techniques with polymer clay.

We know so little about those artists of the distant past. Yet understanding them helps us understand ourselves, our innate drives, desires, and fears that still shape our actions today (though some no longer serve us)—the desire to belong, the desire to be seen as an individual, the fear of the other, who we love, how we live our life, how we cope with loss, and how we face our death.

As a woman born mid-century, I saw no place for me in art, in prehistory or history. So I imagined a place for myself in prehistory. Decades later, science and history has "caught up." Now we can see those "invisible" women artists, along with artists of other races, other beliefs, other countries. By finding a place for myself, I created work that speaks the same for others, here, in our modern time.

From the very beginning, I wanted my artifacts to look truly ancient, to be authentic—not by blind reproduction, but by diligence and attention to detail. I use a faux ivory technique similar to samurai sword-making, to imitate the grain of real ivory. I shape each animal one at a time, by hand. I use a scrimshaw technique to bring up the markings, to mimic the look of an artifact lost to us until excavated in our modern times. Each one is hand-sanded and buffed, so they look like they've been polished by the constant touch of human hands. It's a time-consuming process—each artifact has to look right to me—but it's important to me, and it works. Archeologists, anthropologists and geologists have all remarked how authentic these look.

Many times, people are drawn to one animal over another they actually initially preferred. When I share the story of that animal, I'm amazed how often they say it makes perfect sense to them. So my story is taken up by that person, and carries on with them.

Maker: Luann Udell | **Title:** *Sea Lion Woman Shaman Necklace* | **Materials:** Polymer clay, leather cord, sterling silver findings | **Size:** 460 mm × 200 mm (pendant drop) | **Image credit:** Charley Freiberg

Narrative: This was the second in a series of shaman necklaces inspired by my desire for a female creation myth. I used the song "Sea Lion Woman" as inspiration for this ocean goddess, and played the music constantly in my studio while I made it. The circular pendant represents the heavens (inspired by ancient Chinese *bi* discs), and the otter represents the oceans, and Gaia, the earth. Bears, sea birds, otters, people, all held in wonder as Gaia sings them into being. Of course, minutes later, all became their innate selves, and all heck broke loose. But just for that handful of minutes, all were at peace with the world and each other. And someday, perhaps, we will achieve that again.

ALEKSANDRA VALI

Aleksandra Vali is a recognized studio jeweler and silver-smith. Her work has been distinguished with national awards and featured in international publications and exhibits. Aleksandra is also known as an international art teacher with over fifteen years of professional art and teaching experience. She is currently based in Chicago, USA.

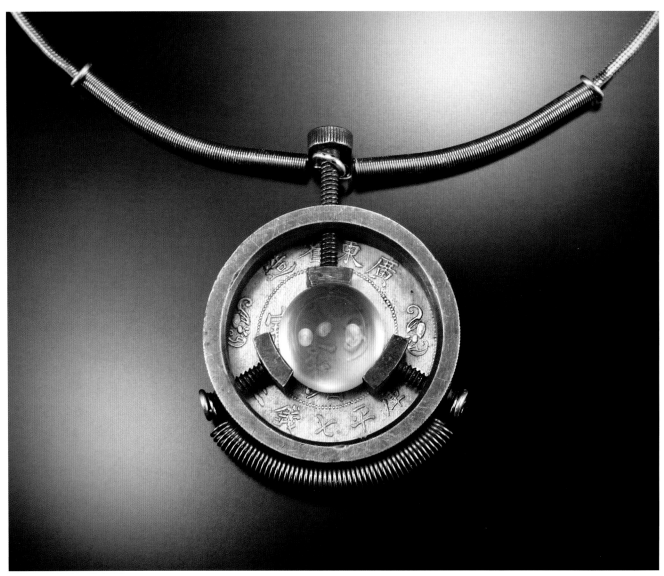

Maker: Aleksandra Vali | **Title:** *Grace of Caishen* | **Materials:** Ancient Chinese coin, old brass watchmaker's holder, stainless steel springs, silver chain, rose quartz | **Size:** 55 mm × 42 mm × 15 mm | **Image credit:** Aleksandra Vali

Narrative: Some of the most ancient coins known to us today come from China, and this is a very precious one. Through the prism of centuries, currency is a measure of value . . . time's continuum wraps into coils and as patterns fade away, true values that form our soul are here to stay. The Chinese god of wealth and prosperity, Caishen, promises luck if obedience is shown through loyalty and perseverance.

Maker: Aleksandra Vali | **Title:** *Testament of Inari Ôkami* | **Materials:** Spring mini caliper vintage, rise, key, glass jar, silver | **Size:** 93 mm × 38 mm × 12 mm | **Image credit:** Aleksandra Vali

Narrative: In Japanese mythology, one of the main prosperity and agriculture gods is portrayed as a rice grower, called Inari. According to one legend, every spring, he descends from the mountains to cultivate rice and, after the harvest, climbs back to the mountains for winter. The delicate rice grain has been a symbol of life and the key to prosperity. The path to prosperity is through hard work and perseverance, which are the true attributes of value, recognized and admired by generations.

Maker: Aleksandra Vali | **Title:** *Tsukuyomi-no-Mikoto's Mystery* | **Materials:** Watchmakers tool-antique mini caliper, ball bearing, silver chain, moonstone | **Size:** 58 mm × 38 mm × 21 mm | **Image credit:** Aleksandra Vali

Narrative: Since the earliest times of Japan, *Tsukuyomi-no-Mikoto* has been connected to the magic of the moon. As the moon rotates in cyclic perfection, it influences our behaviors, emotions and spiritual growth. In ancient Asia, some believed that this gem was a solid ray of moonlight filled with good energy. Asia has been leading in technological advancement and helping uncover new sophisticated technology. As we peer into the future with crystal-clear focus, we base our view on cultural and spiritual depth acquired through centuries.

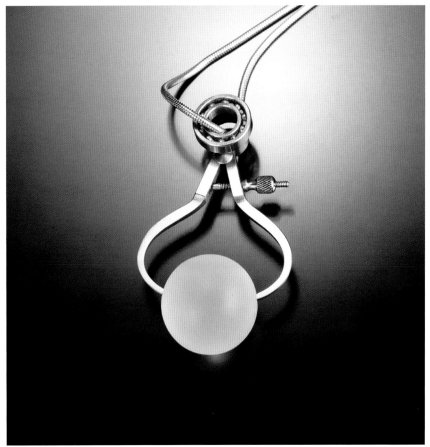

ANNE-SOPHIE VALLÉE

Anne-Sophie Vallée is a jewelry artist from Sherbrooke, Canada.

The act of collecting is where the history of my own work begins. Documenting my daily life encounter with objects, thoughts and ideas is an essential preliminary process. A simple gesture to store memory fulfills the necessary-to-recall experiences. It seems that stories begin and end around us constantly, leaving traces speaking of their existence. I am interested in how those realities overlap and breed.

As an artist, I feel compelled by those personal archives that initiate self-constructed fiction and take me from the rational to the non-rational world. In parallel, I find the process of making to be storytelling in itself. All action leaves its footprint in the work like a recorded dialogue between the mind, the hand and matter. Jewelry stands in a privileged position as a communicative object because of its relation to the body and its transportability. To me, a piece of jewelry belongs as much to the personal as to the public space, in that way, integrating art into everyday life.

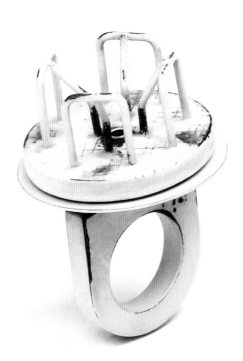

Maker: Anne-Sophie Vallée | **Title:** *I Have Spun (Yellow Ring)* | **Materials:** Powder coated steel | **Size:** 35 mm × 42 mm × 35 mm | **Image credit:** Anne-Sophie Vallée

Narrative: "I Have Spun" is a series of rings in the form of derelict playground equipment placed in the fantastical setting of a pink colored sandbox. The top parts of the rings offer a rough rotational movement as with a miniaturized merry-go-round.

The work suggests an unresolved narrative that relies on one's personal relationship to the past to reveal its complete identity in a present context. The work is about how a miniature object has the potential to encapsulate a space of interiority at the convergence of reality and imagination, emerging through self-constructed fiction. The body as a platform for interaction with objects operates as a catalyst that connects physical and emotional dimensions. Because the idea of play enables communication of experience in a sensitive way, it carries the potential to link and harmonize the personal and the social body at the non-rational level. The miniaturized merry-go-round brings to mind the essence of spontaneous childhood free play. As a counterpart, the state in which it is found might recall metaphorically the loss of such impulse in adulthood.

CAROLINA VALLEJO

The objects I create are expressive prolonging of the body, more than attachments. I use them to tell stories about ourselves, derived from philosophy and psychology. I challenge myself through my projects. I question everything and try to find the essence. The objects thus become an approach to an understanding on the plane where words do not reach, or a simplification of all the information gathered. A concentrate. *I use my background, but at the same time I know, as Federico Garcia Lorca says, that "describing your own village is describing all villages." Only by starting out from what has been personally experienced can I express myself truthfully. I use contrasts to provide character and to provoke reflection.*

Maker: Carolina Vallejo | **Title:** *Justice, from "The Gesture of the Virtues"* | **Materials:** Silver and oxidized Silver | **Size:** 12 mm × 6 mm × 6 mm | **Image credit:** Mikkel Heriba

Narrative: One of the basic conditions for righteous behavior is respect for the equality of all human beings. Tool: a black/white balancing bar which sits on the point of the forefinger. It requires quiet calm to hold the judging finger in just balance. (The forefinger symbolizes the Divine Justice.)

The virtues are conditions of emotions when these are controlled by common sense.

MARION VAN CRUCHTEN

Marion van Cruchten is a jewelry designer, a silversmith and an artist. Marion often works with waste but also with gold, silver and gems in her own studio on her narrative and contemporary designs and customers' orders. She has participated in many exhibitions nationally and internationally. For 8 years Marion was a tutor in jewelry design and silversmithing teaching adult students. She lives in really nice small village in the southern Netherlands.

Values and norms are the starting points of my work. Values and norms can vary a lot with faith, our upbringing and sociocultural environment. Norms can provide comfort but can also have quite a restraining effect.

Out of these values and norms I try to develop jewelry that makes a strong statement about evaluation, about overcoming prejudices, about appreciation and opening someone's eyes. Appreciation? It is something that we all need. It is pure, genuine and gives you comfort. What's better than to receive a little compliment, and knowing that you are appreciated!

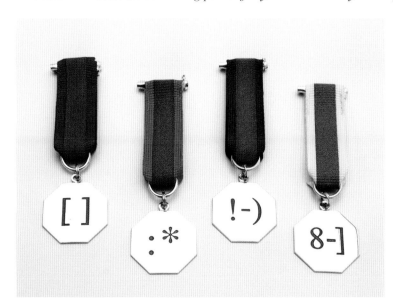

Maker: Marion van Cruchten | **Title:** *Appregards* | **Materials:** Metal, ribbon | **Size:** Approx. 88 mm including the ribbon; the medal is: 26 mm × 26 mm | **Image credit:** Henk Kentjens

Narrative: A compliment from the teacher about your workbook was something you were extremely happy about as a kid. You were proud as a peacock when you came home with your medal of a sporting event. I designed a piece from these past experiences and translated it to this contemporary time.

The well-known emoticons which are commonly used in messages sent by PC or mobile phone are shown on these jewels.

A hug [ ]
A big kiss :*
A well deserved wink !-)
Wow, great job 8-]

FELIEKE VAN DER LEEST

Felieke van der Leest is a trained metalsmith.

One of my favorite materials is plastic toy animals. Every year, new animals are produced, so my collection of animals grows and grows. They keep inspiring me because there is such a large variety, and yet they give me some boundaries to work within.

I like to tell a story, but rather to let it end with a dot, I try to let it end with a question mark. When the story is too obvious the work is getting very easy, boring, and that, for me, is the worst thing that can happen to a piece.

Maker: Felieke van der Leest | **Title:** *Incognitos Anonymous (Object with Necklace)* | **Materials:** Textile, plastic toy animals, silver, glass beads, leather | **Size:** Object 165 mm × 165 mm × 85 mm; Pendant (cluster of animals) 80 mm × 80 mm × 80 mm | **Image credit:** Eddo Hartmann

Narrative: At first I wanted to make a "totem pole" piece. I tried and I tried but having to work with already existing toy animals has its limits. So I stopped putting them on top of each other and they ended up sitting in a circle having a meeting, I have no idea what kind of meeting, but it must be quite a secret one because they wear masks. The bucket and pan masks relate to the faces of carved pumpkins seen at Halloween.

Maker: Felieke van der Leest | **Title:** *African Caucasian Indian (Brooch/Necklace)* | **Materials:** Textile, Argentium®, gold, silver, moonstone | **Size:** 80 mm × 80 mm × 40 mm | **Image credit:** Eddo Hartmann

Narrative: The origin of the piece started years ago when I travelled for the first time to the USA. I had to fill in an official form on the plane. The question of which race I was puzzled me (and shocked me also, to be honest). I was not African, American, Asian, Latin American, Native American . . . I had to ask because I saw nothing familiar on the list. The flight attendant answered me that I was Caucasian. I had never heard of this type of human being, and always thought I was a white European.

Maker: Felieke van der Leest | **Title:** *Sharky Boy (Brooch)* | **Materials:** Textile, plastic toy animal, gold, galvanized glass beads, topaz | **Size:** 100 mm × 100 mm × 45 mm | **Image credit:** Eddo Hartmann

Narrative: Sometimes penguins can be scary when wearing a black coat with water wings, a shark fin, and XL flippers.

From the series "F.I.B.S. (Festival International des Bêtes Sportives)" (2008–2009).

NELLY VAN OOST

Born in France, Nelly Van Oost now lives and works in Brussels, Belgium.

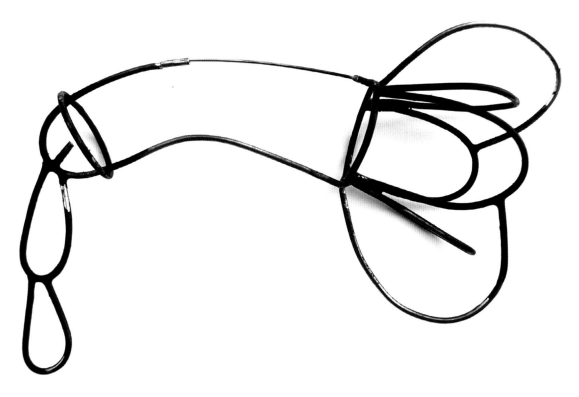

Maker: Nelly Van Oost | **Title:** *Incipit #2* | **Materials:** New silver, paint, steel | **Size:** 140 mm × 60 mm × 40 mm |
Image credit: Carlos Monreal

Narrative: Who hasn't drawn pictures of willies on tables or even on the door of a public toilet? That's what got me thinking . . . . These penises are spontaneous and a bit provocative, but they are an essentially funny representation of the male sex. Through this series I evoke memories of common spaces. I want the viewer to recall stories. Stories that will make them remember a personal anecdote, or a mental image. I would like my penises to evoke a sense of humor, as something that they can easily connect with.

INGEBORG VANDAMME

My work tells about our experiences, thoughts and memories leaving traces in a visible and invisible world. The practice of recycling paper, often combined with cotton and pigments, is found throughout my work: a material carrying our thoughts, our language, and our presence.

Usually, I combine hard materials like aluminium and silver with softer, more temporary ones like paper and other natural fibers, which represent a valued impermanence. Consequently, natural processes with an focus on imperfection are translated into pieces of jewelry, thereby giving materials, like for instance weathered wood and damaged shell, a new life.

Maker: Ingeborg Vandamme | **Title:** *Tearcatcher (Necklace)* | **Materials:** Paper, silver | **Size:** 200 mm; Each element 30 mm × 30 mm × 5 mm | **Image credit:** Conor Vella

Narrative: The use of tear bottles in Victorian times, showing a mourner's remorse, guilt, love or grief, has been a starting point for the *Tearcatcher* necklace. In these piece containers made of paper pulp will get soaked with the tears, turning them into transitory elements affected by grief. The practice of recycling paper, often combined with cotton and pigments, is found throughout my work: a material carrying our thoughts, our language, and our presence.

Maker: Ingeborg Vandamme | **Title:** *Memories (Pendant)* | **Materials:** Anodized aluminum, paper, rubber, ribbon | **Size:** 145 mm × 80 mm × 20 mm | **Image credit:** Ingeborg Vandamme

Narrative: In my work as a jewelry designer I want, among other things, to depict the protection and concealment of the vulnerable, and the nurturing of memories. I often express this in my work by combining hard materials like metal and more transitory ones like paper and objects from nature.

Maker: Ingeborg Vandamme | **Title:** *Secrets (Pendant)* | **Materials:** Anodized aluminum, paper, rubber, ribbon | **Size:** 135 mm × 130 mm × 10 mm | **Image credit:** Ingeborg Vandamme

TRUIKE VERDEGAAL

Truike Verdegaal is a gold and silversmith but studied also at the jewelry department of the Gerrit Rietveld Academie in Amsterdam, The Netherlands.

In addition to my free work I have been designing jewelry on assignment since 1992. People ask me to take a jewel or precious item that they have inherited, and integrate this in a so-called "remembrance jewel."

Very often, an inherited jewel is not to the personal taste of the client. It often ends up in the bottom of a drawer. However, for sentimental reasons, clients do have the desire to wear the jewel.

I do not melt down the inherited jewels. Instead, I work with such jewelry and layer it until it's an unusual, new jewel, to the taste of the owner. This is wonderful work because the stories behind the inherited jewels and the possible combinations of forms and spheres really fascinate me.

In order to get to a design I have several conversations with the client. I ask about the relationship with the deceased, what the history of the inherited item is and what the client's wishes are. During the jewel-making process, I invite the client to come to my studio to see the progress. My handing over this new piece once it is finished, is also an important moment for them.

To me, the inherited jewels and the "voice" of the client are elements that show me the way in which to work. The very emotional stories behind the inherited pieces don't scare me. On the contrary, such stories open up a register of images for me with which I can consequently work. The assignments carry my signature because the client gives me the freedom and trust to make the jewel, and the customer can now wear a jewel that is of enormous sentimental value.

Maker: Truike Verdegaal | **Title:** *Brooch for M.v.D* | **Materials:** Silver, ivory, amethyst, iron, textile | **Size:** Approx. 45 mm × 70 mm × 25 mm | **Image credit:** Eddo Hartmann

Narrative: M.v.D. inherited an antique Japanese netsuke. Sawed through it revealed a touching intimacy. The silver brooch also shows what's habitually hidden.

BILLIE M. VIGNE

Billie M. Vigne's work is an ongoing study of traditional decorative and structural metalsmithing techniques found in ethnic and tribal jewelry. The conflation of this with her aesthetic influences—Oskar Schlemmer's Theatre of the Bauhaus and 1980s postmodern design amongst others—is her continuous preoccupation.

Early on in my work, before I began working with metal, I found narrative useful for generating ideas and focusing projects. Preceding X, *my output was mainly concerned with form and finding a blanket aesthetic. I hadn't realized that the underpinning whir of concern I had been feeling was to do with the validity of my production—the absence of narrative. Narrative provides context for work, gives theatre and complexity to it, and has made my purpose as a maker feel less ambiguous.*

Maker: Billie M. Vigne | **Title:** *X: The Bomb, the Whale and the Phallus* | **Materials:** Oxidized brass, copper and silver hand-pierced, hollow forms with layered figurative detail; carved and cast X-shaped bronze finials; cold connected and soldered hollow formed bails; twisted and bound cord in wool, cotton and bin liners | **Size:** Approx. 530 mm × 320 mm laid flat | **Image credit:** Ollie Harrop

Narrative: *X* is a neckpiece and nuclear dowry bequeathed to a future generation. It tells the murky tale of an unstable nightmare-scape in which the whales know and wait; on the cusp of nuclear warfare, the phallus rises and the bomb is dropped. Structurally, *X* is a study of Tamil Nadu marriage necklaces, distinctive in their reconfigurable order and layered, highly decorative construction.

X is a kiss, X marks the spot, X is the black of the bomb, of machine, and precedes the atomic whiteness of ZERO.

NANCY MELI WALKER

Nancy Meli Walker is an artist, jewelry designer and fabricator who utilizes chasing and repoussé and a variety of other ancient and modern metal techniques to create her jewelry.

I work with narrative as a way to connect and communicate metal jewelry and other elements such as gems and pearls to haiku poetry, a concept, or a story. The wearer then transfers the idea to the public as an illustrative canvas.

Maker: Nancy Meli Walker | **Title:** *War and Peace Choke Her* | **Materials:** Argentium silver, 22k gold, pearls, garnets, plastic toy guns | **Size:** 510 mm × 110 mm × 8 mm | **Image credit:** photographer wishes to remain anonymous

Narrative: The work is a collection of symbols: Chain maille necklace—war throughout history. Pure white bullet pearls—the innocent life lost in war. Plastic toy guns—exposing our children at an early age to war as if it was a game. A 22k gold peace sign—the preciousness and high value of peace. Blood red teardrop garnets—loss of life/blood and tears cried from war. Chasing and repoussé medieval shields—we should shield ourselves from confrontation and war.

ROGER "ROTSCH" WEBER

I've now been working for over 28 years as a trained goldsmith.

Under the label rotsch-o-mat, I produce unique jewelry pieces, motion figures, automatons, and poectic machines. I also create pieces as individual commissions for private customers, museums and theatres. I exhibit my work as part of two or three exhibitions per year and work as a tutor for trainee goldsmiths.

I make pieces of jewelry for confident people who want more than just to wear something shiny with a precious stone in it. My work should make you stare, think or produce a smile.

Maker: Roger "Rotsch" Weber | **Title:** *Tamarotschi* | **Materials:** Metal, wood, paint, circuit boards, Perspex | **Size:** 105 mm × 75 mm × 15 mm | **Image credit:** Oliver Lang

Narrative: Inspired by the Tamagotchis that make small children addicted, I've created a more harmless mechanical version as a pendant.

The animal can be fed metal balls by means of a magnetic stick. Its mouth is operated with a button. Then it can be stroked by means of a crank system on the back and finally emptied again with another button. Afterwards you can leave it for days without fear that it will go hungry.

KAROL WEISSLECHNER

Karol Weisslechner is a senior lecturer in the S+M+L_XL Metal and Jewelry Studio at the Academy of Fine Arts and Design in Bratislava, Slovakia. Apart from lecturing and managing the Academy he regularly takes part in creative symposia in Slovakia and abroad. He also organizes international symposia, conferences on artistic jewelry, exhibitions, expert colloquia, and study tours.

Jewelry has been a part of mankind since ancient times. Apart from its decorative function, it can become a symbol of identity or even a communication tool. Art jewelry conveys the essential features of human emotionality in a wider connotation and this is what I find intriguing about its creation. I consider a personal story as the ultimate base for all artistic creation.

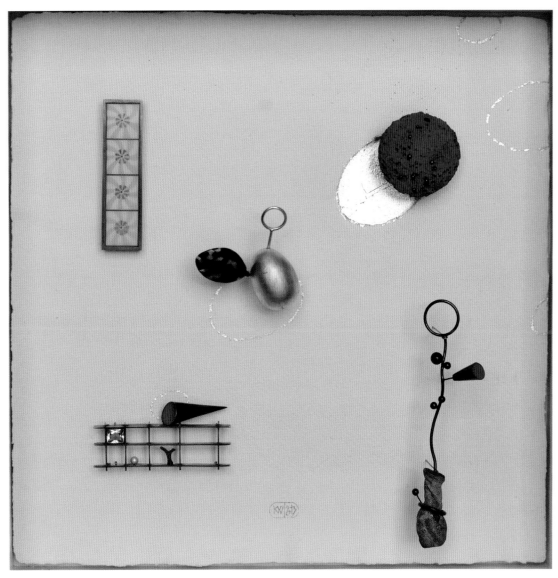

Maker: Karol Weisslechner | **Title:** *Build a House, Plant a Tree (Composition of Brooches and Pendants)* | **Materials:** Silver, wood, pigment, amethyst, plastic, silver and gold plated | **Size:** Various dimensions | **Image credit:** Simona Weisslechner, author's archive

Narrative: They say: "Build a house and plant a tree." It means you should live your life. I enjoy building compositions of my jewels . . . every composition is like a new story . . . new artwork . . . new tale . . . .
While building, I know I am alive.

LEONIE WESTBROOK

Leonie Westbrook is a jeweler and metalsmith. Currently Leonie works out of a studio based in the Adelaide Hills of South Australia.

Since my childhood on a sheep farm in rural arid Australia I have always felt the need to communicate the influence and intensity of my experiences. An extremely harsh environment where everything exists in a quiet isolation, and the uneasy relationship between industrial and organic was always evident. There was an overwhelmingly quiet and intense beauty about the landscape, yet horrific occurrences were often inflicted on anything living in that environment.

These memories have a profound influence on my practice, although now my daily reality is far removed from these early experiences. Always present in my practice are the notions of impermanence, resourcefulness and the process of adaptation, exploring the vulnerabilities and limitations of human, material, and form. Working with the narrative is a way of imploring the viewer / wearer to connect with the work.

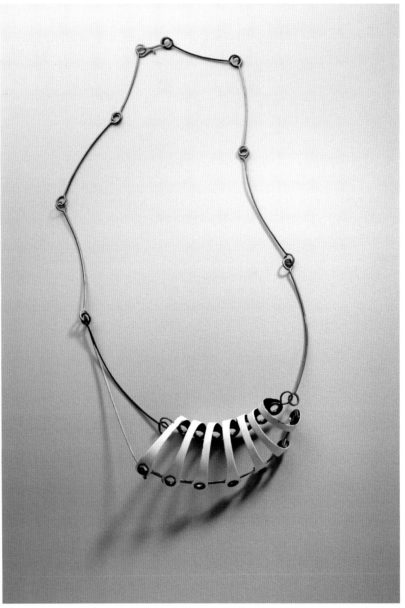

Maker: Leonie Westbrook | **Title:** *A Fine Line (Neckpiece)* | **Materials:** Sterling silver, paint | **Size:** 90 mm × 250 mm × 30 mm | **Image credit:** Grant Hancock

Narrative: Amongst eroding landforms and corroding relics on farming properties where the industrial and organic are almost indistinguishable from the other, remains such as bones are not unusual and are left to bleach and deteriorate in the harsh environment. There always seems an abundance of discarded multiples, piles of scrap metal, machinery that is gradually and quietly disintegrating, becoming something reminiscent of the original form.

Farmers often talk about a good year or bad year in terms of what it means for their livelihood. I always wondered how much real difference a good or bad year made to the animals responsible for producing this livelihood. Through the use of precious material, and in the form of jewelry with its connotations of preciousness, *A Fine Line* exists as an attempt to see the dead and forgotten animal that existed only for someone's profit as still having value.

DAVID AND ROBERTA WILLIAMSON

Roberta and David Williamson are studio jewelers and jewelry, sculpture and design professors at Baldwin Wallace University in Berea, Ohio. They can be seen in the PBS documentary *Craft in America*.

The narrative has been the focal point of our collaborative work since 1967 when we were 18 years old. Telling stories through our work has been a way of expressing ourselves in order to connect with people seeing our pieces. We love the interaction as a work stirs a

long ago memory, a longing, or even a loss. We listen as we are told stories about a childhood monkey, a lost key to a toy box, a royal English relative, a mother's charm from a charm bracelet or how butterflies are their good luck icon.

Over the years the actor Robin Williams bought numerous pieces from us. We love that we connected with him with our work. He once wrote to us "your magical work makes my heart tap dance." For us, that moment of connection is why we create what we do.

Maker: David and Roberta Williamson | **Title:** *Longing* | **Materials:** Vignette, slate, copper, sterling silver, fine silver, wood, watchmaker's crystal, glass, quartz crystal, altered scissors, antique prints, vintage key, fern | **Size:** 400 mm × 200 mm × 30 mm | **Image credit:** Dan Fox

Narrative: Even though we have been together for so many years we seem to always have a sense of longing, not for someone else but for another place and time. Through our pieces we create a story of that place. While working in the studio on our pieces we often play the same historical movie or music over and over, absorbing the essence of that time— the colors, the images, the forms, the interest, the intrigue, the look in the eyes, the secret lovers, the idyll hours. This is the world we longed for in our youth. This is a world we long for in our hearts.

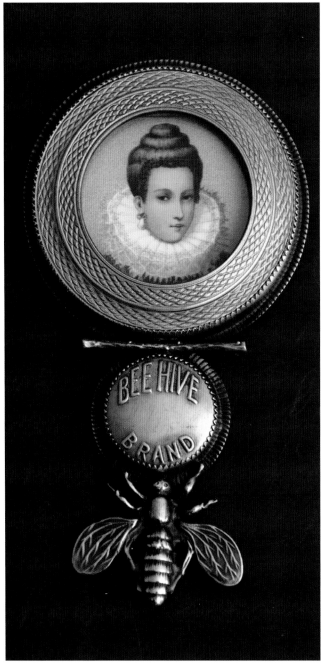

Maker: David and Roberta Williamson | **Title:** *BEES!* | **Materials:** Sterling silver, fine silver, brass, watchmaker's crystal, brass button, antique print | **Size:** 90 mm × 60 mm × 30 mm | **Image credit:** David and Roberta Williamson

Narrative: We bought the beehive button from an elderly lady who collects old buttons. She always has treasures for us to see. We love to think about why someone made a button saying *BEEHIVE*. When we found this print in New York City, the memory of that button in a little box in our studio popped into our heads. Of course, this is the missing button from this lady's dress! Bees do bring good luck!

Maker: David and Roberta Williamson | **Title:** *His Lips Sought the Morning Dew* | **Materials:** Sterling silver, moonstones | **Size:** 170 mm × 80 mm × 30 mm | **Image credit:** Dan Fox

Narrative: Early in the morning the dew on the leaves is magical. The spherical droplets defy reason. We love the idea of insects being refreshed by these wonderous orbs.

Maker: David and Roberta Williamson | **Title:** *A Walk in the Woods* | **Materials:** Sterling silver, fine silver, abalone, turbo shell, rutilated quartz, on a dried magnolia leaf from Williamsburg, Virginia, vintage specimen box | **Size:** Box 300 mm × 180 mm × 80 mm | **Image credit:** Dan Fox

Narrative: We were teaching a summer session at Penland School of Crafts. A student walking in the woods spotted a huge beetle missing part of his rear leg, making it difficult to walk. The beetle's path became large circles because he could push forward with only one leg. He brought us the beetle to see and the class thought to euthanize the beetle to take it away from its misery. Roberta and I took the opportunity to teach a lesson: from sterling silver wire and tubing we fabricated a prosthetic leg for the beetle. After buffing and polishing the prosthesis, we epoxied the perfectly fitting tubing in place on the little leg stump! We took great care to not injure or harm the giant insect. Eventually, as a group, we took the beetle back to the woods for a releasing ceremony. Everyone cheered with sheer delight as the beetle moved ahead, in a straight line mind you, over the bright green moss, back into its home, the woods. We all felt the beetle was very proud of his shiny new leg.

JOE WOOD

Joe Wood is currently Professor of Art at Massachusetts College of Art and Design in Boston, MA. He has been teaching Jewelry, Metalsmithing, Computer techniques for object-makers and other classes at "MassArt" since 1985.

The first European portrait miniatures were made as early as the sixteenth century. British royalty bestowed the tokens to favorite confidants, exchanged them for diplomacy, or made them to commemorate engagements and weddings. Influenced by Flemish illustration, these small images gained popularity among the affluent middle class around the eighteenth century in Britain and then the United States. Miniatures were commissioned to mark important life milestones and soon took on the symbolism of family, romantic love, and childhood innocence—they could be carried daily and had intimate, personal meanings.

In this newest work, Joe Wood transforms these historically personal tokens of affection, meant to be adored and kept close, into grotesque portrait miniatures. A departure from his typical ornamental work, "Dialogues" takes the current political state as its source of inspiration. The nameplates that adorn each brooch—Discourse, Discord, and Disgust—relay the contemporary political narrative: front-running candidates have, rather than addressing real issues, focused their efforts on quarrelsome misdirection and spectacle, generating a hostile political climate that is causing American citizens to distrust and, at times, detest politics. By making these portrait miniatures as brooches, which are traditionally worn on the lapel, Wood envisions them as modern-day political buttons, akin to publicly reflecting the wearer's personal affiliations but instead reflecting the current state of political discourse.

Text by kind permission of the Curatorial Staff, Massachusetts College of Art and Design
Lisa Tung
Chloe Zaug
Darci Hanna

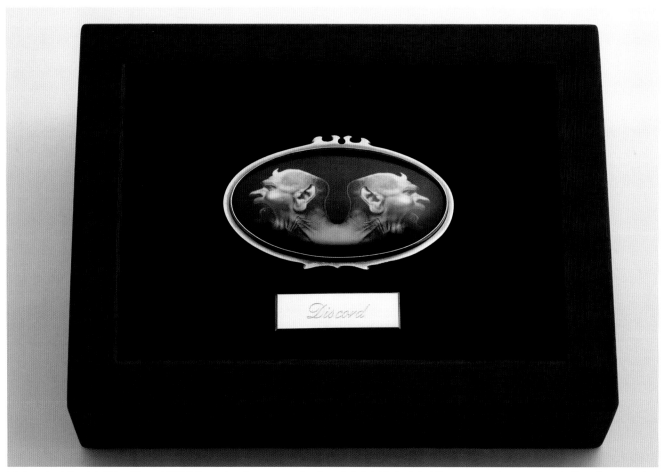

Maker: Joe Wood | **Title:** *Discord (2016 Campaign Commemorative Brooch Set)* | **Materials:** Vitreous enamel on copper, sterling silver, wooden boxes with velvet | **Size:** Brooch 57 mm × 95 mm × 12 mm; Box 60.3 mm × 200 mm × 160 mm | **Image credit:** Joe Wood

Title: *Discourse (2016 Campaign Commemorative Brooch Set)* | **Materials:** Vitreous enamel on copper, sterling silver, wooden boxes with velvet |
Size: Brooch 57 mm × 95 mm × 12 mm; Box 60.3 mm × 200 mm × 160 mm | **Image credit:** Joe Wood

Title: *Disgust (2016 Campaign Commemorative Brooch Set)* | **Materials:** Vitreous enamel on copper, sterling silver, wooden boxes with velvet |
Size: Brooch 57 mm × 95 mm × 12 mm; Box 60.3 mm × 200 mm × 160 mm | **Image credit:** Joe Wood

NANCY LEE WORDEN

Nancy Lee Worden'sjewelry can be found in major public collections. She lives and works in Seattle, Washington.

I am an artist who makes jewelry about human behavior. Most of my work implies a narrative behind it and is often a response to something that has happened to me or that I have observed. While the content of my artwork is very personal, *I have tried hard to distill the essence of each topic so that other people can see their own story in my story. My intent is to provide insight, comfort and perhaps some humor for myself and my audience to help us deal with the crazy stuff life throws at us.*

Maker: Nancy Lee Worden | **Title:** *The Family Reunion* | **Materials:** Gold-plated sterling silver, brass, copper, onyx, acrylic, photographs and scorpions cast in resin | **Size:** 265 mm × 35 mm × 50 mm | **Image credit:** Rex Rystedt

Narrative: I was inspired to create this work after a particularly difficult family reunion. This necklace combines snarky remarks I overheard from my grandmother growing up with images of family prototypes; the tomboy, the mama's boy, the family ne'er-do-well. None of the people in the images are related to me. I had to wait for my parents and my grandparents to pass away before I could make a piece like this. The scorpions set the tone.

The Family Reunion text on the reverse reads, clockwise from clasp: A nice young man and such a comfort to his mother! / He was strict and expected his women to obey. / Mary always was one for the boys. / Trouble followed him wherever he went. / After the war, Fred just kind of wandered. / It's time to settle down and start acting like a lady.

ERQIANG WU

Erqiang Wu believes that contemporary jewelry art—its ideas, form, material, and technical means—is very different from traditional jewelry, paying more attention to the expression of creative thinking. His works emphasize weakening the traditional jewelry value of wealth. He combines themes of realism and romantic expression, to enrich people's spiritual world.

His works place attention on social and human ecology as well as natural environment ecology. As he works to express personal views, he doesn't rigidly adhere to traditional materials like gold, silver, or jade; he brings to use anything that can be suitable to express creative ideas.

Maker: Erqiang Wu | **Title:** *Township Love* | **Materials:** 925 silver, cliff wood | **Size:** 70 mm × 30 mm × 60 mm | **Image credit:** Erqiang Wu

Narrative: The work expresses my living of the daily life of the metropolis, along with the infinite love and yearning for the rural life of my childhood. In fact, in the rapid change of urban and rural areas of China today, the township is not only a person's emotional home, but also a generation or even a few generations of universal feelings. The development of society is in some ways a departure from the original simple feelings of the people. Through this work, I want to retain not only the landscape, but also the pure emotion.

HELEN WYATT

Helen Wyatt is a jewelry artist currently undertaking a masters degree by studio led research in jewelry and small objects at Queensland College of Art. Helen's practice is informed by the intersection of nature and development in the environments within which she lives—both in Sydney and Brisbane, Australia.

Maker: Helen Wyatt | **Title:** *Mrs. Fraser* | **Materials:** 925 silver, brass, Perspex, acetate, aquamarine, stainless steel | **Size:** 50 mm | **Image credit:** Helen Wyatt

Narrative: This piece represents a point of tension for Fraser Island, Australia—in this case the interface of a colonial and an indigenous engagement with the island. Mrs. Fraser's highly contested account of her time there led to repressive policies in the management of the local people. The brooch captures the preciousness of the island and the early nineteenth century newspaper report questioning her story—a story she sold on her return to England.

MEIYI YANG

Meiyi Yang is a jewelry/accessories designer/maker who has studied industrial design. She was born and raised in Shenzhen, the biggest jewelry market in China, so she has a longheld deep interest in jewelry design. She also has a deep interest in fashion design and the relationship between jewelry and clothing as they complement each other.

I enjoy observing. I believe that everything has its own stories. Much inspiration for my works comes out of the exploration of folktales or true stories. Jewelry, in my opinion, is an article which, though it cannot talk itself, may communicate with people. It can diffuse signals, the origin of which is thoughts, concepts, and notions. These elements breathe and collide continuously, and communicate with each other.

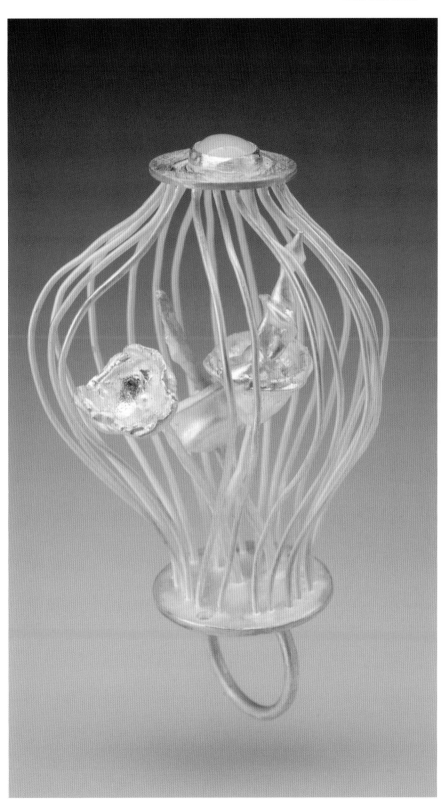

Maker: Meiyi Yang | **Title:** *Escape* | **Materials:** Sterling silver, moonlight stones | **Size:** 68 mm × 115 mm × 75 mm | **Image credit:** Elizabeth Lamark

Narrative: I believe the most desirable thing in the world is freedom. So I made a ring and named it *Escape*. It shows my hope to get out of pressure, fleeing to freedom. However, when people try so hard to escape from their "undesirable" situations, they only end up finding themselves running into other unsatisfactory situations. Hence there is no real freedom.

A good example is marriage. There is a book called *Fortress Siege* by the famous Chinese writer Qian Zhongshu, in which he wrote "Marriage is like a fortress besieged: those who are outside want to get in, and those who are inside want to get out." As another example, children want to grow up when they are young, because in most young people's minds, growing up equals cutting loose from their parent's control or school's discipline.

People are never satisfied with their current situations and continuously pursue higher goals, and that cycle repeats. They believe that whatever's next will be better, but the present—which could become wonderful memories years later—is often ignored. I want to constantly remind myself through this ring: no matter what life you are chasing, cherishing what's in front of you is equally important.

LIAUNG CHUNG YEN

Liaung Chung Yen is an award-winning goldsmith based in upstate New York in the USA. He was born and raised in Taiwan and his jewelry and artistic aesthetic is influenced by both Chinese culture and art. Yen sees his work as an expression of the mind, as well as small sculptures documenting the time and emotion in which he lives. Yen's work is also an exploration of sculpture form in jewelry by using geometric shapes and architectural structures.

I am always interested in reading comic books and watching movies. The similarity between them is that they both consist of frames. Each frame can be seen as a fragment of the movie. By connecting all the fragments together, the story has unfolded. I always have a picture in my mind after seeing a movie. I remember the silhouettes of children riding bicycles across the sky with ET in the basket. I also remember "Don" Vito Corleone sitting in a chair with

a cat in his hand and listening to people's requests in The Godfather. *These pictures in my mind provide me memories of the stories and the movie-going experience.*

I am also drawn to the daily objects that have been used by people. Usage presents the history of the object as well as the trademark of the people who used it. I have always liked a teapot that belongs to my father. It has a lotus root-shaped body with a vine-like handle and pourer. There are a couple of lotus seeds on the lid that make jingling sounds while pouring the tea. Every time I see this teapot it reminds me of the lifestyle and culture I am living in. With this teapot also come memories of teatime with my family. By connecting all the experiences, I have my own story with the teapot.

I think of my jewelry as fragments, carrying stories by using metaphor in my design. It also presents the imagination of the mind as well as the story and history of the making process.

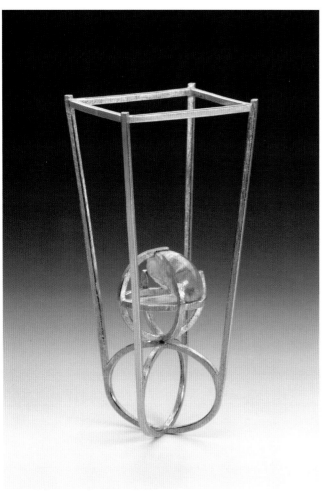

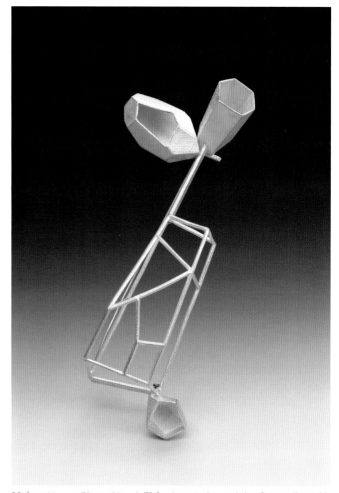

Maker: Liaung Chung Yen | **Title:** *A Space for a Broken Heart (Ring)* | **Materials:** 14k yellow gold, fluorite | **Size:** 30 mm × 70 mm × 30 mm | **Image credit:** Shu Ching Yang

Maker: Liaung Chung Yen | **Title:** *Love Is Around the Corner (Brooch)* | **Materials:** Sterling silver, steel pin | **Size:** 115 mm × 50 mm × 25 mm | **Image credit:** Shu Ching Yang

Narrative: We describe a human heart as made of glass. It is beautiful, pure, shaped by the heat but fragile at the same time. The fluorite bead was broken during shipment. I found it to be just like the glass heart. I then created a space for it.

Narrative: People always have their routines. Some people make a right turn all the time, and some always make the left. We are too often used to what we are familiar with. Sometimes, a little change makes the new discovery. Love is just around the corner.

Maker: Liaung Chung Yen | **Title:** *Opposites Attract (Brooch)* | **Materials:** 22k and 18k yellow gold, sterling silver, citrine, druzy, steel pin | **Size:** 115 mm × 70 mm × 25 mm | **Image credit:** Shu Ching Yang

Narrative: They are completely opposite. The round shape with soft texture and the clean line with hard edge, the shiny with polished facets and the dark with the rough surface; they are drawn to each other because of unfulfilled desires and qualities in their lives.

Maker: Liaung Chung Yen | **Title:** *In the Mood for Love (Brooch)* | **Materials:** 22k and 18k yellow gold, sterling silver, quartz, steel pin | **Size:** 60 mm × 135 mm × 27 mm | **Image credit:** Shu Ching Yang

Narrative: Every time I see her, I have the butterfly in my stomach. It seems that I have developed a special feeling for her, but I am not sure if she feels the same. What I can do is to find a tree with a hole and tell the secret of love to the tree, just like the old tale. Hopefully, the tree will keep the secret, or tell her the secret.

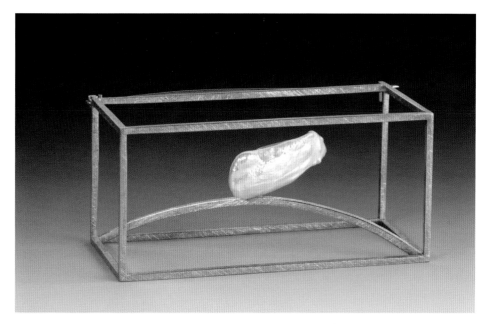

Maker: Liaung Chung Yen | **Title:** *A Space for Self-content* | **Materials:** 14k yellow gold, pearl | **Size:** 30 mm × 65 mm × 30 mm | **Image credit:** Shu Ching Yang

Narrative: ". . . I like to stay in my place with my favorite music playing, the candles lit, and a drink. It doesn't matter if I am in a sad mood with a broken heart or in a joyful moment, I feel content and I am the treasure in my space. I enjoy this environment and the atmosphere that I have created. This is my place."

ANASTASIA YOUNG

Anastasia Young is an independent jewelry artist, author and lecturer, whose jewelry has been exhibited internationally. She uses fictional narrative as a starting point for works, but is also fascinated by the inherent narrative qualities and cultural significance of archetypal objects (for example, spiders, teeth, or mechanical machinery) and their ability to create narrative merely by their symbolic interpretation by the viewer.

I have always been drawn toward working with figurative and representational forms, and these naturally lend themselves to fictional interactions between each other as well as with the real world. From the start of my time as a jeweler, I was writing fictional scenarios and creating jewelry pieces that were sometimes characters from my stories, or pieces which related to events that affected the characters. This method of working then became the most useful way for me to design, as the interplay between elements could be justified through the narrative (sometimes after the fact!). This makes it sound like a well-planned and reliable process, which it is not; recurrent themes crop up in my work uncontrollably because this is the visual language which best expresses my ideas.

Maker: Anastasia Young | **Title:** *Trophy Wife Trophy (0 67251047e)* | **Materials:** Sterling and fine silver, 18k yellow gold, diamond, moonstone, epoxy resin, buffalo horn | **Size:** 70 mm × 40 mm × 30 mm | **Image credit:** Anastasia Young

Narrative: This brooch follows the construct of a Bachelor Machine (similar to Duchamp's artwork, "The Bride Stripped Bare by Her Bachelors, Even"). It is therefore dictated that the Bachelor (the spider) will be executed and that the Bride (the hand) will be instrumental in the process. The engraved inscriptions are also an important part of the narrative.

The piece takes its form from a traditional Scottish grouse foot brooch, popular in the nineteenth century, but the hand of a doll has been mounted as the trophy rather than the foot of a bird. The figurative elements interact to produce a complex tension within the piece, accentuated by the use of mixed materials.

KEE-HO YUEN

Kee-ho Yuen employs an eclectic use of contemporary and traditional technologies and materials, ranging from advanced 3-D computer modeling to traditional fabrications and enameling.

Maker: Kee-ho Yuen | **Title:** *Time Out* | **Materials:** Gold plated silver, bronze, anodized aluminum, bird eye maple wood, graphite and rock | **Size:** 75 mm × 62.5 mm × 100 m | **Image credit:** Kee-ho Yuen

Narrative: The pig often symbolizes stupidity, but I believe pigs are actually smarter than we think. In this piece, a pig is taking a moment to decide whether it should take a chance and cross the stream by walking over a tree branch. We all have big decisions to make.

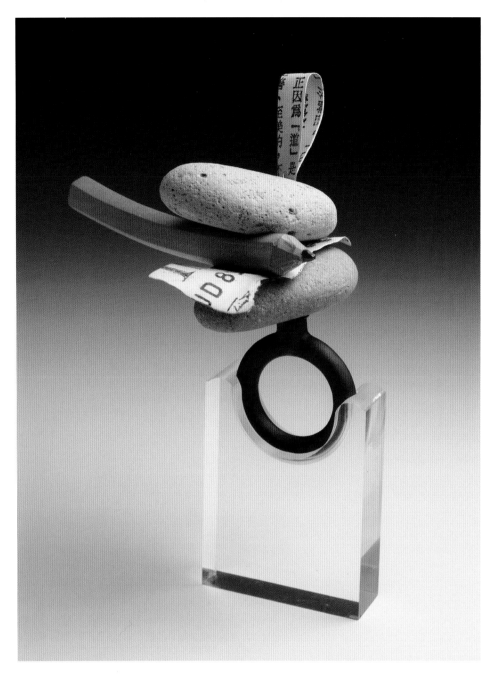

Maker: Kee-ho Yuen |
Title: *Bending Power* |
Materials: Anodized aluminum, rock, cedar wood, lead, brass, acrylic paint, and laser printer ink |
Size: 80 mm × 80 mm × 100 mm |
Image credit: Kee-ho Yuen

Narrative: I believe in the power of writing. The yellow strip is the writing of Laozi, a famous Chinese philosopher, teaching us not to focus too much on the materialistic world. The white structure under the pencil is a dollar bill.

Maker: Kee-ho Yuen |
Title: *The Story Never Ended* | **Materials:** Bronze, anodized aluminum, bird eye maple wood, plastic, cotton thread | **Size:** 80 mm × 26 mm × 80 mm | **Image credit:** Kee-ho Yuen

Narrative: This piece is about the race between a hare and a tortoise. It is a very popular children's story that teaches us the virtue of endurance. However, many people have developed a parallel universe for this story. For example, what if the hare did not take a nap, or the race course crossed a stream? Imagination and creativity can reinterpret a well-known fable to reflect our changing culture. Things revolve and evolve like a yo-yo. Whether we nap or run, we all take our chances.

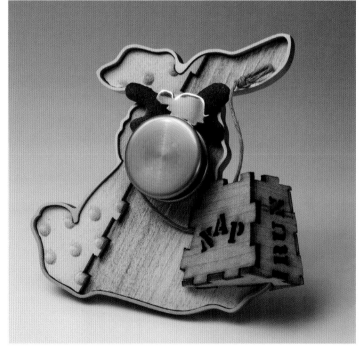

CRISTINA ZANI

Cristina Zani is an Italian-born jewelry artist. After living and working in several countries, she established her workshop in the Lake District in 2012. In 2016 she moved to Edinburgh where she is currently based.

My work is influenced by Italian literature. I approach the creation of my jewelry in the same way I would compose a story.

Maker: Cristina Zani | **Title:** *Infinite Maps (Brooch)* | **Materials:** Oxidized copper, enamel, steel | **Size:** 85 mm × 50 mm × 10 mm | **Image credit:** Cristina Zani

Narrative: This brooch is part of a collection titled "Infinite Maps," inspired by Italo Calvino's novel *Invisible Cities*. The pieces in this series stem from my fascination with maps and are a reflection on the concept of invisibility. I am intrigued by the patterns drawn by intersecting roads and by the idea that, by taking sections of maps out of context, the city becomes invisible and the focus shifts to the intricate designs created by the lines.

Maker: Cristina Zani | **Title:** *Uno, Nessuno e Centomila (One, No One and One Hundred Thousand)* | **Materials:** Oxidized copper, 24k gold leaf | **Size:** Approx. 60-25 mm × 20 mm × 10 mm | **Image credit:** Cristina Zani

Narrative: Inspired by the homonymous novel by Luigi Pirandello, this series of rings symbolizes the gradual disintegration of the main character's fictitious personas and his struggle to find his true hidden self.

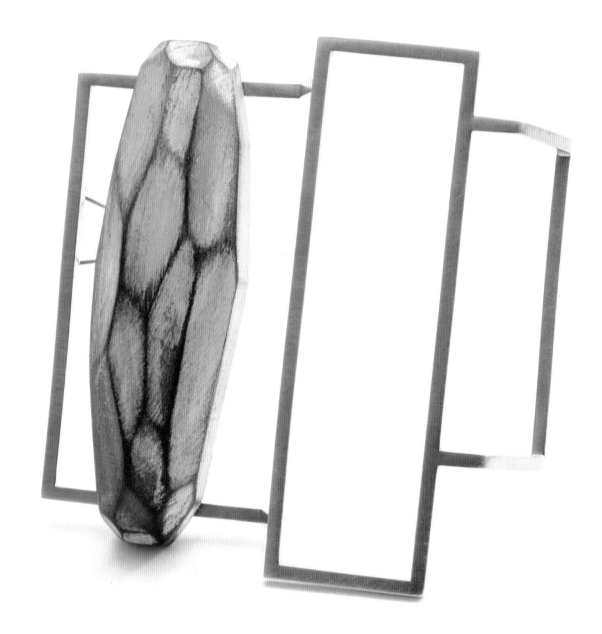

Maker: Cristina Zani | **Title:** *My Seoul (Turquoise and Gold Brooch)* | **Materials:** 24k gold plated silver, steel, wood, paint |
Size: 80 mm × 90 mm × 25 mm | **Image credit:** Cristina Zani

Narrative: Like Marco Polo of *Invisible Cities*, I borrow elements from the city's landscape to visually describe it and subtly suggest it to the viewer.

The choice and juxtaposition of materials, shapes and colors echoes its somber modern buildings intertwined with bright, ancient wooden temples and vibrantly painted palaces. Like those buildings, my pieces show the vulnerability of materials when exposed to time and elements; the layers and colors that slowly transform with the passing of years. Simple in form, but rich in stories and complexities.

CONTRIBUTING MAKERS